THE MULTILINGUAL LEXICON

THE MULTILINGUAL LEXICON

Edited by

Jasone Cenoz
*University of the Basque Country,
Victoria-Gasteiz, Spain*

Britta Hufeisen
*Technical University of Darmstadt,
Darmstadt, Germany*

and

Ulrike Jessner
*University of Innsbruck,
Innsbruck, Austria*

KLUWER ACADEMIC PUBLISHERS

DORDRECHT / BOSTON / LONDON

A C.I.P. Catalogue record for this book is available from the Library of Congress.

ISBN 1-4020-1543-7

Published by Kluwer Academic Publishers,
P.O. Box 17, 3300 AA Dordrecht, The Netherlands.

Sold and distributed in North, Central and South America
by Kluwer Academic Publishers,
101 Philip Drive, Norwell, MA 02061, U.S.A.

In all other countries, sold and distributed
by Kluwer Academic Publishers,
P.O. Box 322, 3300 AH Dordrecht, The Netherlands.

Printed on acid-free paper

Printed in the Netherlands.

TABLE OF CONTENTS

ACKNOWLEDGEMENTS

We are deeply grateful to the contributors for their time and encouragement. We also wish to thank Patxi Gallardo (University of the Basque Country) for his work on the editing and preparation of the camera-ready copy of this volume and Martha Gibson for her collaboration on the editing of the book. The book's appearance would have been seriously delayed without their labours.

Jasone Cenoz
Britta Hufeisen
Ulrike Jessner

CONTRIBUTORS

Jasone Cenoz
University of the Basque Country
Spain
e-mail: fipceirj@vc.ehu.es

Ton Dijkstra
Nijmegen Institute for Cognition and
Information
The Netherlands
e-mail: dijkstra@nici.kun.nl

Peter Ecke
University of Arizona
United States of America
e-mail: eckep@u.arizona.edu

Rita Franceschini
Saarland University
Germany
e-mail: r.franceschini@mx.uni-saarland.de

Martha Gibson
Technical University of Darmstadt
Germany
e-mail:mgibson@spz.tu-darmstadt.de

Christopher Hall
Universidad de las Américas Puebla
Mexico
e-mail: chris@mail.udlap.mx

Britta Hufeisen
Technical University of Darmstadt
Germany
e-mail: hufeisen@spz.tu-darmstadt.de

Ulrike Jessner
University of Innsbruck
Austria
e-mail: ulrike.jessner@uibk.ac.at

Michael McCarthy
University of Nottingham
United Kingdom
e-mail: michael.mccarthy@nottingham.ac.uk

Andreas Müller-Lancé
University of Freiburg
Germany
e-mail: muelance@uni-freiburg.de

Cordula Nitsch
University of Basle
Switzerland
e-mail: cordula.nitsch@unibas.ch

Ute Schönpflug
University of Halle
Germany
e-mail: u.schoenpflug@psych.uni-halle.de

David Singleton
Trinity College
Ireland
e-mail: dsnglton@tcd.ie

Carol Spöttl
University of Innsbruck
Austria
e-mail: carol.spoettl@uibk.ac.at

Longxing Wei
Montclair State University
United States of America
e-mail: WeiL@Mail.montclair.edu

Daniela Zappatore
University of Basle
Switzerland
e-mail: daniela.zappatore@unibas.ch

JASONE CENOZ, BRITTA HUFEISEN & ULRIKE JESSNER

WHY INVESTIGATE THE MULTILINGUAL LEXICON?

Multilingualism both as an individual and social phenomenon is very common in the world considering that there are approximately 5,000 languages and speakers of different languages which have contact with each other in everyday life. Some specific historical, social, economic and political factors have contributed to the development of multilingualism in recent years. Among these factors we can consider the economic difficulties of some countries that result in immigration or the economic and political power of some English speaking countries that have had important implications for the spread of English. Nowadays, it is extremely common to find individuals who can speak more than two languages.

In spite of its importance as a global phenomenon, multilingualism has not received much attention on part of researchers in linguistics, psycholinguistics and applied linguistics. For many years linguists have tried to describe and explain the way human languages work by focusing on monolingual speakers and have ignored bilingual and multilingual speakers. Bilingualism has received a lot of attention in psycholinguistics and applied linguistics in the last few decades but most researchers have not gone beyond bilingualism and have limited their theoretical proposals and empirical work to two languages. For example, most research on language acquisition focuses on first and second language acquisition. Even in cases in which the term 'second language acquisition' is said to be used for the acquisition of languages other than the first language, no distinction is made between the acquisition of a second language and additional languages (see for example Sharwood-Smith, 1994). Similarly, the extensive research on the effects of bilingualism on cognitive development devotes very little attention to the effects of bilingualism on the acquisition of additional languages.

So apart from its limited tradition of research, the study of multilingualism has not benefited from the statements made by some researchers about including situations involving the use of more than two languages as part of bilingualism (see for example Schreuder & Weltens, 1993, 3).

Furthermore, the word 'bilingualism' which includes the Latin prefix 'bi' (two), is not appropriate to refer to more than two languages. In contrast, the term 'multilingualism' encompasses not only 'bilingualism' but also additional

J. Cenoz, B. Hufeisen & U. Jessner (eds.), The Multilingual Lexicon, 1—9.

languages, three, four or more, and is the most appropriate term to be the cover term for phenomena involving more than one language.

The need to use the term 'multilingualism' and to conduct specific research that goes beyond bilingualism has a theoretical and empirical basis. Bilingualism is a phenomenon that may have a lot in common with multilingualism, but research on the acquisition and processing of two languages cannot explain the specific processes resulting from the interaction between the languages that may result from the simultaneous presence of more than two languages in the multilingual person's mind. Research on multilingualism is more complex than research on bilingualism. Apart from all the factors and processes involved in bilingualism, it has to take into account the implications that the knowledge of more than the first language has on the acquisition of an additional language or the multiple relationships between the different linguistic systems in language comprehension and production. Theoretical models of multilingualism (see for example Herdina & Jessner, 2002) emphasize these differences, and recent research on different aspects of multilingualism provides additional evidence of the differences between second and third language acquisition (Cenoz & Genesee, 1998b, Jessner, 1999; Cenoz, Hufeisen & Jessner, 2001a). Furthermore, specific research on the cross-linguistic influence of previously acquired languages on third language acquisition has reported interesting patterns that indicate that third language production has specific characteristics that distinguish it from second language production (see Cenoz, Hufeisen & Jessner, 2001b).

This volume focuses on a specific aspect of multilingualism, the multilingual lexicon, and aims at contributing to develop our knowledge of the way multilingual individuals acquire and process language. To date, books on the mental lexicon have mainly been concerned with the processing of one or two languages. The present volume goes beyond this and provides an additional theoretical and empirical basis to justify the development of multilingualism as a specific area of research.

A multilingual individual can be defined as a person who is able to communicate in two or more languages. As is the case with definitions of bilingualism, the ability to communicate covers a broad spectrum of proficiencies from having a native-like command of more than one language to the general ability to function and communicate in more than one language at almost any proficiency level. Balanced bilingualism is highly infrequent and a balanced level of proficiency in several languages is not to be expected if we take into account the different dimensions of communicative competence including linguistic, pragmatic, sociolinguistic, discourse and strategic competence (Celce-Murcia, Dörnyei & Thurrell, 1995). As has been proposed by Grosjean (1985) and Cook (1992), a multilingual speaker has a specific type of competence which is different from monolingual competence in each of the languages s/he speaks. This volume provides interesting insights into the analysis of one of the areas of multicompetence, the multilingual lexicon.

1. THE MULTILINGUAL LEXICON

The lexicon has always been at the centre of interest in studies on bilingual individuals and/or second language learners. Discussions on the nature of the acquisition of the lexicon have concentrated on questions concerning similarities and differences between lexical operations in L1 and L2 learning and the relationship between form and meaning in processing one or two languages. One of the main questions in research on the mental lexicon is still formed by the discussion on the L1/L2 interdependence/dependence – linked to the classic compound/coordinate dichotomy. But researchers dealing with the question of separation/integration have now shifted their attention to the degree of interconnectivity. Many of the studies on bilingual representation and processing focus on the conceptual and lexical or associative links in the bilingual mental lexicon (several studies in Harris 1992 and Schreuder & Weltens 1993; Singleton 1999, 167ff.).

Processing models which have been developed so far are models adapted from monolingual processing models such as de Bot's (1992), which is based on Levelt's production model (e.g. 1989) where lexical knowledge including lemmas and forms, i.e. sematico-grammatical and morphophonological knowledge, is a part of declarative knowledge.

Other studies on the nature of the lexicon often stem from acquisition studies which were originally motivated by classroom research and concentrate on the connections between the languages which are in contact in a language learning situation. In these studies of cross-linguistic influence the prominent role of the lexicon in language acquisition becomes very obvious. Investigations of codeswitching and –borrowing have formed another research area where the bilingual lexicon has always been a crucial part of the discussion.

To find out whether there are interconnections between the various lexicons in the multilingual's mind is certainly a burning question for research on multilingualism. Other related issues deal with the way the various lexicons are organized and can be accessed and under which conditions they appear. Whereas many scholars, depending on their theoretical approach and scientific background tend to subsume multilingualism under bilingualism and/or second language acquisition (e.g. Singleton, 1999: 130), others have started to concentrate on specific aspects of third language acquisition in order to pinpoint the differences between the processes involved in the acquisition and processing of two or more languages. Some important indicators for the activation of languages in a multilingual individual include recency of activation and use of different languages together with the role assignment of specific languages in an individual (Williams & Hammarberg, 1998). The role of typological factors in a more complex language contact situation where more than two languages are involved has also to be reassigned (Cenoz, 2001).

Furthermore, studies employing trilingual or multilingual subjects not only offer the opportunity to investigate the acquisition and processing by testees representing the majority of the world's population but also offer new perspectives on the study of language acquisition in general. For instance, a study by Abunawara (1992) showed that the number of connections between the lexicons is higher at lower levels of proficiency. The employment of trilingual versus bilingual participants made very clear that the focus on more than two languages offers invaluable insights not only into multilingual processing but also into psycholinguistic aspects of language learning in general (see also Herdina and Jessner, 2002).

2. OVERVIEW OF CHAPTERS

This volume brings together contributions from international scholars who in their research have focused on various aspects of the multilingual lexicon. The various chapters deal with multilingual processing (Dijkstra, Schönpflug), transfer in multilinguals (Jessner, Wei, Hall & Ecke, Gibson & Hufeisen, Cenoz), specific aspects of multilingual learning (Müller-Lancé and Spöttl & McCarthy) and the neurolinguistics of multilingualism (Franceschini, Zappatore & Nitsch). At the end of the volume David Singleton offers a critical overview and synthesis of the enormous number of perspectives represented.

The first two chapters focus on the question of how multilinguals process their different languages during perception, production and related tasks.

Ton Dijkstra's contribution "Lexical processing in bilinguals and multilinguals: The word selection problem" deals with word selection during visual word recognition in multilinguals and compares it with that of bilinguals (and monolinguals). For Dijkstra the consequences of an increased lexicon are at issue: Does the increased word density of words mean stronger competition between words? What happens to the neighbourhood effect when foreign words are added to the lexicon?

He employs the Interactive Activation Model (by McClelland & Rumelhart, 1981) as a starting point for a multilingual model of visual word recognition, which has three hierarchical, yet interconnected, levels of linguistic representation: features, letters, and words. Dijkstra shows how the model can be used to explain phenomena such as the neighbourhood effect or the recency effect. When extended to the bilingual domain, it looks as if the Bilingual Interactive Activation Model must be linked to a language nonselective access hypothesis with an integrated lexicon consisting of a mix of words from two languages. When extended to three (or more) languages, the more general multilingual variant of the BIA model includes the greater number of words in the lexicon as new lexicons (languages) are added. He concludes that there is no need for a specific multilingual model as multilinguals do not require any special processing mechanisms during word selection and therefore suggests simply extending an existing monolingual or bilingual model.

The second chapter "The transfer-appropriate-processing approach and the trilingual's organisation of the lexicon" deals with the effects of active and passive competence in a second or third language on word fragment completions in either language. *Ute Schönpflug* argues that the more languages a speaker knows, the more alternatives there are and the longer the decision process will take; the higher the competence level in one of the languages, the more conceptually driven the word fragment completions will be (and conversely the lower the competence in one of the languages, the more perceptually driven).

Schönpflug discusses language processing as it takes place at different levels: a prelinguistic and (language independent) conceptual level and a functionally different semantic-conceptual-lexical level. Schönpflug tests the uniqueness point of word completions in trilingual Polish speakers of German (L2) and English (L3) and correlates it with their (self-rated) active and passive knowledge in the two languages. Results indicate that the higher the active and passive competence in their L3 English is, the later the uniqueness points for English and German words occur.

The next set of chapters deals with various issues of transfer by exploring different mechanisms and directions on the interaction between the languages of a multilingual.

In her chapter "The nature of cross-linguistic interaction in the multilingual system" *Ulrike Jessner* concentrates on transfer phenomena which are characteristic for a multilingual setting and which do not occur in bilinguals as such. She emphasizes that these characteristics must be linked to individual variability in multilingual proficiency due to changes in language use.

Basing her findings on the Dynamic Model of Multilingualism (Herdina & Jessner, 2002), which takes a holistic approach to multilingualism as a non-linear, reversible and complex process, Jessner argues that multilingualism cannot be explained using extended monolingual acquisition models because the complexity of a system with parameters unique to the multilingual speaker cannot be found in monolingual or bilingual speakers. Jessner pleads the case for joint investigations of transfer and interference, borrowing and code-switching, thus bringing together typical areas of investigation in second language acquisition research and bilingualism research. She suggests using the umbrella term cross-linguistic interaction to account for various phenomena in multilingual research.

In this chapter she shows that the concept of transfer is more diverse than originally thought and that it includes much more than simple cases of interference. As an example for metalinguistic thinking involving all three languages she reports on several think-aloud-protocols by German-Italian bilinguals learning English as their L3 while writing texts in an academic setting. She describes how subjects use their different languages as supplier sources for their target items, how they employ avoidance and simplification strategies, and how they might over-monitor, especially when cognate words are involved.

After discussing interlanguage transfer effects in general terms in multiple language acquisition, *Longxing Wei* deals specifically with the L2-L3 transfer phenomenon in the activation of lemmas in his chapter "Activation of lemmas in the multilingual lexicon and transfer in third language learning". To some extent he employs Levelt's model of speech production process (1989), as in his view, a monolingual model cannot account for bilingual or even multilingual settings, acknowledging that there is a single mental lexicon for multilinguals with lemmas assigned to each language.

He reports on a study of two L3 speakers, which investigated interlanguage transfer in lexical-conceptual structure, predicate-argument structure, and morphological realization patterns. He assumes that if the L3-specific entries in the lexicon are not sufficient to express the speaker's intentions, s/he might turn to other interlanguage items which serve the same communicative purpose. The result is inappropriate lexical choices. Wei shows that a participant with Chinese L1, Japanese L2 and English L3 resorts to the Japanese lemma in order to produce an English lexical item.

Christopher Hall and Peter Ecke introduce a thought-provoking explanation for the default mechanism in L3 vocabulary acquisition in their chapter "Parasitism as a default mechanism in L3 vocabulary acquisition". They hypothesise that the parasitic learning strategy constitutes a default cognitive procedure in which the similarity between novel lexical input and prior lexical knowledge is recognized and used in vocabulary acquisition. In the case of similarity or overlap, new lexical representations will be integrated into the rest of the network with the help of connections to pre-existing representations. If these connections occur between different languages, the result is lexical transfer or cross-linguistic/lexical influence. Hall and Ecke emphasize that this mechanism is not by any means the sole source of erroneous production but that it is a very useful language acquisition procedure.

Hall and Ecke test their hypothesis with students whose native language is Spanish, with English as their L2 and German as their L3. They find that the interconnections of the multilingual lexical network allow cross-linguistic influence at all levels from all possible source languages in any possible target language, yet at various levels of intensity. With regard to L3 acquisition they find that cross-linguistic influence at the form level comes mainly from within the L3, at the conceptual level mostly from the L2, whereas the L1 functions as the source at the frame level, with the L2 exerting the heaviest influence.

The next chapter "Investigating the role of prior foreign language knowledge: translating from an unknown into a known foreign language" by *Martha Gibson and Britta Hufeisen* investigates the role of prior second language knowledge in a translation study with multilingual learners of English and German. As part of a larger long-term project, this study triangulates results from a questionnaire on language background and metalinguistic awareness with production results from a translation task from an unknown foreign language (Swedish) into a known second language (German or English as L3, L4 or L5). They discuss the instances of transfer and cross-linguistic interaction with respect to the roles the previous languages play in the production process, be they facilitating or hindering.

Gibson and Hufeisen base their experiments on the hypothesis that it is a learner's L2 which exerts a particularly strong influence on following foreign languages in the framework of a dynamic language acquisition model. This model accounts not only for variables in language systems and learner-inherent factors but also extra-linguistic factors. Gibson and Hufeisen find that good results in the translation task correlate with a high degree of metalinguistic awareness but also with a distinct ability and interest in deriving, deducing, and (successful) guessing and top-down processing techniques.

In "The role of typology in the organization of the multilingual lexicon" *Jasone Cenoz* touches upon a topic that has not yet received a great deal of attention in the discussion on cross-linguistic influence and transfer. Cenoz discusses the potential of existing models to account for different language systems with respect to language selection in multilingual processing, e.g. the language node(s). She argues that it is the similarity or distance between languages that is responsible for the usage of procedural and lexical knowledge on the one hand, and the joint or separate storage on the other, in a kind of continuum. It is not the absolute distance of languages but the relative distance (this also includes the subjective impression of closeness or distance) in comparison to the respective L1 that seems to be one of the major predictors of cross-linguistic influence together with the factors recency, proficiency, and L2 status. To explain the concept of cross-linguistic influence, Cenoz proposes a continuum ranging from interactional strategies, where intentional switches into languages other than the target language are employed, to transfer lapses which are non-intentional switches and thus automatic.

In her study with children who are native speakers of Spanish living in the Basque country and were exposed to Basque as an early immersion language (L2), and are learning English as their L3, she found that while speaking English the subjects mainly used Basque when employing interactional strategies.

The third set of contributions in the volume highlights various learning issues, including strategies and vocabulary acquisition:

Johannes Müller-Lancé in "A strategy model of multilingual learning" derives a model of multilingual learning after an extensive discussion of the applicability of existing models to the factors. He identifies factors such as inferencing strategies, various levels of proficiency, and learning conditions as crucial for multilingual language processing and concludes that existing monolingual models or their derivations which have been extended to bilingual or multilingual acquisition do not adequately account for the particularities of multilingual processing. He especially emphasizes factors such as inferencing strategies, individual variation, and cognitive control. He develops a sophisticated (synchronic) connective model incorporating the mental lexicon, language comprehension, and language production.

For the two versions - production and comprehension - of his strategy model, Müller-Lancé follows Levelt's monolingual speaking model (1989), integrating the problem of identifying second language items, the use of inferencing strategies, and the distinction between graphic and phonetic input and output. He identifies three types of multilinguals, the monolinguoid, the bilinguoid, and the multilinguoid, the latter having strong cross-linguistic connections between the mental representations of all her or his languages and who at the same time seems to be the most vivacious and daring language learner of the three types.

The chapter by *Carol Spöttl* and *Michael McCarthy* "Formulaic utterances in the multilingual context" deals with lexical units consisting of more than one word, known as formulaic utterances. These utterances can be idiomatic combinations, metaphors, or collocations based on syntagmatic patterns which are neither irregular nor infrequent. Spöttl and McCarthy report on their ongoing research into the questions of whether the processing of formulaic utterances differs from that of single-word vocabulary items, whether such processing is more problematic for the multilingual learner, how these items are linked in the various lexicons the multilingual learner can access, and which role formulaic utterances play in a multilingual context. They argue that formulaic utterances are worthy of intensive research given the assumption that they are stored, accessed and retrieved not as single lexical items that must be constructed and re-constructed syntactically, but as chunks.

For the empirical part of their chapter formulaic utterances from the five-million word CANCODE spoken corpus of British English were taught to various groups of learners in order find evidence for the claim that formulaic utterances are a difficult feature of language acquisition, whether they are processed phonologically, and whether and how cross-linguistic influence can be detected. The focus was on semantically opaque chunks. Students were to find L3 or L4 (Spanish, Italian, or French) equivalents of the given English L2 chunks, and despite frequent reports by the students that they understood the L2 utterance, they nevertheless found it difficult to produce L3 or L4 equivalents. This task became more and more difficult the more idiomatic the L2 string.

The next chapter in this volume concentrates on neurolinguistic issues of multilingualism. In "Lexicon in the brain: what neurobiology has to say about languages" *Rita Franceschini, Daniela Zappatori* and *Cordula Nitsch* set out to explain what neurobiological experiments can tell us about the acquisition of languages in relation to the multilingual lexicon. Although the authors caution that new neuroimaging techniques to make brain activity visible are not yet very precise concerning localization and the dimension of time and development, linguistic research can still benefit from interesting insights into what happens when we speak, hear, or think about language. The question of whether parts of different languages are "stored" together or separately is an especially crucial one which might be solved via brain imaging studies. From earlier studies we know which brain areas are active, for instance, in language production and comprehension, when lexical or semantic decisions are being made, and syntax structures are being processed but the exact correlation between linguistic components and brain structures continues to be debated.

As almost all imaging studies deal with bilinguals, the authors report on these and try to link the results to questions concerning multilingualism. It seems that language activities such as word generation basically call for the same type of brain activation, even if the languages under investigation are as far apart typologically as Chinese and English. For some linguistic tasks, the age factor seemed to play a decisive role such that it usually resulted in increased activity, and with certain tasks, in differing areas than for younger participants and the speakers who had acquired their language(s) early in life.

Franceschini et al. also report that early multilinguals tended to integrate other languages learned later in life into their existing networks, whereas late multilinguals displayed higher variability for early and late languages, and new neural substrate had to be recruited. Together with the main functional principle of automatization - not a language-specific mechanism - language proficiency was identified as another critical determinant of the representation of a second language in the brain. Linguistically relevant entities such as language typology were found to play no decisive or even minor role in any of the studies. These results, however, must be considered against the backdrop of variables such as experimental task and the individual language biography of the subjects. The authors caution that many other influencing factors have not yet been tested in isolation and/or in experimental situations.

The volume concludes with a recapitulation by *David Singleton* "Perspectives on the multilingual lexicon: a critical synthesis" of the main ideas presented in the other chapters. He discusses questions of lexical storage, how they are being dealt with in the various contributions and in which direction current research seems to be going. Singleton then concentrates on the important question of interdependence and independence.

All in all we hope that this book will stimulate further interest in the worldwide phenomenon of multilingualism, which we feel should be treated as the norm in linguistics and not as the exception.

J.C./B.H./U.J.

University of the Basque Country (Spain)
Technical University of Darmstadt (Germany)
University of Innsbruck (Austria)

TON DIJKSTRA

LEXICAL PROCESSING IN BILINGUALS AND MULTILINGUALS: THE WORD SELECTION PROBLEM

1. INTRODUCTION

Some multilinguals understand and speak many different languages. A lecture at the Second International Conference on Third Language Acquisition and Trilingualism (Leeuwarden, the Netherlands, September 13-15, 2001) discussed the linguistic abilities of a person who mastered 17 different languages at least reasonably fluently. Such multilinguals must have stored vast numbers of words in their mental lexicon, and it would appear to be as difficult to retrieve just the right word from such a large database as it would be to find a needle in a haystack. Still, these multilinguals appear to be able to communicate rather smoothly, without suffering from many misperceptions of words or cross-linguistically based speech errors. How can their word retrieval system operate so efficiently? We will refer to this issue as the *word selection problem*.

Derailments of language processing in multilinguals might especially be expected if one realizes that already monolinguals are capable of selecting/identifying a word within a third of a second from a lexicon of 50,000 words or more (see Aitchison, 1987: 5-7). If they are reasonably fluent in their L2, proficient bilinguals must have 10,000s of additional word forms for use in their second language, and the number of extra words from yet other languages in multilinguals must be considerable. This implies that during reading and speaking, thousands of extra words are possible targets for recognition or articulation. And yet, the cost associated to the ability of processing more than one language seems to be relatively mild. In their comparison of bilingual and monolingual performance in different tasks, Ransdell and Fischler (1987: 400) concluded that "Becoming fluent in a second language appears to have only slight impact on the ability to process the first". They observed, for instance, that bilinguals made English (L1) lexical decisions on words that were only about 125 ms slower than those of monolinguals (given RTs of 700-900 ms), but just as accurate. In all, multilinguals thus appear to perform an amazing feat when they recognize and produce words from their many

J. Cenoz, B. Hufeisen & U. Jessner (eds.), The Multilingual Lexicon, 11—26.
© 2003 *Kluwer Academic Publishers. Printed in the Netherlands.*

languages, not (just) in the sense that they are able to store so many words, but especially in that they are able to retrieve the right ones so quickly and without flaw.

This chapter considers which factors may help multilinguals to solve their word selection problem during visual word recognition. Basing ourselves upon evidence from the bilingual domain, we will evaluate a number of solutions to the problem of word selection in the multilingual:

(a)   Multilinguals are able to access just the task-relevant language (language selective access) and to switch between their languages when needed.

(b)   Word candidates from different languages are automatically activated during lexical selection (language nonselective access), but multilinguals can control their relative language activation in a top-down way (i.e., if they want to).

(c)   The characteristics of lexical items from different languages suffice to account for the word selection process in multilinguals. Word candidates from different languages are activated during lexical selection, and multilinguals have no top-down control over the activation of words from different languages.

During our evaluation, we will contrast available models of word recognition with respect to their basic underlying assumptions, and extend their views from monolinguals and bilinguals to multilinguals.

2. THE INTERACTIVE ACTIVATION MODEL FOR MONOLINGUAL WORD RECOGNITION

As a starting point, let us consider what we know about word selection in monolingual language comprehension (see also de Bot, in press). A well-known monolingual model for visual word recognition is the Interactive Activation (IA) model (McClelland & Rumelhart, 1981, see Figure 1). This model comprises units (nodes) corresponding to linguistic representations at three hierarchically arranged levels: features, letters, and words. Feature nodes detect the presence or absence of visual features (i.e. line segments) of letters at different positions in a word. Facilitatory connections exist between nodes from adjacent representation levels and inhibitory connections between nodes at the same level. An input letter string "switches on" particular features at each letter position, which subsequently excite letters that contain them and inhibit letters for which they are absent. Each activated letter then excites in parallel all words having that letter at the correct spatial position, while all other words and letters in that position are inhibited. Subsequently, all activated words inhibit each other (lateral inhibition) while they excite their component letters (top-down feedback). After a number of processing cycles, an asymptotic activation value is reached in some word and letter units. Word recognition can be assumed to take place if an activation threshold set at the word level is crossed. When the input is turned off, activation gradually decreases towards initial or resting level values due to activation decay.

In the first stages of word recognition, many word candidates are activated in parallel (see also Schönpflug, this volume). Especially words that differ from the presented target word in only one letter become activated, because they match the target to such a large extent. Words that differ from a target word at only one letter position are called *neighbors*. For instance, upon presentation of a four-letter word like WIND, words that share three letters with the target word become relatively active because of the bottom-up support from the three activated letter units. Examples of neighbors of WIND are BIND, KIND, WAND, WILD, and WINK. (Further note that WIND is a homograph, implying that without context several meanings could become available). These neighbors subsequently inhibit other less activated words, thus helping each other (gang effect). Over time, they also start to affect each other's activation and that of the target word negatively through lateral inhibition. The IA model has been able to account for many neighborhood effects reported in the literature (for a discussion in the context of bilingualism, see Van Heuven, Dijkstra, & Grainger, 1998).

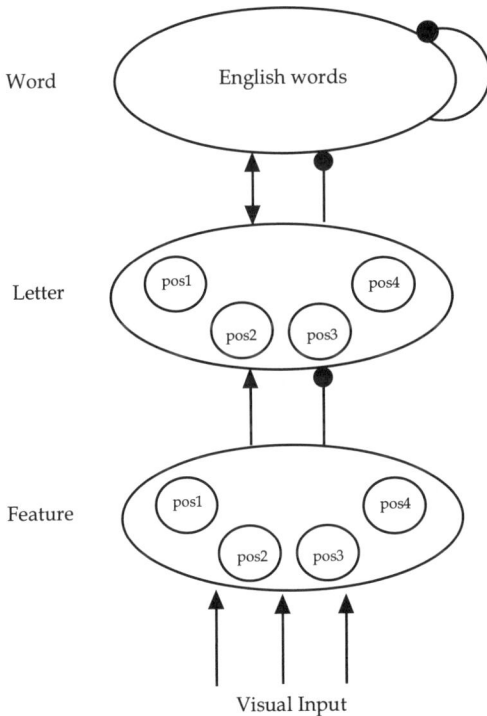

Figure 1. The Interactive Activation model of visual word recognition. Normal arrows indicate excitatory connections, lines with ball heads indicate inhibitory connections.

In the model, higher frequency words are generally recognized faster than lower frequency words because their representations have a higher resting level activation. During recognition, this results in a headstart plus extra inhibitory power for higher frequency items. One may further assume that recently recognized items have a slightly heightened resting level activation, which would explain their faster recognition if they are repeated (recency effect).

3. LANGUAGE SELECTIVE VERSUS LANGUAGE NONSELECTIVE ACCESS

The monolingual IA model can be extended towards the bilingual domain in accordance with either a *language selective* or a *language nonselective access* hypothesis (see Dijkstra & Van Heuven, 1998; see also De Bot, in press). According to the language selective access view, there are separate lexical networks for different languages and words from each language can be separately accessed. A selection mechanism, called an "input switch", guides all incoming visual or auditory information to the lexical system of the bilingual that is relevant for performing the monolingual task at hand (e.g., reading English). The system can operate at such a high level of selectivity that the linguistic input initially (i.e. at the orthographic or phonological level) only contacts representations in the active (target) language. Only if the lexical representation corresponding to the input is not found in the lexicon of the target language, is contact established with the other lexical system. This viewpoint provides a simple solution for the word selection problem in multilinguals, because they would simply switch to the language relevant to a particular situation without being disturbed by all the "extra baggage" of their other languages.[i]

Early studies collected evidence that was interpreted as support for the language selective access hypothesis. For instance, Gerard and Scarborough (1989) had Spanish-English bilinguals and English monolinguals perform an English lexical decision experiment, in which they pressed a "yes" button if a presented letter string was a correct word in English (e.g., HOUSE), and a "no" button if it was not (e.g., FOUSE). No significant latency differences arose between bilinguals and monolinguals with respect to the processing of cognates, interlingual homographs, and control words. Cognates are words that overlap across languages in their orthographic form and meaning (e.g., FILM), while interlingual homographs only have the same orthographic form across languages (e.g., RED in English and Spanish, where it means "net"). In addition, word latencies varied primarily with the frequency of usage in the target language. These findings suggested that all participants were effectively operating in a language selective manner.

These results seemed to contradict the alternative view on bilingual word recognition proposed above, that of language nonselective access. According to this view, lexical candidates from different languages become activated in parallel, leading to the prediction of slower RTs for interlingual homographs than for matched monolingual control items. However, later studies have revealed that the lexicon of other languages *is* activated under the circumstances that Gerard and

Scarborough examined after all. For instance, even though Dijkstra, Van Jaarsveld, and Ten Brinke (1998) replicated Gerard and Scarborough's null-results, a recent additional analysis of their data (Dijkstra & Van Heuven, 2002) indicated that, despite the over-all null results, responses to the homographs slowed down as Dutch frequency increased and they became faster for higher frequency English readings. More convincingly, De Moor (1998) and Van Heste (1999) showed that the semantics of the L1 reading of the interlingual homographs was activated even though this was not evident from the result pattern for homographs and control words. This was demonstrated by the finding that in an English lexical decision task performed by Dutch-English bilinguals, the word FIRE was semantically primed by the presentation of the word BRAND (the Dutch word for "FIRE") on the previous trial. Several other studies have shown that language nonselective effects also occur with other types of stimulus materials and different tasks (e.g., neighborhood density studies, Van Heuven et al., 1998), that they occur not only from L1 on L2, but also in the opposite direction, and that they also occur in trilinguals (e.g., Van Hell & Dijkstra, 2002).

Van Hell and Dijkstra selected Dutch-English-French trilinguals, who were most fluent in L1, less fluent in L2, and least fluent in L3. These participants performed a Dutch word association task and a Dutch lexical decision task. The words in the stimulus list belonged exclusively to Dutch (e.g., the Dutch word TUIN, meaning "garden" in English) or had a cognate relationship with their English translations (e.g., Dutch BAKKER, meaning "baker" in English) or with their French translations (e.g., Dutch MUUR, which is MUR in French, meaning "wall"). The majority of the cognates were non-identical cognates, and hence they were unambiguous with respect to the language they belonged to. In the word association task, mean association times to L1 cognates with English (L2) were found to be shorter than those to L1 noncognates (1641 ms vs. 1845 ms). The mean association times to L1 cognates with French (L3) were also somewhat shorter than to L1 noncognates (1809 ms vs. 1845 ms), but this difference was not statistically significant. In the Dutch lexical decision task, latencies to L1 cognates with English were shorter than for noncognates (499 ms. vs. 529 ms). Again, a nonsignificant cognate advantage was obtained, however, for L1 cognates with the trilinguals' third, and weakest, language (French) (519 ms. vs. 529 ms) (see also Schönpflug and Franceschini et al., this volume).

Next, Van Hell and Dijkstra replicated the lexical decision experiment with trilinguals who were more proficient in French (L3). The fluency levels of these participants were comparable in L2 and L3 (as assessed by an independent test after the experiment). Now not only a cognate advantage arose in words that were cognates with their L2 (English) translation (489 ms for English cognates vs. 541 ms for noncognate controls), but also in words that were cognates with their L3 (French) translation (520 ms for French cognates vs. 541 ms for controls). These results indicate that foreign language knowledge (from L2 and L3) can affect lexical processing in the native language (L1) even under circumstances in which the participants are unaware their knowledge of other languages is relevant. At the same time, a comparison of the two lexical decision experiments by Van Hell and Dijkstra indicates that the L3 proficiency had to be high enough to exert an observable effect on the RTs to L1 target words.

In sum, in the last decade, several studies have demonstrated that there is language nonselective access rather than selective access in many experimental circumstances (for an overview, see Dijkstra & Van Heuven, submitted). Bilingual word recognition apparently involves a parallel activation of word candidates from different languages. The classical idea of setting a "language input switch" to force language selective access to words from only one language is not tenable. Multilinguals apparently do not solve the word selection problem they are faced with by means of this kind of cognitive mechanism.

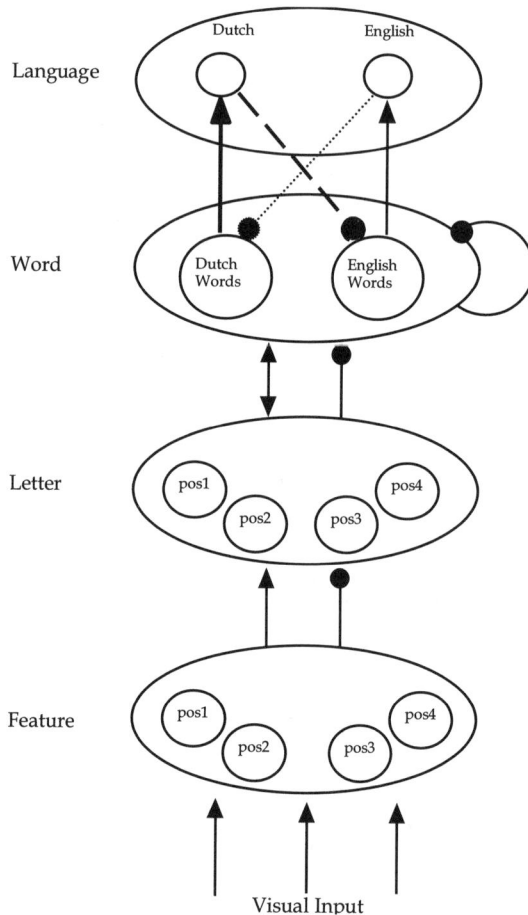

Figure 2. The Bilingual Interactive Activation model. The bold arrows between word and language node levels reflect strong activation flows during Dutch word input.

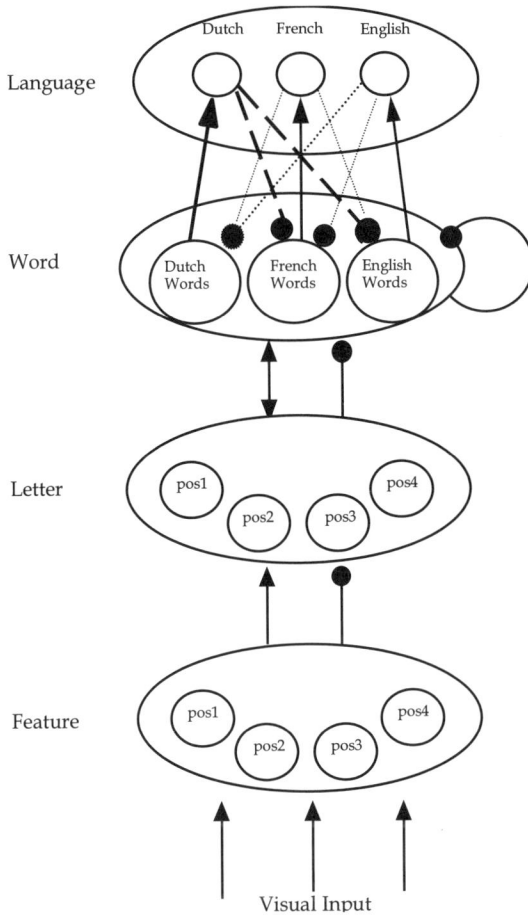

Figure 3. The Trilingual Interactive Activation model. The bold arrows between word and language node levels reflect strong activation flows during Dutch word input.

4. MODELLING BILINGUAL AND MULTILINGUAL WORD RECOGNITION

In line with the available evidence we need to extend the monolingual model towards the bilingual domain as in Figure 2. This figure represents the Bilingual Interactive Activation (BIA) model (Dijkstra & Van Heuven, 1998; Van Heuven et al., 1998). It incorporates an integrated lexicon that consists of a mix of words from two languages (for instance, from English and Dutch). In Figure 3, the model is extended to trilinguals (and it can easily be extended further). We will refer to the more general multilingual variant of the BIA model as the Multilingual Interactive

Activation (MIA) model. With the addition of each new lexicon, the number of words in the lexicon increases.

What happens to the word recognition performance of the model if the size of its lexicon increases? With a larger density of words, the competition between words (lateral inhibition) becomes stronger, and the moment in time that the presented word can be identified is delayed. Note that this is the case irrespective of whether the newly acquired words are from the same language or from another language. Indeed, when we grow up, we acquire many new words from our native language as well. For instance, if we become biologists specializing in botany, we may learn hundreds of words for little plants. Recognizing these new words from the same language may be similar to recognizing newly learned words from another language. In both cases, there are on average more words that are similar to an input string, making the recognition of this string more difficult.[ii]

The processing consequences of adding words from other lexicons can be examined more precisely by using the Interactive Activation framework. We will first evaluate what happens to the neighborhood characteristics of target words when words from other languages are added to the lexicon. Next, we will present some simulations with the BIA model to assess how much the recognition process is slowed down in multilinguals as a consequence of adding foreign-language words.

Table 1. Mean number of neighbors from Dutch, English, and French for 3-5 letter Dutch target words, and the size of the lexicon added for each language.

	3-letter words		4-letter words		5-letter words		mean
	Neighbors	*Lexicon*	*Neighbors*	*Lexicon*	*Neighbors*	*Lexicon*	
Dutch	10.41	393	5.27	984	2.13	1251	4.54
English	7.47	436	3.63	1323	0.83	1846	2.66
French	5.52	301	1.72	782	0.78	1728	1.55

Suppose one is a trilingual reading and speaking Dutch, English, and French. Computations on a Dutch lexicon of 2628 words of 3-5 letters (lemmas) with a frequency larger than 1 derived from the CELEX database show that there are on average less than five Dutch words that differ in only one letter of a given target word (see Table 1). Adding words from other lexicons, of course, leads to an increase in neighbors. For a multilingual with a native-like knowledge of all 3-5 letter words from English and French, presentation of a Dutch word would be accompanied by the additional activation of three English neighbors (as a rough estimate) and two French neighbors (Table 1). However, I hasten to add that these numbers should be taken as rough estimates only, because the precise outcome of the computations on neighborhood density depends critically on several assumptions with respect to the lexicons in question. For instance, the number of neighbors depends on the size of the lexicons used and on the representation of intralingual and interlingual homographs, diacritical markers, and morphologically complex words.

Table 2. Mean number of processing cycles (NC) required to recognize a Dutch target word when the lexicon contains only Dutch words, Dutch and English words, or Dutch, English, and French words. Recognition is assumed to take place if a word activation threshold of .70 is surpassed.

	Mean NC Dutch	Mean NC Dutch-English	Cycles difference with Dutch	Mean NC Dutch-English-French	Cycles difference with Dutch
3-letter words	19.13	19.88	0.73	20.22	1.09
4-letter words	19.63	19.74	0.11	19.83	0.20
5-letter words	19.63	19.78	0.15	19.86	0.23

<u>Note</u>: The size of the Dutch, English, and French lexicons was that given in Table 1. However, Dutch-English, Dutch-French, and French-English interlingual homographs were excluded in computations for multiple lexicons.

What are the consequences of these extra neighbors for processing? An indication can be obtained by conducting simulations with the BIA model including one or more lexicons. Table 2 provides simulation results obtained with a model incorporating only a Dutch lexicon (i.e., a Dutch selective-access or SAM model, see Dijkstra & Van Heuven, 1998), an integrated (mixed) Dutch-English lexicon (a bilingual non-selective access or NSAM model), or a Dutch-English-French lexicon (a trilingual non-selective access model). The simulations indicate that the addition of a whole new lexicon leads to a relatively small slowing down in model performance! This becomes clear if we linearly transform the cycle times necessary for recognition by the model into reaction times. Assuming that 20 cycles in the model corresponds (very) roughly to about 600 ms, this implies that one cycle corresponds to about 30 ms. There are many possible objections to this kind of direct linkage between computer model and empirical data, but a tentative conclusion is that adding a new lexicon to the L1 word recognition system may have only limited effects on lexical processing in L1. One explanation for this is that when target words have many competing neighbors, these competitors will also interfere with each other (through lateral inhibition) and not just with the target.

We further note that not all words will suffer equally strongly from their competitors. Empirically, the strongest effects appear to be exerted by high-frequency neighbors on low-frequency target words (Grainger & Segui, 1990). Because foreign language words are probably lower in subjective frequency, their effect on the native language will be smaller than that of within-language neighbors (cf. Van Hell & Dijkstra, 2002). At the same time, cross-linguistic competition will be stronger in the other direction (from L1 on L2-L3). Competition with the native language will increase when the multilingual becomes more proficient in other languages. Similar kinds of reasoning may hold for phonological in addition to orthographic neighborhoods.

Thus, the implementation of the interactive activation framework allows us to more precisely assess the word selection problem in multilinguals. It also helps us to obtain a better insight into how this problem may be solved by the multilingual. A number of possible helpful factors suggested indirectly by the model are discussed in the following sections.

5. BOTTOM-UP FACTORS FACILITATING WORD SELECTION IN MULTILINGUALS

The neighborhood density and simulation analyses in the previous section suggest that the word selection problem may be facilitated by differences in the characteristics of lexical items across languages. This suggestion is based on the observation that in this type of model the input stimulus itself is the most important cue for selection. Even some of its orthographic characteristics already restrict the number of possible words in a drastic way. The recognition of one letter in a 3-letter word implies that scores of possible words from the lexicon are excluded as possibilities. Language-dependent stimulus factors that may help to reduce the number of lexical candidates upon target word presentation are language-specific cues, language distance, and script type.

Even when two languages are closely related and are represented by the same script, words may contain *language-specific cues*. Examples are the diacritical markers (accents) of French and the onset capitals for nouns in German. In such cases, the use of these cues might quickly reduce the number of competitors of an item to those of the target language. (Note that this implies a bottom-up mechanism, not necessarily a top-down mechanism.) There is some preliminary evidence that language-specific bigrams and other cues may indeed affect the selection process, but much more study is necessary here (see Kroll & Dijkstra, 2002; Schwartz, Kroll, & Diaz, 2000). For French, it has been shown that the monolingual neighborhood competitor set of target words does indeed depend on the presence or absence of diacritical markers (Mathey & Zagar, 2000, p. 200).

Furthermore, the analysis in the previous section indicates that lexical distance depends on *language distance*. If two languages become more different in their orthotactics and phonotactics, the number of cross-language neighbors will decrease. In general, the neighborhood densities within languages will be larger than across languages, and newly acquired other-language words are mostly grouped together in previously less dense areas of the mental lexicon. Learning other-language words leads to an increase in the number of neighbors of L1 target words, but this increase is less than in the case of new L1 words, because the other-language words are positioned somewhat more distant in lexical space. As a consequence, words from more distant languages having the same script will interfere less than words from closely related languages (see Cenoz, but also Franceschini et al., this volume).

So far, we have spoken about language pairs that share their *scripts*, i.e. their orthographic lexical and sublexical representations. For such language pairs, the word selection problem must clearly be the most severe. According to a multilingual Interactive Activation framework, distinctions in script will help the word selection process considerably. For languages with different scripts and for language specific phenomena, the selection problem will be similar for monolinguals and multilinguals, because it will depend on the target language only. For instance, Chinese-English bilinguals can select words from their lexicons via language-specific orthographic input representations. In this case, script differences can be considered to induce a language-specific orthographic activation mechanism. Thus, while multilinguals need to spend considerable effort in learning the scripts of different languages, precisely those distinctions in scripts may be helpful later in reducing the number of word candidates that become activated during stimulus presentation.

6. NON-LINGUISTIC TOP-DOWN CONTROL AND RELATIVE LANGUAGE ACTIVATION

Not only characteristics of the items themselves, but also properties of the context in which the items appear might be important in solving the word selection problem. In principle, both non-linguistic and linguistic types of context information could modulate word activation. Examples of non-linguistic context effects are top-down effects of participant expectations and instructions with regard to the experimental situation at hand. Examples of linguistic context effects on target item recognition are bottom-up lexical effects of previous items in stimulus lists (cf. Dijkstra et al., 1998) and syntactic/semantic effects of sentence context. In this section we will examine to which extent especially non-linguistic types of context may provide effective constraints on multilingual word recognition; in the next section we will focus more on linguistic context effects.

The underlying idea is that context might be used for a deactivation of lexical candidates from a non-target language as soon as they become active. This option is different from language switching in that the *relative activation of word candidates from different languages* is modulated not before (proactively) but after word candidate activation (reactively). This possibility is available in the BIA/MIA model in the form of top-down inhibition exerted by the *language nodes* (see Figure 2). Activated language nodes of one language suppress word candidates from the other language (e.g., the English language node will suppress the activation of Dutch words). If the activity of the language nodes can be modulated by factors external to the word recognition system, this provides a mechanism for context effects to influence the activation of words from different languages.

The concept of relative language activation has also been used by Grosjean (1985, 1997, 1998, 2001) in his notion of a "language mode", referring to the relative state of activation of a bilingual's two (or more) languages and language processing mechanisms. Depending on non-linguistic and linguistic factors such as the person spoken to, the situation, the content of discourse and the function of the interaction, one language (the base language) may be active while the state of the other language may vary from deactivated (monolingual language mode) to relatively active (bilingual language mode). According to Grosjean the bilingual's language mode affects perception and the speed of access to one or two lexicons, and the language mode itself is affected both by the readers' expectations and by language intermixing. As has been shown by Grosjean (2001) and Dewaele (2001), the language mode view can easily be extended to multilingual processing.

Similarly, Green (1998) in his IC model assumes that language users can control (regulate) their language processing by modifying levels of activation of (items in) language networks. A key concept in this model is the *language task schema* that specifies the mental processing steps (or "action sequences") that a bilingual takes in order to perform a particular language task. A language task schema regulates the output from the word identification system by altering the activation levels of representations in that system and by inhibiting outputs from the system.

In sum, the concept of relative language activation can in principle account for both non-linguistic (expectation, instruction) and linguistic (syntactic, lexical) effects of context. If relative language activation can be controlled by the multilingual, word candidates from different languages could be differentiated more quickly, leading to a faster lexical selection process.

As we have seen, the BIA model assumes that words from different languages differ in their resting level activation, because they differ in terms of their subjective frequency (which is related to the relative proficiency of the multilingual in the different languages) and their recency of use. Frequency and recency effects are empirically well-established phenomena, so these assumptions seem reasonable. However, much less is known about the extent to which non-linguistic and linguistic context factors can modulate relative language activation. In several papers, Dijkstra and colleagues have argued that there is only little evidence supporting *non-linguistic context* effects on bilingual word recognition (e.g., Dijkstra & Van Heuven, 2002). Their arguments are based on studies involving the presentation of isolated target words in stimulus lists (such studies avoid the linguistic effects of syntactic/semantic context).

As an example, consider the three experiments by Dijkstra et al. (1998). In the first English lexical decision experiment of this study, already mentioned above, no RT differences were observed between interlingual homographs and one-language control items for Dutch-English bilinguals. However, when Dutch words were added to the stimulus list in Experiment 2, the null-effects for interlingual homographs turned into robust inhibition effects. When the task was changed into generalized lexical decision in Experiment 3 (where participants respond with "yes" to any word they encounter, irrespective of its language), the effects turned into strong facilitation.

The experiments demonstrated that both stimulus list composition and task demands affected the result patterns, but what was the underlying mechanism? Because the stimulus materials in the second and third experiment were (almost) identical, it appears that the relative activation of L1/L2 lexical candidates generated by the stimulus list alone cannot explain the variation in results. However, the conclusion that non-linguistic top-down effects modulated the activation of Dutch lexical candidates in Experiment 2 does not seem viable either, because strong inhibition effects occurred in this experiment for interlingual homographs relative to monolingual controls. More likely, the differences in results between Experiments 2 and 3 were due to the differences in task demands (language-specific vs. generalized lexical decision). Other studies that suggest relatively small non-linguistic context effects on word activation are those by Dijkstra, De Bruijn, Schriefers, & Ten Brinke (2000), and Van Hell & Dijkstra (2002).

In sum, currently there is little convincing evidence that in bilingual visual word recognition the activation of the word candidates from different languages can be affected by non-linguistic top-down operating contextual factors. It is more likely that non-linguistic context effects influence the way in which word decisions come about (strategic aspects of performance). In the next section, we will consider the effects of linguistic context effects on multilingual word recognition.

7. LINGUISTIC TOP-DOWN CONTROL AND RELATIVE LANGUAGE ACTIVATION

A different possibility is that the word recognition process is speeded by the use of higher-level types of *linguistic context* information, such as morphological representations, sentence level information, or language membership information.

Morphology must provide an important source for distinguishing words from different languages. Seventy percent or more of the English and Dutch word types that we encounter in reading are multimorphemic, and although this percentage becomes much lower (perhaps 30% or less) if one takes into account the word frequency of the different word forms (tokens), we are still talking about a large number of words (Baayen, personal communication, January 11, 2002). Languages exploit a variety of means for creating morphologically complex words (see, e.g., Baayen & Schreuder, 1996), leading to very different word forms across languages. During reading, these complex forms must either be retrieved from the lexicon (if they are listed there) or they must be parsed according to language specific principles in order to be recognized. Application of the morphological principles of the wrong language will only seldom result in intelligible representations (e.g., Dutch-English readers might perhaps misparse a word like "bootstrap", assuming that it refers to a staircase on a boat, cf. *bootsman* or *monnikskap*). The longer the complex words are, the fewer neighbors there will be. Moreover, if affixes are stored, their language specific nature will restrict the selection process even further.

For words in *sentences*, syntactic, semantic, and language information provided by the sentence context could also provide a source of serious constraints on lexical selection. In fact, it is quite possible that the word selection problem is quickly solved by using such information. For instance, with respect to within-language homophones, cross-modal studies in the monolingual domain have found that alternative meanings may be activated in parallel in a constraining sentence context (Swinney, 1979; Tanenhaus et al., 1979). However, the alternative meanings do not seem to be activated to the same extent: The more frequent (dominant) meaning appears to be more accessible than the other one (e.g., Duffy, Morris, & Rayner, 1988), and sentential context appears to be able to make the non-dominant meaning as accessible as the dominant one (Lucas, 1999). Under some conditions, only the contextually appropriate meaning appears to be activated (Tabossi & Zardon, 1993). If these results can be generalized to the multilingual, they imply that sentence context will reduce or even solve the word selection problem the multilingual is faced with. Hardly any evidence is available with respect to this issue. One of the few studies investigating the combined effects of sentence and language context in bilinguals is that by Elston-Guettler and Williams (submitted).

A final solution to the word selection problem is to use a word's *language membership* information as a selection criterion as soon as it becomes available. This possibility is also incorporated in the MIA framework, where word candidates that are activated by the input feed activation to the language node they are linked to. As soon as one language node becomes more activated than the other (to some predetermined extent set on the basis of the stimulus list context, instruction, and so on), it starts to send down inhibition to all activated lexical candidates from the non-target language(s).

This theoretical viewpoint predicts that, for instance, the recognition of interlingual homographs could be speeded using such language information. However, a study by Dijkstra, Timmermans, and Schriefers (2000) provides some evidence against this view. These authors examined the role of language information as follows. In three experiments, each with a different instruction, bilingual participants processed the same set of homographs embedded in identical mixed-language lists. Homographs of three types were used: high-frequent in English and low-frequent in Dutch; low-frequent in English and high-frequent in Dutch; and low-frequent in both languages. In the first experiment (involving language decision), one button was pressed when an English word was presented and another button for a Dutch word. In the second and third experiments participants reacted only when they identified either an English word (English go/no-go) or a Dutch word (Dutch go/no-go), but they did not respond if a word of the non-target language (Dutch or English, respectively) was presented. The overall results in the three experiments were similar to those obtained by Dijkstra et al. (1998, Experiment 2) for lexical decision. In all three tasks, inhibition effects arose for homographs relative to one-language controls. Even in the Dutch go/no-go task for Dutch-English bilinguals performing in their native language, participants were unable to completely exclude effects from the non-target language on interlingual homograph identification.

These results indicate that participants cannot use the language membership information of the target word to aid their word selection process. In fact, it was found that target-language homographs were often "overlooked" (i.e., not responded to), especially if the frequency of their other-language competitor was high. In the Dutch go/no-go task, participants did not respond to low-frequency items belonging to their native language Dutch in about 25 percent of the cases! Apparently, if the higher-frequency English counterpart was first detected and recognized, the subsequent recognition of the Dutch reading was substantially delayed. These results also suggest that language membership information is available only after word recognition has taken place. If this is true, such information will be able to help multilingual word recognition only on limited occasions.[iii]

To summarize, it is quite likely that both non-linguistic and linguistic context effects may help to speed up the recognition of words by multilinguals. It appears, however, that while linguistic effects may operate on the word representations themselves, non-linguistic effects may be effective especially during later stages of processing having to do with task and decision components. In all, there are often strong selectivity-inducing constraints available in the input stimulus and its context, and it seems likely that the multilingual will exploit these as soon as possible.

8. CONCLUSIONS

The theoretical analysis in this chapter suggests that multilinguals do not require any special processing mechanisms to solve the word selection problem they are faced with during reading. A straightforward extension of a bilingual model of word recognition to multilinguals (or of a monolingual model to a bilingual model) seems to suffice. It is possible to add such mechanisms as non-linguistic control over relative language activation to facilitate word selection in multilinguals, but the empirical evidence supporting such mechanisms is at present either unavailable or weak. As we have seen, characteristics of the input items and languages already provide many cues that can be used during selection in multilinguals, making the selection problem in fact less rather than more severe than that in monolinguals who acquire special jargon terms within their own language.

Assuming that the theoretical frameworks that have been proposed for monolinguals and bilinguals also apply to multilinguals is the most simple theoretical viewpoint, and for reasons of parsimony we should adhere to that view unless new evidence shows it is not psychologically valid. Language processing in general is so complex, and multilingual processing even more, that this may be the best research strategy to follow until we have collected more evidence.

We have considered a number of linguistic factors that appear to help the word selection process in visual word recognition by multilinguals: item related characteristics having to do with neighborhood density, language-specific cues, language distance, and script type, and linguistic context aspects having to do with morphological, syntactic, and language membership information.

Most of the reviewed selection-constraining factors for visual word recognition would seem to hold for auditory word recognition and for word production as well. However, there may yet turn out to be some interesting differences that are modality-dependent. For instance, in auditory word recognition, sublexical cues due to differences in phoneme repertoire, aspiration, tone, and so on, might facilitate word selection relative to the visual domain (for evidence that auditory lexical access may be language nonselective nevertheless, see Schulpen, Dijkstra, Schriefers, and Hasper, submitted). And in word production, in contrast to the visual word recognition domain, the retrieval of language information (via the lemmas) appears to be fast enough to allow multilingual speakers to exert considerable control over the language of their intended utterance. All in all, the word retrieval system seems to be organized so efficiently that the selection-inducing factors are just strong enough to help multilinguals not to become slow readers, misperceiving listeners, or stuttering speakers. Rather than taking our admiration away for the language processing feats of multilinguals, these observations may stimulate our wondering about the complexity of the human word identification system.

Nijmegen Institute for Cognition and Information (Netherlands)

NOTES

* The author wishes to thank Walter Van Heuven for his computations on the data presented in Tables 1 and 2.

[i] However, the solution may not be so simple after all, because to avoid interactions between the two lexical systems, one needs to assume that not only the word level, but also the feature and letter levels are specific to each language. This assumption does not seem to be attractive, considering the amount of reduplication of units it would lead to in multilinguals.

[ii] In *word production* every new language will lead to the addition of translation equivalents or near-synonyms to express the same concept (e.g., for an object). However, whereas the basic problem for the multilingual is to distinguish these possible words with respect to the language they belong to, monolingual speakers would need to distinguish the various plants they know both in terms of their conceptual or visual characteristics and with respect to their names.

[iii] Given this empirical evidence, it is proposed that language membership information is derived via so-called "lemma representations", or at least becomes available only after word identification.

UTE SCHÖNPFLUG

THE TRANSFER-APPROPRIATE-PROCESSING APPROACH AND THE TRILINGUAL'S ORGANISATION OF THE LEXICON

1. INTRODUCTION

A critical question with reference to the theoretical basis of multilingualism is whether the trilingual speaker's total lexicon represents different sets of lexica depending on the similarity of the languages involved. The languages given have different similarities or distances from each other, and thus interconnections have different strengths when they are derived from phonological, morphological and syntactical features of the given languages. In addition, the issue of semantic or conceptual interconnections between languages has to be considered and associated with the question of semantic similarity. The aim of this research is to clarify the issue of conceptual interconnections between second and third language.

2. BILINGUAL AND TRILINGUAL LANGUAGE PROCESSING

Both Paradis and Goldblum (1989) and Perecman (1989) see language processing as taking place on different levels: a prelinguistic conceptual level which reflects properties of the human mind and is common to both of the bilingual's languages because it is independent of language, and then the functionally different semantic – conceptual - lexical level. Perecman (1989) outlines a neurolinguistic model for language processing in bilinguals and then accounts for language variation. The model assumes a hierarchy of processing, at the top of which there is the conceptual level with shared processing of language independent information. Below that there are various linguistic strata – the lexical-semantic, the syntactic, the phonological and the phonetic articulatory levels. Perecman assumes that for monolinguals where the conceptual systems feeds into only one linguistic system, the processing routines from the conceptual down to the phonological forms have become automatized. For the bilingual and the trilingual speaker less routine can be expected: The conceptual level feeds into more than one linguistic system, and the distinction between levels of representation will be more marked (see also Dijkstra, and Franceschini et al., this volume). Perecman stipulates that multiple languages are unified in a single system at the prelinguistic conceptual level, that they are strongly linked at the lexical-

J. Cenoz, B. Hufeisen & U. Jessner (eds.), The Multilingual Lexicon, 27—43.
© *2003 Kluwer Academic Publishers. Printed in the Netherlands.*

semantic level, and that the links get progressively weaker as processing moves from the lexical-semantic to the articulatory-phonetic level. This may explain the observation frequently made that interference is more likely to occur at the conceptual-lexical level than at levels further down where the links between systems are weaker. The larger the number of linguistic systems at work the more interactions between the various levels of the system are to be expected. Hence, trilingual language processing is more complex than just the doubling of the interactions of a bilingual system. In a trilingual system one or two language systems may be dominant, thus offering the unique opportunity to observe two dominant and one weak system.

The transfer-appropriate-processing approach states that people are generally faster or more efficient in performing a task on a stimulus when there has been previous experience in performing the same task on the same stimulus. The approach applies specifically to memory processes. The degree of overlap between processes engaged during a first study exposure and those engaged during a second test exposure (Bransford, 1979). More recently, the framework has been extended to implicit memory phenomena (Blaxton, 1989; Graf & Ryan, 1990; Roediger & Blaxton, 1987; Roediger, Weldon & Challis, 1989; Srinivas, 1996).

Dissociations between explicit and implicit memory tests are now documented in memory research. Explicit memory tasks are those in which instructions are given to subjects to retrieve the items from the study episode. Standard examples of some explicit tasks are free recall, cued recall and recognition. In implicit memory tasks, subjects are simply asked to complete the tasks with the first solution that comes to mind, to identify speeded presentations of stimuli, or to respond as quickly as possible. For example, in an implicit memory task such as word fragment completion, subjects complete fragments of studied and non-studied items with the first solution that comes to mind. Explicit tasks such as free recall and recognition greatly benefit from conceptual elaboration of material compared to encoding that focuses on perceptual features. In contrast, in implicit tasks such as speeded word identification, word stem completion, and word fragment completion, this conceptual advantage is not obtained; priming on these implicit tests is usually equally facilitated following conceptual or perceptual encoding of the target word (Roediger et al., 1992). Roediger postulated that explicit memory tasks are conceptually driven whereas most implicit memory tasks depend on perceptual processes. Implicit memory tasks such as word fragment completion appear to be relatively insensitive to semantic elaboration at encoding (Srinivas & Roediger, 1990). But Weldon and Roedinger (1987) and Challis and Brodbeck (1992) show that word fragment completion is also subject to manipulations concerning the activation of concepts. In tasks like the word fragment completion task in absence of a biasing context, dominant alternatives of possible meanings are activated. In the case of trilingual persons the search strategies for fragment completion include the priority of finding words in the dominant language(s). Furthermore, Basden's et al. (1994) experiments yielded also support for a revised transfer-appropriate-processing framework involving three processes: conceptual processing, lexical access and perceptual overlap.

A study reported by Schönpflug (2000) dealt with the same problem employing the word fragment completion test method to explore the processes used for completing words in a trilingual context. The relationship between the first and the second and the first and the third and the second and the third language are seen as the results of developmental processes. According to Dufour and Kroll (1995) bilingual language competence is a development in the direction of an independent conceptual system for the two languages. Novices in a second language process semantic information through the semantic-conceptual store of their first language.

A recent study by Hamilton and Rajaram (2001) tested the concreteness effect on implicit and explicit memory tests. The rationale of introducing this variable is that concreteness effects indicate that conceptual processes are involved in word fragment completion.

On the other hand, concrete and abstract words have a different number of translation equivalents (Schönpflug, 2000). Concrete words tend to have one translation equivalent whereas abstract ones tend to have more than one. This is the case when translating German words into English and English words into German. Word completions may also be influenced by the number of translation equivalents as Schönpflug's study shows. The study finds differential uniqueness points (number of letters given when correct target word was found) for concrete and abstract words, words with either one or more than one translation equivalent, and long and short words in the subjects second and third language, German and English, respectively. Generally, concrete words have a later uniqueness point than abstract words, words with more than one translation have a later uniqueness point, and words from the third language, English, have a relatively later uniqueness point than words from the second language, German. The subject took more letters to correctly complete word fragments of short words as compared to long words.

3. THE PRESENT STUDY

This study aims at exploring the effects of second and third language active and passive competence on word fragment completions of words of either language. It may be hypothesized that

> H1: A trilingual speaker's active and passive competence in their second and third language have an effect on word fragment completions: The more competent the speakers are in their second and third language, the later their uniqueness points in word fragment completions in the respective language. The argument is based on decision theory: The more alternatives there are in the decision-making process the longer takes the process of finding the right alternative.
>
> H2: Trilingual speakers with greater competence in the second than the third language will reveal in their second language more conceptually driven word fragment completions than in their third language. Conceptually driven processing is indicated by effects of concreteness and number of translation equivalents on word fragment completions. The weaker the speaker's

competence of a language, the more s/he will tend to process word fragments in that language on a perceptual level.

H3: The number of incorrect word fragment completions in either the second or the third language will decrease with a speaker's competence in the respective language.

H4: Differential effects of either active or passive competence in the second or third language on word fragment completions are expected: Completions should depend more on active than passive language competence as in word-completion tasks words are "generated" by finding the correct endings of the words.

These hypotheses were tested in a study involving trilingual speakers' word-completions of a mixed list of English and German target words. The words were selected either concrete or abstract, and had one or more than one translation equivalent. The analyses to be presented complement the results of a previous study involving the same trilingual group of students and their word fragment completions.

3.1. Method

3.1.1. Sample
From a study of larger scope 21 trilingual students with Polish as their first, German as their second and English as their third language were selected as a homogeneous sample. The students were all born in Poland and had Polish passports, they had spent most of their life time in their home country (average 18 years). They studied cultural sciences at a binational University with one campus on the Polish and another on the German side of the Polish-German border. Half of the 21 students had previously spent on the average up to 8 years in Germany, the other half stayed all their life in Poland until they started their university studies. The average number of visits to an English-speaking country was 7.93 times; 50% of the 21 students had spent up to six years in an English speaking country. All students had learned German as their first (8-9 years) and English as their second foreign language (mostly 5-7 years) at school.

The trilinguals' self-rated competence in their second and third language in terms of the four aspects of language competence comprehension, reading, speaking and writing was on the average rated as 'good' (59%), 'very good' (28%) and 'like a native speaker' (13%) for German, whereas 52% assessed their competence in English as 'little', 31% as 'good', 14% as 'very good' and only 3% as 'like a native speaker'. When their mother tongue was excluded from the spectrum of choices, they preferred to spell and count in German rather than English.

3.1.2. Material and Procedure

Biographical Questionnaire. An English translation of the German biographical questionnaire is published in Schönpflug (2000). The questions covered sociodemographic information, the history of language learning, current language use, self-ratings of language use in various contexts and language use preferences.

Word fragment completion test. The word fragment completion test comprised 32 words (see Table 1) which had been selected from a word list of 256 English and German words previously calibrated for translations and number of translations given in a pretest study including 403 bilingual (English-German, German-English) and trilingual participants with English and German as two of their languages. The words were selected according to word frequency counts and concreteness ratings. They were all high-frequency words, occurring – in English – 100 and more times per million words (Thorndike & Lorge, 1957 for English words; Baschek et al., 1977 for German words). Concreteness ratings were taken from the Paivio et al. (1968) norms for English and the Baschek et al. (1977) norms for German words. Concrete words had concreteness ratings of 6 and higher, low concrete (abstract) words of full range from 3 and lower (full range from 1 to 7). Long and short words were distinguished for the Schönpflug (2000) study and are not of relevance here. There were 16 German and 16 English words. According to the pretest 16 had only one translation in the other language and 16 had more than 1 translation. Disregarding the long and short words each combination of word category and language had four examples.

Table 1. Word list for word fragment completion test

Type of Word	Language			
	German		English	
	Short	Long	Short	Long
Concrete/ 1 Translation	Harfe Buch	Bleistift Kartoffel	harp book	potato bottle
Concrete/ >1 Translation	Vieh Puppe	Fahrkarte Schlinge	bowl flag	streamer ticket
Abstract/ 1 Translation	Stolz Tod	Wahrheit Notwendigkeit	thought truth	advantage freedom
Abstract/ >1 Translation	Tugend Anschein	Ehrfurcht Vertrauen	awe anger	confidence virtue

Procedure. The subjects first answered the biographical questionnaire. Then they completed the list of 254 abstract and concrete English and German nouns by giving as many translation equivalents (German to English; English to German) as they could think of for each word. After this procedure was finished they were given the word-completion test.

The 32 word fragments, presented in a random order, changing for each subject, were given first with their initial letter and a blank marked for each of the following letters (P_ _ _ _ for PUPPE). The participants were asked to fill in the remaining letters of the word they had in mind that would meet the requirement of the final number of letters given by the blanks. They were told that it could be either a German or an English word. If their first choice was not correct, a second letter was given, e.g. PU_ _ _, and they were asked again to complete the word. The correct letters were provided one by one until the last but one letter was given. If the subjects did not complete the word until this stage a failure was recorded. Each new letter added to the previous ones was presented in a separate line with neither previous nor subsequent lines visible. The presentation of each line was self-paced but interrupted after one minute. If completion was not achieved within this time limit, the participants were advised to start with the next line. At the end of each word test, marked blanks equivalent to the word length were provided to give some idea of what alternative words the students might have in mind (e.g. angel/anger/Angel/Anger). The uniqueness point of the word completions was the critical dependent variable. Uniqueness point is the number of given letters necessary to complete the word correctly divided by the total number of letters in the word. Errors, i.e. the number of incorrectly completed words, divided by 32, were also recorded.

3.2. Results

3.2.1. Aspects of L2 and L3 competence

Self-rated language competence. The subjects' self-rated language competence in their second language (German) was superior to the third language (English). Table 2 gives the means, standard deviations and the results of the tests for significance of mean differences for the various measures assessed..

Table 2. *Mean self-ratings (M) and standard deviations (SD) of trilingual students' self-ratings of language competence in their second (German) and third (English) language*

	Language	
Competence Domain	German (L2) M (SD)	English (L3) M (SD)
Speaking	2.39 (0.70)	1.61 (0.70)***
Writing	2.44 (0.62)	1.50 (0.51)***
Comprehension	2.83 (0.71)	2.22 (0.73)**
Reading	2.72 (0.67)	2.06 (0.73)***
Active[1]	2.42 (0.60)	1.56 (0.48)***
Passive[2]	2.78 (0.60)	2.14 (0.70)***

** Significant mean difference at p <. 01
*** Significant mean difference at p<. 001
[1] Average of speaking and writing values.
[2] Average of comprehension and reading values.

Significant differences between the two languages were observed in all aspects of L2 and L3 competence. Thus, the observed L2 dominance was general (see also Gibson & Hufeisen, this volume). Self-ratings of passive competence (comprehension and reading) were higher than of active competence (speaking and writing) (t = 6.64; df = 20; p<.00) for the difference between active and passive German competence and t = 6.38, df = 20, p<.00 for active and passive English competence, respectively). The active competencies showed greater discrepancies between the two languages than the passive competencies. Furthermore, a distinct characteristic of the third language is its greater discrepancy between self-rated active and passive language competence as compared to the trilinguals' second language.

The correlations between the two main aspects of language competence, active and passive knowledge, were very high, also across languages as Table 3 reveals.

Table 3. Pearson r bivariate correlations of active and passive language competence in the trilingual speakers second (German) and third (English) language

Language Competence	Passive English	Active German	Passive German
Active English	.80	.63	.87
Passive English		.73	.76
Active German			.80

The least similarity between a trilingual speaker's second and third language is on the level of active competence (r = .63). The other correlation coefficients are quite high indicating that those trilinguals who have high second language competence also think they have relatively high third language competence. Active and passive knowledge within one language are highly associated within the second as well as the third language. This result does not contradict the greater discrepancy of the means of active and passive competence observed for L3. A high correlation coefficient does not inform about the absolute level of the values of the variables involved.

Number of years spent in L1, L2 or L3 countries and language preferences / language competence. Number of years spent in home country where the first language or mother tongue was spoken was not significantly related to speaking, writing, reading or listening preferences of the Polish mother tongue. Number of years spent in Germany, however, was positively associated with preference of writing in Polish (*r* = .56; p<.01) and negatively with preference of writing in German (*r* = -.55; p<.01). Number of years spent in an English speaking country was negatively related to preference of reading in English.

Number of years spent in Poland correlated negatively with all measures of self-rated German and English language competence: significant negative correlations were found between number of years spent in Poland and speaking competence in German (*r* = -.44; p<.05), writing competence in German (*r* = -.49; p<.05) and competence to understand while listening in English (r = -. 43). Number of years spent in Poland seems to affect active knowledge of L2 and L3 more than passive knowledge in both foreign languages (r = -.46; p<.05 for active German competence and r = -.44; p<.05 for active English competence). The respective correlations with passive L2 and L3 competence was not significant. These results indicate that staying in mother tongue contexts impairs foreign language competence, especially active competence. On the other hand, staying in an L2 country enhances speaking and reading competence in L2 (i.e. German) (r = .49; p<.05 and r = .55; p<.05, respectively). Number of years spent in an English speaking (L3) country did not relate to English competence.

3.2.2. Uniqueness points and type of words
In four univariate analyses of variance with one aspect of language competence (active knowledge of English, passive knowledge of English, active knowledge of German, passive knowledge of German) as the independent grouping factor (dichotomised, high and low groups, respectively) and three within-subject-factors: 'language' (English vs. German), 'concreteness' (concrete vs. abstract) and 'number of translation equivalents' (1 vs. >1 translation) were performed. The results of the four analyses of variances are included in Table 4 and significant higher order interactions are depicted in Figures 1, 2, 3, respectively. Table 4 reveals that a main effect of language competence was only found for active German (L2) competence. High active knowledge of German led to a later uniqueness point for the word types differing in language and number of translation equivalents: ($M_{low active German competence}$ = .40; $M_{high active German competence}$ = .45). This is one conformation for hypothesis 1 as far as L2 is concerned. For number of translation equivalents main effects were observed for all four types of language competences: for active German competence $M_{1 translation}$ = .40; $M_{>1 translation}$ = .47; for passive German competence $M_{1 translation}$ = .41; $M_{>1 translation}$ = .43; for active English competence $M_{1 translation}$ = .41; $M_{>1 translation}$ = .45; for passive English competence $M_{1 translation}$ = .41; $M_{>1 translation}$ = .43. These main effects and the first order interactions (Language x Number of Translation Equivalents and Language x Concreteness) have to be related to the higher order interactions involving the terms given. These are for active and passive L3 competence the Language Competence x Language x Number of Translation Equivalents and for active L2 competence the Language Competence x Number of Translation Equivalents x Concreteness. The means of these triple interactions are depicted in Figures 1, 2, and 3.

Figure 1 reveals that high competence of active English as compared to low competence has later uniqueness points for English and German words with 1 or greater than 1 translation equivalents. Hypothesis 1 is thus corroborated for L3 as well. Low active competence of English, however, leads to earlier uniqueness points for only English words and words with more than one translation equivalent.

High and low passive knowledge of English have the same effects as reported for active competence of English. The similarity is not surprising as the correlations between these two measures is very high (Pearson r = .80). The common results require some further thoughts. It seems that the better the trilinguals' competence in their third language English, the more letters they need to recognize the word hidden in the word fragments. Competence in the third language may lead to the activation and competition of more alternatives for possible solutions, so that trilinguals need more information (letters) to decide which of the alternatives is a match to the target word. Low competence leads to the activation of fewer alternatives, and therefore, earlier word fragment completion. This is plausible as long as the words analysed are only the correctly completed ones. The false solutions will be presented and commented later.

Table 4. Results of the analyses of variances of the uniqueness point in word fragment-completion (correct completions)

Factor	German (L2) Competence				English (L3) Competence			
	Active		Passive		Active		Passive	
	F-value[1]	Effect size[2]	F-Value	Effect size	F-value	Effect size	F-value	Effect size
LC	3,90	0,17						
N	4,96	0,21	5,92	0,24	4,79	0,20	5,46	0,22
L x N			4,90	0,21				
L x C	3,96	0,17			3,86	0,19	5,25	0,22
LC x L x N					3,71	0,16	5,04	0,21
LC x N x C	4,44	0,19						

[1] *Only significant effects below p < .06 are reported.*
[2] *Effect sizes are presented because of the relatively small number of subjects. The values are Eta^2, i.e. multiplied with 100 they represent the percentage of variance explained by the factor given.*
LC = Language Competence; L = Language of words; N = Number of Translation Equivalents of words; C = Concreteness of words

Active knowledge of the second language German, however, shows a different pattern of influence on types of words (see Figure 3). Again, high competence in active German leads to a generally later uniqueness point than low active competence, but there is one word category that is an exception: concrete words with 1 translation equivalent. They have a slightly earlier uniqueness point when word fragments are completed by highly competent speakers and writers of German than when students had lower active German competence. With both high and low competence groups of subjects, the abstract words with more than one translation equivalent were processed fastest.

Hypothesis 2 predicted that when L2 is dominant over L3, L2 word fragment completions are more concept driven in L2 as compared to L3 completions. As the Language Competence x Number of Translations x Concreteness interaction is only significant for active German competence, this interaction confirms hypothesis 2. But the hypothesis has to be reformulated in a more narrow way: Active L2 competence is predominantly concept driven.

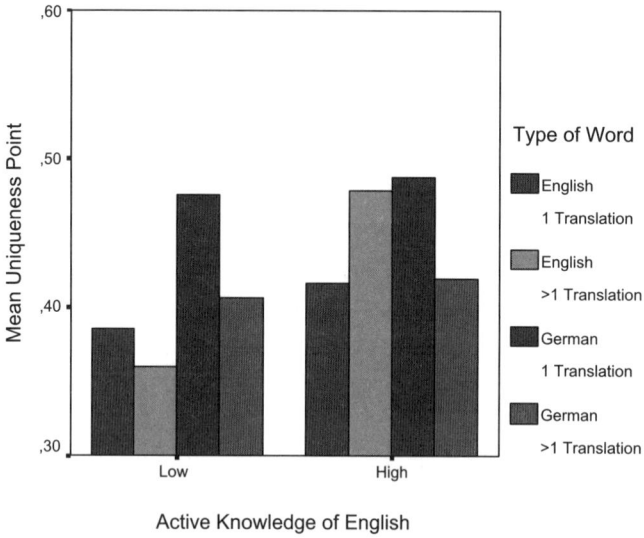

Figure 1 The influence of active competence of English and type of words on the uniqueness point in word fragment completion (correctly completed word fragments)

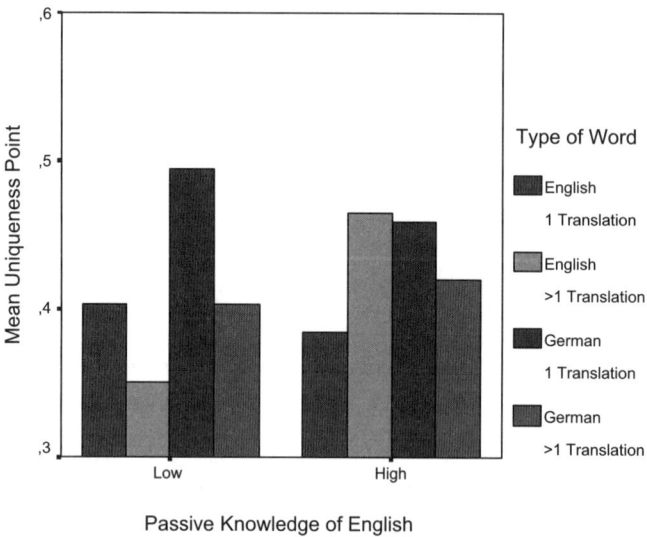

Figure 2 The influence of passive competence of English and type of words on the uniqueness point in word fragment completion (only correctly completed fragments)

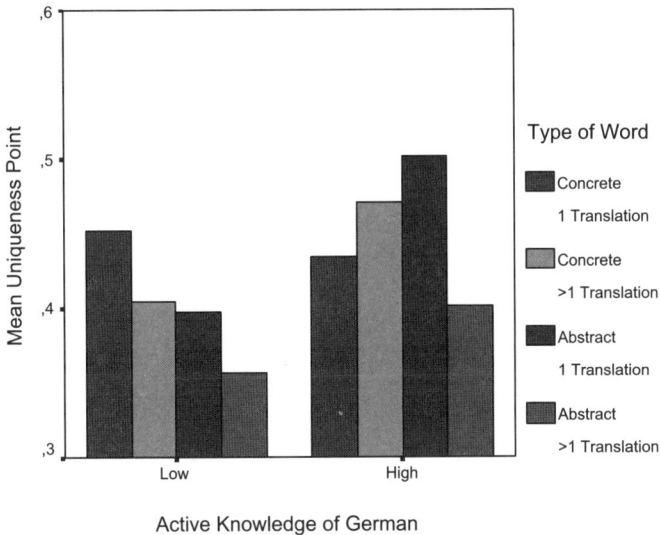

Figure 3 The influence of active competence of German and type of words on the uniqueness point in word fragment completion (only correctly completed fragments).

Hypothesis 4 says that word fragments are better completed by persons with higher active competence than passive competence in that language. This predicted result was not found. Uniqueness points of active and passive competence within L2 and L3 are close together ($M_{active\ German} = .43$, $M_{passive\ German} = .41$; $M_{active\ English} = .39$, $M_{passive\ English} = .38$), although there were slightly higher uniqueness points for the active language competence groups, these differences were not significant.

3.2.3. Mean error rate of word completions

The incorrectly completed words for each word category and the two (low and high) language competence groups were analysed equivalent to the uniqueness points. Table 5 gives an overview of all the significant effects for the four univariate analyses of variance with repeated measures including low and high active/passive language competence as between group factor and language, concreteness and number of translation equivalents as within-group factors. Language competence alone did not yield any main effect no matter what language and whether active or passive competence was under consideration. Language and number of translation equivalents seem to be decisive factors for the error rate, however; for number of translations: $M_{1\ translation}$ = .17; $M_{>1\ translation}$ = .34; for language: M_{German} = .19; $M_{English}$ = .32.

Furthermore, the simple interaction between the two factors is significant for three of the four competence groups, whereas the Number of Translations x Concreteness interaction is significant for all four language competence groups.

Table 5. Results of the analyses of variances of the mean error rate in word fragment-completion as dependent on language competence

Factor	German (L2) Competence				English (L3) Competence			
	Active		Passive		Active		Passive	
	F-value[1]	Effect size[2]	F-Value	Effect Size	F-value	Effect Size	F-value	Effect Size
L	9,38	0,33	10,17	0,37	7,91	0,29	10,68	0,36
N	40,42	0,68	46,56	0,71	38,31	0,67	42,20	0,69
L x N	5,95	0,24	5,27	0,21	4,54	0,19		
L x C	4,62	0,20					4,50	0,19
N x C	7,69	0,29	5,38	0,22	8,70	0,31	6,50	0,26
L x C x N			7,29	0,28	5,47	0,22	7,36	0,78
LC x L x N	7,70	0,29			5,13	0,21	10,62	0,36
LCx L x C x N							5,09	0,21

[1] *Only significant effects below p < .06 are reported.*
[2] *Effect sizes are presented because of the relatively small number of subjects. The values are Eta², i.e. multiplied with 100 they represent the percent of variance explained by the factor given.*
LC = Language Competence; L = Language of words; N = Number of Translation Equivalents of words; C = Concreteness of words

But as there are also significant higher order interactions the interpretation has to be based on these. For reasons of comparability with the analyses involving uniqueness points the Language Competence x Language x Number of Translation Equivalents are in the focus of interest. It is significant for three of the four language competence groups; it is not significant when passive knowledge of German (L2) is the between-group factor.

The three significant triple interactions are depicted in figures 4, 5, and 6. The error rate for English words with >1 translation equivalent is the highest of all word types. This is evident for three of the four language competence groups.

The error rate for German words with 1 translation equivalent is also higher for low competent active and passive speakers of German as a second language.

There is no significant interaction or main effect involving passive knowledge of German. The highest order interaction is a Language x Concreteness x Number of Translations effect. It indicates that the mistakes made in word fragment completions by trilinguals with high passive knowledge in their second language are concept driven: In their second and third language mistakes in word fragment completions depend on concreteness and number of translation equivalents of the target words.

The quadruple interaction for passive knowledge of English will not be commented in this context. It indicates that errors made by low and high passive English (L3) competent persons are subject to all other factors involved in this analysis: language, concreteness and number of translations of words to be completed.

The fourth hypothesis suggests that word fragment completions are more successful when the active knowledge of a language than when passive competence is given. This hypothesis was not confirmed by significant results: Uniqueness points were similar for active and passive German and English competence: M = .43, M = .42, M = .43, M = .42 , respectively. Active competence also tends to decrease the error rate slightly but not significantly so as compared to passive competence in both languages: M = .25, M = .26, M = .25, M = .25, respectively.

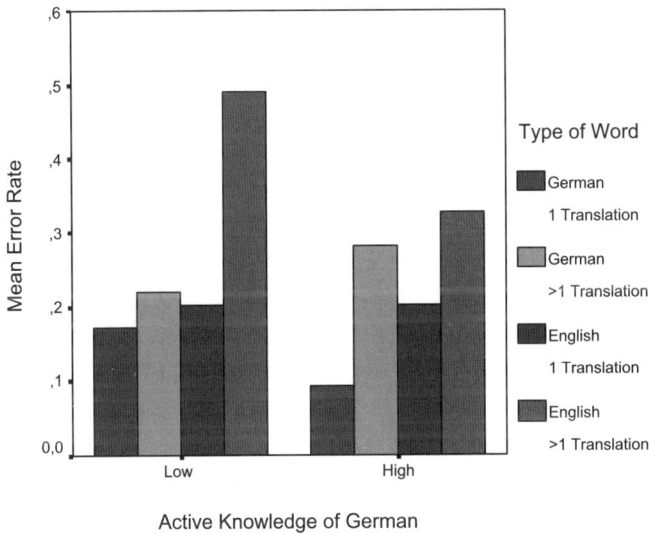

Figure 4 The influence of active competence of German and type of words on the error rate in word fragment completions

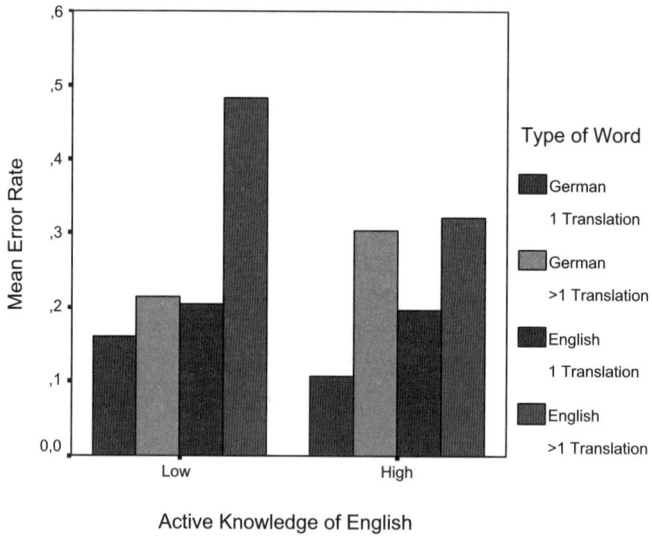

Figure 5 The influence of active competence of English and type of words on the error rate in word fragment completions

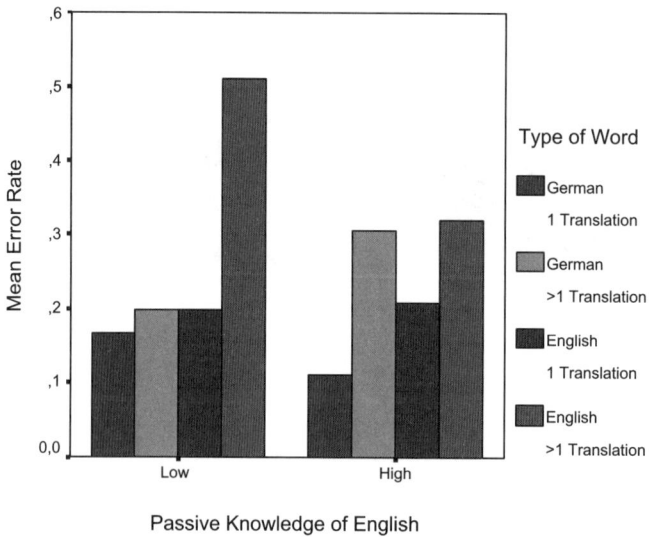

Figure 6 The influence of passive competence of English and type of words on the error rate in word fragment completions

4. DISCUSSION

The research on word fragment completions provides a method that helps to clarify various issues in multilingual word processing (see also Dijkstra, and Franceschini et al., this volume). Word fragment completions indicate the importance of data-driven processing as opposed to concept-driven processing and what roles formal parts of the word play in order to identify the correct target word. Word fragment completions are part of language production achievements, but still seem to be ruled by implicit and data driven language processing. However, as Schönpflug (2000) was able to show, they are also concept driven as they are affected by the number of translation equivalents the target words have with regard to another language involved and by their concreteness. As may be concluded from Dufour and Kroll (1995) language processing in the second language should be more concept driven than in the third language. This conclusion, however, is only warranted when the trilingual speaker has a dominant second language over the third.

The trilingual Polish university students included in our study characterize themselves as more competent in their second language than in their third. However, the four self-ratings of either active or passive knowledge of German and English are highly correlated. Thus, according to the self-ratings of the trilingual students, foreign language competence is a common factor that expresses itself in the second and third language alike. In the third language, however, the discrepancy between passive and active competence is evaluated as being greater than in the second language.

The results obtained in the word fragment completion tasks used in this study indicate that self-rated active and passive knowledge of the second and the third language differentially influences speed with which word fragments are completed correctly. Speed is measured in terms of the number of letters necessary to find the correct target word *(uniqueness point)*. Active and passive knowledge within the second or third language yield similar results in terms of correct word fragment completions and error rates, because they are highly correlated. Across languages the results are different for high and low active and passive competence in their second and third language. Trilingual speakers with high competence in their second language have later uniqueness points irrespective of language and active and passive competence. This is also observed for the third language. Thus, the first hypothesis was corroborated. The higher a speaker's competence, irrespective of whether active or passive, the more information s/he needs to complete the words correctly (see, however, Dijkstra, this volume). As competent persons have a larger lexicon, they need more information to choose the right alternative. This global result has to be looked at differentially, however. Types of words (German/English) and 1 or more than 1 translation equivalent do not matter for the group with a high self-rated competence of English (L3), but it does matter for those with low competence. English (L3) words are earlier recognized than German (L2) ones. Also this confirms the first hypothesis as L2 dominant speakers have more alternatives in their better foreign language and, therefore, need more information to discriminate between the activated alternatives.

Words with more than 1 translation equivalent tend to have earlier uniqueness points than those with just 1 translation equivalent. This raises the question in what way the number of translation equivalents enhances the discrimination between the possible completions at a smaller size of the fragment given. One may argue that the higher number of translation equivalents of a word helps to decide at an earlier point whether the fragment presented could be either a German or an English word. This cuts down the number of possible alternatives for word fragment completion decisively.

According to hypothesis 2 either number of translation equivalents or concreteness or both indicate conceptually driven processing. Dufour and Kroll (1995) claim that progress in language competence is characterized by conceptual processing. Hence, the dominant second language should be processed conceptually whereas the non-dominant third language should be processed in a data-driven mode. The results corroborate the second hypothesis. Concreteness and number of translation equivalents together tend to significantly determine active competence of the second language German, but none of the other active or passive competencies. Number of translation equivalents makes a strong contribution to all language competencies alike: active and passive German and English.

Only for high and low active German competence, competence makes a difference for word fragment completions of concrete or abstract nouns and nouns with 1 or more than 1 translation, but language of the words does not matter. This seems to partly confirm the fourth hypothesis claiming that active more than passive language competence enhances word completions. Word fragment completions are 'generating' tasks which require an activated representation of the lexicon. But, abstract words with more than 1 translation are processed earlier by the low as compared to the high active competence group. This was also observed for two other word categories: concrete with more than 1 translation and abstract with 1 translation but not for concrete words with one 1 translation, here the reverse relationship is found.

This diverse spectrum of results shows that active or passive language competence alone is not a decisive factor for the correct solutions of the task chosen. A direct test of comparisons of the mean uniqueness points for active and passive competence of L2 and L3 did also not corroborate hypothesis 2. Furthermore, the language of the words alone or in interaction with the second or third language competence does not explain correct word fragment completions. Rather, conceptual features of the words like concreteness and number of translation equivalents play at least an equally decisive role in correct word completions and error rates but more so for the stronger second than the weaker third language.

Those word categories that have the earliest uniqueness point tend to have the highest error rate, the most prominent example are English words with more than 1 translation for the low German and English competence groups. In general, however, low competence groups do not have the highest error rates neither in the language the competence is measured in nor in the other foreign language of the trilingual speakers. Errors depend on concreteness and number of translation equivalents as much as on the language of the words and language competence. This means that the third hypothesis does not reflect the complicated interactions observed. Errors seem to depend on all the factors considered here.

The differential results for low vs. high competence in the second and third language may not be attributed to an automatization efficiency. Low competent subjects accumulate a set of organized procedures for word fragment completions that lead to less extensive target feature analysis. For a more unfamiliar language those specialised procedures are lacking. There will be relatively more perceptual implicit processing in the weaker third language and less conceptual processing than in the stronger second language. A higher probability of errors is to be expected but was, indeed, not observed.

Fewer errors and an earlier uniqueness point were observed for words with more than one translation equivalent. With the data available this cannot be explained in a conclusive way. One possible explanation looks at this finding from a cross-linguistic semantic network perspective: The more links of the cross-linguistic network of translation equivalents are activated the more alternative possible solutions are part of the process of finding the correct target word.

5. SUMMARY

The transfer-appropriate-processing framework looks at advantages in processing from study trials to test trials through similarities in subprocessing. The study trial in this investigation was searching for translation equivalents of German and English words in the respective other language. In the test trial subjects knew that the word fragment to be finished could be either a German or an English word. With this openness with regard to language of the target word a greater number of translation equivalents is activated and are highly functional to find a correct solution. The number of translation effect dominated over all other factors. Bilingual study and test contexts of the second and the third language, therefore, activate simultaneously both lexica and the connections between the two as represented by the possible translations. But obviously in this processing the first, strongest, language was not involved as there were no intrusions or interferences reported or observed. To conclude: The research on word completions reveals that the organization of the trilinguals' lexica depends as much on conceptual features of words in the lexica as on the speakers' language competence. The language of the target words, i.e. the second or the third language of a trilingual speaker, is only relevant for word fragment completions in interaction with conceptual features as far as speed of completion is concerned. There are more errors in the third than in the second language, however. High self-rated language competence either in the second or in the third language has an effect on performance in the second and the third language.

University of Halle (Germany)

ULRIKE JESSNER

THE NATURE OF CROSS-LINGUISTIC INTERACTION IN THE MULTILINGUAL SYSTEM

1. INTRODUCTION

This chapter is intended to offer new perspectives on the characteristic features of transfer phenomena occurring when three languages are in contact. Cross-linguistic influence in multilinguals – in contrast to second language learners – has turned out to be characterised by certain features as recent research on speech production in third language acquisition (henceforth TLA) and trilingualism has shown. This chapter suggests that there are other aspects, which are linked to research on individual variability in multilingual proficiency due to changes in language use, involved in the contact between the language systems that should be taken into consideration.

2. CROSS-LINGUISTIC CONTACT IN BI- AND TRILINGUAL SYSTEMS

Cross-linguistic influence (henceforth CLI) coined by Kellerman and Sharwood Smith in 1986 has been the common term used for "phenomena such as 'transfer', 'interference', 'avoidance', 'borrowing', and L2-related aspects of language loss" (Sharwood-Smith and Kellerman, 1986: 1). This concept is predominantly related with studies of second language acquisition (henceforth SLA). Obviously cross-linguistic aspects also form an important part of the topics discussed in studies of TLA and trilingualism. But in contrast to SLA and bilingualism where we have two systems influencing each other and where over the years it has been made clear that we should note a bidirectional relationship of a multifaceted nature (see Kellerman 1995), in TLA we have two more relationships to investigate, that is the influence of L1 on L2, L1 on L3, L2 on L1, L2 on L3 and L3 on L1 (see also Cenoz and Gibson & Hufeisen, this volume).

2.1. Two Languages in Contact

The vast literature on the various contact phenomena between two languages ranges from studies discussing transfer and interference in SLA research (e.g. Odlin, 1989; Gass and Selinker, 1992) to code-switching and related phenomena in studies on

45

J. Cenoz, B. Hufesien & U. Jessner (eds.), The Multilingual Lexicon, 45—55.
© 2003 *Kluwer Academic Publishers. Printed in the Netherlands.*

bilingualism (e.g. Jacobson, 1990; Milroy and Muysken, 1995). The difference in research goals which did not exist in the early days of work on transfer, as a look at Weinreich (1953) shows, is strongly related to the acquisition – learning dichotomy and the definition of bilingualism based upon.

A look at the history of research in SLA studies also makes clear that transfer is a much more diversified phenomenon as originally expected in early studies of contrastive analysis where the mainly negative influence of the L1 on the L2 formed the dominant object of investigation. Nowadays it is well-known that transfer studies in SLA research also concentrate on the effects that the L2 shows on the L1 and that these effects include various phenomena as described in Cook (in press). Furthermore Kellerman (1995) has pointed out that there are cases where the L1 can influence the L2 at a level where cognition and language touch and that these cases may be beyond individual awareness.

2.2. Three Languages in Contact

Although for many SLA researchers the contact between two languages is taken to include more than two languages (Perdue, 1993: 48) over the last decade an increasing group of linguists have begun to look beyond SLA and concentrate on the contact between three languages to find out about the differences in quality between SLA and TLA (e.g. Cenoz, Hufeisen and Jessner, 2001a and b). It is important to note here that the study of TLA is methodologically based on studies on SLA and bilingualism, that is research on TLA combines two fields of investigation which hitherto have ignored each other in many respects.

As already pointed out above the relationship between three languages presents a much more diversified issue than the contact between two languages. Williams and Hammarberg (1998) and Hammarberg (2001) present several criteria which they consider influential in the relationship between the languages in L3 production and acquisition: typological similarity (see also Cenoz, this volume), cultural similarity, proficiency, recency of use and the status of L2 in TLA studies.

The role of L2 in TLA has turned out to be of greater importance than originally suggested and several attempts have been made to discuss this issue. De Angelis and Selinker (2001) have defined interlanguage transfer as the influence from a non-native language on another non-native language, that is the influence from L2 on L3 and vice versa, and introduced it into the multilingualism discussion. They note that language transfer theory cannot be comprehensive if its principles are based on two languages only (see also Cusack, 1993 and 2000). In his analysis of inventions produced by French L3 speakers, Dewaele (1998) also shows that the speakers relied more on their English as their L2 whereas French L2 speakers relied more on their L1. Ringbom (2001) focuses on the differences in form and meaning and finds that the transfer of form is more common across related languages whereas the transfer of semantic patterns and word combinations is nearly always based on the L1. His studies of the types of transfer produced by Finnish students in their L3, English, show that L2-transfer, in this case from Swedish, on L3-production is clearly manifested in the lexicon.

2.3. Other Evidence

At the same time we have to take a phenomenon into consideration which was termed "The Paradox of Transfer" (Herdina and Jessner, 1994). This concerns conflicting evidence which first was identified by Peal & Lambert (1962) who found out that bilingual children not only outperformed their monolingual counterparts in linguistic tasks but also showed cognitive advantages and concluded that this evidence of a kind of positive transfer taking place between the bilingual's two languages facilitates the development of verbal intelligence. Thus this phenomenon does not only refer to linguistic competence but seems to affect cognitive skills as well (see also Baker, 2001: 140-142).

In Herdina and Jessner (2002: 26-27) it is therefore argued that the paradox of transfer "is attributed to two factors: (1) a terminological confusion concerning the type of phenomena to be classified as transfer phenomena and (2) a theoretical confusion relating to the nature of transfer phenomena, which cannot be restricted to specific modules." It is furthermore stated that transfer is of an intermodular nature and that a large number of transfer phenomena are not transfer phenomena at all but are to be attributed to cross-linguistic interaction as discussed later in this chapter (compare the discussion of shades of meaning attributed to language transfer as described by Dechert and Raupach, 1989b: xi-xii).

Cummins' Interdependence Hypothesis based on the assumption of a common underlying proficiency (e.g. 1991) has to be seen in relation to the paradox of transfer as was found in the seminal Peal & Lambert study. His investigation into the influence of L2 on L1 in academic tasks shows that children transfer academic knowledge from L2 learning contexts to their L1. Similarly, in their recent publication on the multifaceted relationship between L1 and L2 Kecskes and Papp (2000) relate the results of their studies to a common underlying conceptual base linking the constantly available systems which make up the multilingual language processing device to explain the positive influence of foreign language learning on the L1 and vice versa as they point out. The processes as described in their and Cummins' studies can be interpreted as cross-lingual transfer phenomena and it is also these processes that contribute to our understanding of cross-linguistic interaction in multilinguals as postulated in the dynamic model of multilingualism (Herdina and Jessner, 2002).

3. CLIN: A DYNAMIC SYSTEMS APPROACH TO CROSS-LINGUISTIC INTERACTION

In dynamic systems theory which has been studied and applied in other sciences such as meterology, physics, mathematics and economics for some decades and has become widely known as chaos theory, the focus is on the development of systems in time and the interaction of the systems involved as pointed out by Van Geert in the following:

"A system [...] is more than just a collection of variables or observables we have
isolated from the rest of the world. It is a system primarily because the variables
mutually interact. That is, each variable affects all the other variables contained in the
system, and thus also affects itself. This is a property we may call complete
connectedness and it is the default property of any system. The principal distinctive
property - compared to a constant - is that it changes over time. Consequently, mutual
interaction among variables implies that they influence and co-determine each other's
changes over time. In this sense, a system is, by definition, a dynamic system and so we
define a dynamic system as a set of variables that mutually affect each other's changes
over time" (Van Geert, 1994: 50).

One of the advantages that dynamic systems theory offers are rich metaphors
which can be used in order to understand the complexity of the issues involved.
Researchers working with this approach have mainly tried to predict and model the
activity of time-dependent changes in a system and in order to find out about the
lawfulness in the phenomena, patterns of complex systems are studied and the
responsibility for stability and instability and the nature of structural reorganisation
are attempted to be analysed. In contrast to what reductionist views offer most
biological and many physical systems are irregular, discontinuous and
inhomogeneous and we have adopted this idea for multilingual systems.

In a dynamic model of multilingualism (henceforth DMM) we are not concerned
with languages as systems (L1, L2, L3, etc.) but with the language systems (LS_1,
LS_2, LS_3, etc.) forming part of the psycholinguistic system of the multilingual
speaker. Based on dynamic systems theory we wish to characterise language
development in multilingual systems as a non-linear, reversible and complex process
where the development of the individual language systems is dependent on the
interaction of the pre-existing systems and those systems in development. And it is
only in the understanding of the dynamics of the multilingual system that
multilingual phenomena can adequately be understood.

DMM takes a holistic approach to multilingualism. It is assumed that
multilinguals cannot be measured by monolingual standards and that
multilingualism cannot simply be explained by extended monolingual acquisition
models. Furthermore it is claimed that the language systems within the
psycholinguistic system can be seen as separate systems as often perceived by the
multilingual speaker her/himself who nevertheless often has problems keeping the
systems apart (see also Singleton, 1996). In DMM the multilingual system is not the
product of adding two or more language systems but a complex system with its own
parameters, which are exclusive to the multilingual speaker, that is they are not to be
found in the monolingual speaker or the bilingual speaker (see, however, Dijkstra,
this volume).

In DMM we recognise transfer phenomena as significant features in multilingual
systems. The existence of transfer phenomena in multilingual speakers in addition to
the attempts to suppress the contact between the systems in a monolingual
environment (see also Grosjean, 2001) or the conscious employment of transfer
strategies in language learning constitute prime objects of multilingual investigation.
We would like to suggest that transfer phenomena should be researched as a
coherent set of linguistic phenomena since this methodological separation is
considered a hindrance in studies of multilingual phenomena where a systematic

differentiation is definitely needed. Recently the discussions of codeswitching in the classroom have made this issue become even more apparent. For instance, Lüdi (1996: 242) points out that code-switching can occur in language learners and compensatory strategies can also be found in competent mono- and bilingual speakers.

We have therefore also argued that the interaction phenomena occuring in L3-production should be viewed from a multilingual standpoint (Jessner and Herdina, 1996) and that phenomena of transfer, interference mostly studied in SLA studies and mixing phenomena including code-switching and borrowing mostly studied in bilingualism research should be discussed within a common framework. We argue that such a framework could be offered by DMM which focuses on developed and developing systems, that is systems in different stages of development, and thus provides a bridge between SLA and bilingualism research.

In DMM the concept of cross-linguistic interaction (henceforth CLIN), resulting from the interaction of two or more language systems, can be taken to include not only transfer and interference but also codeswitching and borrowing phenomena and is thus reserved as an umbrella term for all the existing transfer phenomena. And it is not only in this sense that CLIN is a wider concept than that of CLI. CLIN is also intended to cover another set of phenomena such as non-predictable dynamic effects which determine the development of the systems themselves and are particularly observable in multilingualism. Such influences can be interpreted as synergetic and interferential ones. Thus CLIN is not just a category to be added to the existing transfer phenomena but constitutes a significant factor representing the non-reducible dynamic aspect of the multilingual system.

According to a dynamic systems approach we have to view the hypotheses by Cummins and Kecskes and Papp as described above in a slightly different way. Whereas both suggestions describe a kind of overlap between the two language systems, we would rather see the two languages as two liquids, which, when mixed, acquire properties that neither of the liquids had. To use a metaphor one could say that the product is not grey as imagined when you mix the colours of white and black but rather a shade of pink. So these new properties constitute a complete metamorphosis of the substances involved and not merely an overlap between two subsystems.

Furthermore the interaction between three language systems results in different abilities and skills that the learners develop. For instance due to their prior language learning experience L3-learners develop an enhanced level of metalinguistic awareness and metacognitive strategies which considerably contribute to the quality of CLIN taking place in TLA. Thus CLIN is seen as qualitatively and quantitatively different from the concept of CLI. In DMM the concept of multilingual proficiency is defined as the various language systems in contact (LS_1, LS_2, LS_3 etc.), their interaction as expressed in CLIN and the influence that the development of a multilingual system shows on the learner and the learning process. That is, the learner develops skills and qualities that cannot be found in an unexperienced learner. This change of quality in language learning is thus seen in connection with the catalytic effects of third language learning. It should be noted that we have chosen to talk about multilingual proficiency and not multicompetence as suggested by Cook (e.g. 1993), who bases his assumptions on Grosjean's work (e.g. 1985), since the concept of multicompetence does not include a dynamic component focusing on the interaction between the language systems - which is essential in a holistic approach as described in DMM.

4. CLIN IN TRILINGUAL SUBJECTS

In the following some selective data from a study with trilingual learners, that is German/Italian bilinguals studying English at Innsbruck University, will be presented. In the analysis of the data an attempt will be made to identify some of the qualities developed in the multilingual subject which are seen as contributing to the change of quality in language learning in learners with prior language knowledge. This is also to relate the ideas on CLIN, as presented in this chapter, to the empirical investigation of trilingual subjects.

4.1. Method and Data Collection

The research method of this qualitative study that was chosen in order to get access to the mental activities of the students during text production in their third language is an introspection study in the form of thinking-aloud protocols, i.e. the testees were asked to formulate loudly all their thoughts during the writing performance without the use of a dictionary. The thoughts were then tape-recorded, transcribed and analysed. The structure of this investigation is based on Cumming's doctoral dissertation on academic writing in a second language (1988) where he researched into the behaviour of the students during writing a letter, a summary and an essay. Before completing the three tasks for which they were allowed 90 minutes each the respondents were introduced by the author to verbal thinking for about 15 minutes following the suggestions by Ericsson and Simon (1984). The language chosen for this introduction was English.

4.1.1. Participants
The participants of the study were 14 bilingual students from South Tyrol studying English at Innsbruck University. The subjects were chosen according to their linguistic background as members of bilingual families so that they can be described as ambilingual balanced bilinguals, as defined in Herdina and Jessner (2002: 119), with a high level of proficiency in English, that is when the data were taken they had been in contact with English for at least eight years. The fact that they were university students of English guaranteed for a fairly high level of proficiency in the third language as well. On the scale of the Common European Frame of Reference they could be identified as B2 with regard to all the skills described. Their proficiency level in English was lower than their levels in their first languages though. When students from South Tyrol start with their university studies they usually have been in contact with English for 5 years. Information on the language biography of the participants was backed up by a questionnaire.

4.1.2. Pilot Study
A pilot study had also been carried out with a trilingual student from Carinthia in Austria who grew up with Italian and German in the family. In contrast to the students from South Tyrol at the time of the study he had studied English for eight years at school. Results of this study were presented in Jessner (1999; 2000). Example 2 and 3 of the data presented here are taken from that study.

4.1.3. Hypothesis
The data discussed in this introspection study are supposed to give evidence of the metalinguistic thinking involving the usage of all three, typologically closely related languages in the process of writing an essay, a summary and a letter in English (for typological closeness and distance, see also Cenoz, this volume). The data are supposed to show how the candidates search for and assess improved phrasing and how they compare cross-linguistic equivalents and thus give evidence of the connections that are created between the linguistic systems L1, L2 and L3 forming part of the multilingual students' psycholinguistic systems. These cognitive processes could point to a common underlying proficiency (Cummins 1991) in contrast to separate underlying proficiences without transfer(ring) processes between the language systems (see also Dijkstra, Schönpflug and Franceschini et al., this volume; De Bot in press). Such an approach implies that the use of two or more languages results in the development of metalinguistic abilities, i.e. an increased monitoring system for all the languages known by the multilingual speaker, which thus enhances metalinguistic awareness per se.

4.2. Analysis and discussion

The selected data give evidence of the metalinguistic thinking processes involving the usage of all three, typologically related, languages in the process of academic writing. The examples demonstrate how the testees search for and assess improved phrasing and how they compare (seemingly) cross-linguistic equivalents. It has to be kept in mind that the use of all three languages in a single sentence is rather rare but this might be related to the method chosen. So most of the analysed data are bilingual data.

essay
   1. ... they might decide that their job is more important than a family, no, not necessarily, more important than

E: finding, founding, foundations
I: fondare una familia, {founding a family}
E: founding a family,
G: gründen, {finding}
E: than founding a family, finding?founding, foundation,

G: ja, {yes}
E: a family.

letter
    2. I must admit that I like

E: holding
I: tenere
G: Referate halten, hmmm,
E: I like,
I: come si dice? {How do you say this?}
E: I like to present, presentations, to work out presentations and to write research papers, no, I like writing, working out
I: gerundio
E: presentations and writing out research papers.

letter
    3. ... my feeling about the result is not so, not so

E: bad,
I: no, é
E: not so bad, is
I: come si dice mediocre {How do you say mediocre?}no lo so come dire, non son' certo {I'm not sure}, incerto
E: insecure
G: unsicher
E: is not the best.

E: English; I: Italian; G: German
{ }: English equivalent

First of all, it is clearly shown in the data that the language systems interact. The issue of parallel activation of languages in the multilingual has also been discussed by De Angelis and Selinker (2001) and Williams and Hammarberg (1998), for instance, who have shown that the various languages are simultaneously interacting and competing for production. Both languages are thus used as supplier languages. Furthermore the examples give evidence of what Schmid (1993) identified as congruence, that is the identification of interlingual correspondences, correspondence, that is the development of processes to relate similar forms in the related L2 and L3 and difference, that is the identification of contrasts.

From the examples it becomes clear that the interviewee searches for the right word in her/his L1 (if we want to adhere to this terminology) and her/his L2 or s/he looks into both. What is interesting to note here is that according to these data the candidates use both languages for support in contrast to Clyne (1997) who found that most of his Dutch-German-English trilinguals and all of the Italian-Spanish-English ones admitted to using one language as a support to help them with another

– in a different communicative situation though. But it supports evidence from Näf and Pfander (2001) who present examples of what they call "doubly supported" interference where a combined, parallel pressure from both the L1 (French) and the L2 (German) as potential supplier languages for the production in English as L3 has been found (see also Hufeisen, 1991 and Cenoz, this volume).

It is also important to point out that the candidate who looks for the right word in a kind of internalised list of synonyms in all three languages appears rather to be concerned with alternative content than with finding synonyms in his lexical searches (something also detected by Smith (1994) in a similar kind of bilingual study).

As known from various studies on SLA (see e.g. Kasper and Kellerman, 1999) learners develop strategic skills in order to compensate for their lack of knowledge or availability. In TLA the learner has even more alternatives to choose from as interview studies like Hufeisen (2000b) and Missler (1999) have shown. Numerous learners are aware of this choice and use it systematically, which makes it difficult to trace mistakes in the common sense (or in the sense of contrastive analysis hypothesis) on this level of multilingual proficiency.

What we can detect are avoidance and simplification strategies as shown in sample 3. Here the candidate fails to find the equivalent for Italian "mediocre" and decides to avoid the expression by finding an alternative or approximation (Poulisse, 1990). We are confronted with a case of over-monitoring as described by James (1998: 176) who states that "[t]here are situations where the learners believe something to be wrong in their IL system and so decide not to access it but instead either to stay silent or to use an alternative. [...] But their self-assessment of their ignorance is wrong, and they are over-monitoring: the result is error, since they have, in effect, avoided using the right form that they know." This is similar to Clyne (1997: 103) who notes that in the case of careful monitoring people are caused to avoid even those instances that are common to the languages where the language being spoken has an alternative. Avoidance as a communication strategy when the languages in contact are very close is also suggested by Gibson, Hufeisen and Libben (2001) in their study of the knowledge of German as L3. They found that the L2 in the specific task on German prepositional verbs did not turn out to be helpful. Note that even the metalinguistic comments are expressed in three languages before the candidate opts for the right word.

What causes the learner to avoid the identical word in the target language is a complex phenomenon which is very difficult to analyse but offers important insights into the multilingual lexicon. According to Laufer and Eliasson (1995: 36) "[a]voidance is not to be equated with ignorance. Complete ignorance and full-fledged knowledge are states of mind and are seen [...] as the end points of a scale or continuum relating to the amount of mentally stored or memorized information in a given area. Avoidance, on the other hand, is a strategy or process for handling information and can apply anywhere along this scale. It presumes an awareness, however faint, of the target language feature, and it always involves a quasi-intentional or intentional choice to replace that feature by something else." Odlin, for instance, defines avoidance as underproduction related to language distance in the following way only: "If learners sense that particular structures in the target language are very different from counterparts in the native language, they may try to avoid using those structures" (1989: 37) but this has to be seen in contrast to the evidence in sample 3.

The above discussion has shown that a high level of proficiency in all the languages involved in the multilingual learner is not necessarily a predictor of the avoidance of avoidance strategies in multilingual processing. To gain better insight into the avoidance phenonemon my suggestion is to have a closer look at the nature of metalinguistic and metacognitive awareness in multilinguals and in particular the role metalinguistic awareness plays in CLIN since many questions concerning the dynamic nature of cross-linguistic interaction need to be explored. For instance, in the case of typologically related languages: if we agree that metalinguistic awareness in multilingual learners is seen as more enhanced does this also mean that the learner can get more insecure and starts using simplification and avoidance strategies to a higher degree, for instance? Or does this simply show that the input in the three languages is not sufficient to meet the perceived communicative needs of the learner? What exactly are the factors which stimulate and determine the learner's decisions? It might also be advisable to have a close look at the distinction between intuitions and metacognition when discussing the avoidance strategy as suggested by James (1992: 185) who claims that "decisions about whether to avoid or to transfer are not founded on metacognition at all, but on intuition."

We are fully aware of the limitedness of the evidence gained from introspective data but still consider them methodologically valuable enough to include them in the discussion. At the same time it is suggested to compare them with other data such as those stemming from neuroimaging studies (see Franceschini and Zappatore, 2001), for instance, to gain further insight into the metalinguistic awareness of multilingual learners.

In addition to this we should bear in mind that a distinction between preconditions and consequences of multilingualism is difficult to make. Thus it is not quite clear whether parameters such as lateral or creative thinking, metalinguistic awareness or communicative sensibility represent preconditions or consequences of multilingualism (as already noted in Baker, 2001).

5. OUTLOOK AND ISSUES APPLIED

We have only very limited data so far but the discussion has shown that the exact nature of the relationship between CLIN and metalinguistic awareness in multilinguals should be focused on in future research. And based on the suggestions made in DMM an investigation into the links between the dynamic nature of CLIN and metalinguistic awareness in multilingualism research is considered valuable. Such an important area should possibly be explored in large corpora so that parameters can be identified which favour simplification and avoidance in multilingual learning and the results could then contribute to a more general theory of cross-linguistic interaction in multilinguals.

Some current projects on multilingual curriculum planning concentrate on teaching across the language subjects where one of the aims is to activate prior language knowledge in the process of learning a further language (see e.g. Jessner, 2001) or to foster comprehension between typologically-related languages such as Romance languages (e.g. Klein, 1999; Müller-Lancé, this volume). As much as such approaches are welcome we have to be very cautious as to overemphasize the profits of multilingual teaching before we are able to come up with a plausible explanation of common linguistic phenomena as those described in the concept of CLIN and in consequence with a suggestion of teaching methods which, besides the promotion of positive effects of multilingual teaching, are also able to face and integrate contact phenomena between the languages which are mainly considered as errors and therefore non-constructive in language learning and as a consequence tend to be ignored in the preparation of teaching material.

ACKNOWLEDGEMENT

The author is most grateful to Kees de Bot for his comments on an earlier version of this chapter.

University of Innsbruck (Austria)

LONGXING WEI

ACTIVATION OF LEMMAS IN THE MULTILINGUAL MENTAL LEXICON AND TRANSFER IN THIRD LANGUAGE LEARNING

1. INTRODUCTION

This chapter describes the composite elements of the multilingual mental lexicon and explores the nature and sources of transfer in third language learning. Unlike most previous studies of language transfer which identified learner errors by focusing on surface configurations of learner language, this study explains causes of learner errors by describing how language-specific lemmas in the multilingual mental lexicon are activated in language learning and speech production processes. To do so, it adopts some current psycholinguistic models of language acquisition. Multilingual transfer in third language learning is identified and described at several levels of information processing and speech production processes. This study focuses on the nature of lemmas in the multilingual mental lexicon and how they are activated in third language production. In so doing, sources of learner errors are traced to the composite nature of the multilingual mental lexicon and causes of transfer are explained in terms of constraints on third language development, learning strategies and processes. The third language data under this study came from two adult native speakers of Chinese. One has acquired native-like Japanese proficiency as a second language and is learning English as a third language, and the other has acquired native-like English proficiency as a second language and is learning Japanese as a third language. Based on evidence for certain specifications about the multilingual mental lexicon, this chapter presents a model of multilingual lemma activation in third language production.

2. VIEWS ON LANGUAGE TRASFER

It has been commonly recognized that Universal Grammar (UG) is not the only correct mechanism for characterizing the role of grammar in second language acquisition. Although UG is capable of explaining certain language processing mechanisms and learning strategies, it fails to take into account quite basic and widely accepted principles of second language acquisition. To speak of universal

J. Cenoz, B. Hufesien & U. Jessner (eds.), The Multilingual Lexicon, 57—70.
© 2003 *Kluwer Academic Publishers. Printed in the Netherlands.*

principles is to grossly oversimplify the nature of second language acquisition. According to Bley-Vroman (1989), UG parameters that are not fixed in the first language are lost, and those that are fixed are supplemented by general learning strategies, and these two things and only these two things mediate second language learning process. The questions then become apparent: What are the general processing/learning strategies in second language acquisition? How do they operate? What precisely can we explain with them? To answer such questions, we must first note that certain aspects of the second language grammar are initially not accessible to the learner, despite the fact that they may exist in the first language. This concerns especially the organization of lexical material into syntactic categories, which is a crucial prerequisite for speech parsing. It has been observed that initially learners organize their interlanguage around nonlinguistic processing devices and gradually build up language specific and target language specific processing devices (Pienemann, 1984). Huebner (1985) and Johnston (1985) argue that even the most advanced of second language learners will display weakness in certain areas. In other words, the learner's internal representation of the target language is not the same as that of the native speaker although it is highly systematic. Researchers such as Klein (1995), Jessner (1997) and Hufeisen (2000a,b) depart from the view that multilingual learning is the same process as learning a second language. They claim that adult third language learners bring with them a wealth of knowledge and strategies that those of a second language do not. They argue that while adult third language learners make use of similar general cognitive capabilities to those of adult first foreign language or second language learners, they bring their previous foreign or second language learning experience to the new learning process. Although there are different perspectives within UG regarding second or third language acquisition, it has become apparent that the role of interlanguage in further language learning becomes relevant to a discussion of language transfer.

The concept of language transfer in studying the nature of second language acquisition has had a long history in the literature. As early as in 1940s and 1950s, Fries (1945), Haugen (1953), Weinreich (1953), and Lado (1957) claimed that language transfer was one of the major factors affecting foreign/second language acquisition. Lado (1957) discovered some basic principles underlying second language learners' behavior and laid the basis of Contrastive Analysis in the practical need to teach a second language in the most efficient way possible. Therefore, the origins of Contrastive Analysis are pedagogic since it relates learner difficulty to differences between the target language and the native language. That is, on the basis of contrastive analysis of the two languages in question, differences between the language systems at various linguistic levels are determined in order to predict difficulties for the second language learner. Thus, according to Lado (1957), individual second language learners tend to transfer certain forms and meanings and their distribution from their native language and culture to the language and culture they learn to acquire.

There are mainly three criticisms of the Contrastive Analysis Hypothesis. First, there are doubts concerning the ability of contrastive analysis to predict errors or transfer. Second, there are theoretical criticisms regarding the feasibility of comparing languages and its methodology. Third, there are reservations about its relevance to language teaching (Ellis, 1985). Researchers and foreign/second language teachers have become aware that not all that learners produced can be attributed to transfer from their native languages, and they have also found instances when transfer could have expectedly occurred, yet did not. Dulay and Burt (1974) even claim that it is the structure of the second language and not the first language which guides second language learning and acquisition.

    In more recent studies, researchers have examined language transfer from several new perspectives. Zobl (1980a, 1980b) is one of the first who view transfer and developmental influences as interacting processes, rather than two opposing ones. He argues that language transfer does exist and its effect can be manifested in a delay in restructuring an interlanguage rule or in the number of rules traversed on the path from the acquisition of one form to another. Schachter (1983) claims that language transfer is not a process at all, but rather a constraint on the acquisition process (see also Schönpflug, this volume). According to Schachter, previous knowledge includes both knowledge of the native language or other languages known and whatever is acquired of the target language. Similarly, according to Zobl (1992), Cenoz and Valencia (1994), and Klein (1995), learners of a third language and subsequent languages have a linguistic and cultural knowledge base of at least two languages and cognitive language acquisition skills derived from a previously acquired non-native language. Thus, on the one hand, the learner's previous knowledge constrains the hypothesis that he/she makes about the second language, and on the other hand, whatever the learner has acquired of the second language is available for use in his/her further language learning process. The point to be emphasized is that the learner's prior knowledge of his/her native language and of the second language may influence the process of cognitive and linguistic adaptation in third language learning. Tanaka (1987) makes the prediction that the second language learner has strong tendency to pick those that are 'assimilable' into the already existing first language schema than those that require 'accommodation' of the first language schema. Wode (1980) claims that the second language learner will pick examplars through the grid of the prior first language. All this is essentially a transfer-based account of the question of what tends to be acquired earlier and more easily in second language learning process. This notion of language transfer significantly differs from the traditional one which restricted language transfer to cases of carry-over of items or patterns from the native language (also see Kellerman, 1984; Andersen, 1983; Gass, 1984; Schachter, 1983; Tanaka and Abe, 1984; Tarallo and Myhill, 1984). The traditional definition of language transfer is thus insufficient to account for the nature and process of second or further language learning (see also Jessner, this volume).

    According to psycholinguistic explanations of language transfer, it is necessary to consider the degree of processing independence between the two languages in bilingual processing. In his Competition Model, MacWhinney (1987, 1997) assumes that the human brain relies on a type of computation that emphasizes patterns of connectivity and activation in all mental processing. Thus, the early second language learner should experience much transfer from his/her native language to the target language. Because analogy and other types of pattern generalization play an active role in bilingual mental processing, all aspects of the first language that can possibly transfer to the second language are predicted to transfer. Although this prediction is extremely strong and highly falsifiable, it seems to be in accord with what we currently know about transfer effects in second language learning.

3. INTERLANGUAGE TRANSFER

Acquisition of a language beyond the second language has received relatively little attention in the field of second language research. The Contrastive Analysis Hypothesis and most approaches to second language acquisition focus on language transfer between two languages, the learner's native language and the target language. However, language transfer from the learner's second or foreign language to his/her further language is not uncommon. Mägiste (1984), Zobl (1992), Cenoz (2001), Cenoz and Valencia (1994), De Angelis and Selinker (2001), Ringbom (2001) and Gibson, Hufeisen and Libben (2001) provide evidence of language transfer in further language learning from various psycholinguistic perspectives. Thus, any theory of language transfer should capture the phenomenon of competing language systems in multilinguals. This phenomenon is called interlanguage transfer.

"By definition, interlanguage transfer is the influence of one L2 (using the broad sense of this term) over another" (Gass and Selinker, 2001: 132). It is important to note that interlanguage transfer takes place in the context of multiple language acquisition rather than in that of second language acquisition per se. The difficulty in keeping foreign languages apart is noted by Schmidt and Frota (1986). Examples of interlanguage transfer abound (Selinker and Baumgartner-Cohen, 1995; Dewaele, 1998; De Angelis, 1999). The interlanguage transfer phenomena raise several important theoretical issues: What types of transfer may occur in further language acquisition beyond the second language? Why and how is knowledge of a prior interlanguage used or not used in third language learning? What are the principles blocking native language transfer in the domain of multiple language acquisition? What are the principles for the facilitation of interlanguage transfer? Does knowledge of more than one language facilitate the acquisition of additional languages within a UG model of acquisition? What are the positive versus negative effects of interlanguage transfer in terms of mental structuring and organization of the multilingual mental lexicon? Does language similarity induce transfer in multiple language acquisition?

The results of some of the previous studies provide sufficient evidence of the existence of interlanguage transfer effects in multiple language acquisition. However, most previous studies remain at a superficial level by describing surface configurations of interlanguage transfer effects without explaining the mental activities and speech production processes and mechanisms involved in multiple language acquisition. Although this chapter does not attempt to explore all the issues mentioned above, it offers some explanations for the phenomena of interlanguage transfer in the context of third language acquisition.

4. LEVELS AND COMPONENTS IN LANGUAGE PRODUCTION

From psycholinguistic perspectives, language production is viewed as a process that consists of several interrelated levels and autonomous processing components (Dell, 1986; Levelt, 1989; Bierwisch and Schreuder, 1992; De Bot and Schreuder, 1993; Poulisse, 1997a; Myers-Scotton and Jake, 2001; Wei, 2002, see also Müller-Lancé, this volume). At the conceptual level, the Conceptualizer presents the speaker's preverbal messages which select specific semantic/pragmatic feature bundles for his/her communicative intentions. That is, the Conceptualizer presents the speech production system with message fragments. Message fragments containing semantic/pragmatic feature bundles activated at the conceptual level are then used as an input and realizes the mapping Verbalizer, whose task is to map pieces of conceptual structure contained in the preverbal message to lemmas in the mental lexicon in order for the relevant lemmas to be activated (see Figure 1). At the lemma level, the activated lemmas send directions to the speech production Formulator at the functional level for syntactic and phonological encoding, which is followed by phonetic transformation into overt speech by the Articulator at the positional level.

In speech production, the first step for the speaker is to generate preverbal messages by selecting specific semantic/pragmatic feature bundles for realizing his/her communicative intentions. The next step is to retrieve appropriate words from the speaker's mental lexicon. For each item, the mental lexicon contains its lemma information (or 'lemma' for short), that is, declarative knowledge about the word's meaning, and information about its syntax and morphology which is necessary for constructing the word's syntactic environment. For example, the lemma for *she* requires the word to be used of a female and that any following present tense main verb must have the suffix -*s* attached to it; the lemma for *know* requires a subject that expresses the thematic role of EXPERIENCER and an object that expresses that is known, and that these elements appear in a particular order. The lemma also contains information about the word's composition in terms of phonological segments and its syllable and accent structure, and it may contain information about the word's register, the kind of discourse it typically enters into, and about its pragmatics, stylistics, and affect. According to Levelt, "It is in the lemmas of the mental lexicon that conceptual information is linked to grammatical function" (1989: 162). In other words, conceptual information about lexical entries is provided as prelexical feature bundles in the mental lexicon that contain information about the three subsystems of lexical structure: 'lexical-conceptual structure' conflating universally available semantic and pragmatic information, 'predicate-argument structure' specifying the properties of verbs in terms of their subcategorization frames, how many arguments they may take, and what thematic role each argument receives, and 'morphological realization patterns' spelling out surface devices for word order, agreement, tense/aspect marking, and so forth. Lemmas send directions to the speech production Formulator, which transforms conceptual knowledge of lexical entries into linguistic knowledge in language production. Although there is some disagreement about the exact nature of the lemma representation in models of multi-layered levels of speech production (Kempen and Huijbers, 1983; Roelofs, 1992; Levelt, 1989, 1995; Bock and Levelt, 1994; Myers-Scotton and Jake, 2000; Wei, 2002), it is generally assumed that lemmas are language-specific and form interconnections between the lexical features and conceptual features, which map to and from syntax (Kroll and De Groot, 1997).

Conceptual Level

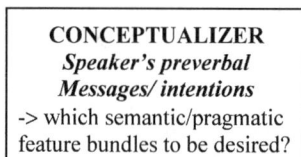

> **CONCEPTUALIZER**
> *Speaker's preverbal*
> *Messages/ intentions*
> -> which semantic/pragmatic
> feature bundles to be desired?

↓

VERBALIZER

⇕(mapping)

Lemma Level

> **THE MULTILINGUAL**
> **MENTAL LEXICON**
>
> ∩
>
> *Lemmas*
> <lexical-conceptual structure>
> <predicate-argument structure>
> <morphological realization patterns>
> -> activation of language-
> specific lemmas

↓

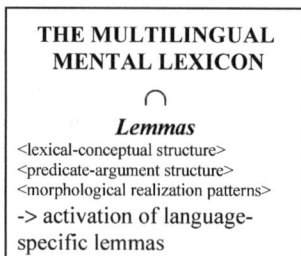

Directions to the formulator

↓

Functional Level

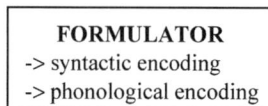

> **FORMULATOR**
> -> syntactic encoding
> -> phonological encoding

↓

Positional Level

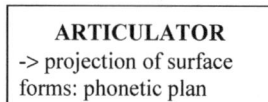

> **ARTICULATOR**
> -> projection of surface
> forms: phonetic plan

Figure 1 A model of multilingual lemma activation

5. THE MULTILINGUAL MENTAL LEXICON AND LANGUAGE TRANSFER

This chapter assumes that although there is a single mental lexicon for multilinguals, this lexicon does not simply contain lexemes, but lemmas from the languages known, and each lemma in the multilingual mental lexicon is tagged for a specific language and supports the realization of an actual lexeme at the positional level. Language-specific lemmas in the multilingual mental lexicon activate language-specific sets of morphosyntactic procedures in the speech production Formulator. Figure 1 represents a model of multilingual lemma activation adapted from Levelt, 1989; Myers-Scotton and Jake, 2000; Wei, 2002).

The first processing component, the Conceptualizer, generates preverbal messages. As generally assumed, preverbal messages generated at the conceptual level are not language-specific. In other words, there are sets of universal concepts available to all speakers of all languages (see also Schönpflug, this volume). However, at the conceptual level, the speaker selects semantic/pragmatic feature bundles to be desired. It involves "selecting the information whose expression may realize the communicative goals" (Levelt, 1989: 5). The Verbalizer then maps the selected information to the multilingual mental lexicon at the lemma level, where language-specific lemmas are activated. The activated lemmas in the multilingual mental lexicon then send directions to the second processing component at the functional level, the speech production Formulator, for syntactic and phonological encoding, which in turn sends information to the third processing component at the positional level, the Articulator, which transforms phonetic plan into overt speech.

In Levelt's (1989) model an incomplete second language knowledge base is accounted for by assuming that some of the second language lexical items are not yet fully specified in terms of the semantic, syntactic, and phonological information they contain, and the lack of automaticity is simply accounted for by assuming serial, step-by-step processing rather than parallel processing at the morphophonological and articulatory levels. "As serial processing is slower, it allows the speaker to replenish the resources needed to carry out nonautomatic, attention-demanding processes" (Poulisse, 1997b: 208). Accordingly, monolingual models of speech production need not be adapted to handle the multilingual or third language learner's incomplete knowledge base and lack of automaticity. However, it will be much more problematic for monolingual models of speech production to deal with language transfer in second or further language learning. Without investigating the nature of the multilingual mental lexicon, sources of interlanguage transfer can not be accounted for. This chapter assumes that an incomplete third language knowledge base also contains language-specific lemmas for the lexical items in the languages known to the learner. In other words, the multilingual's mental lexicon is not the same as the monolingual's because of its composite nature. Thus, it is problematic for existing monolingual models of speech production to deal with the characteristic of second or third language production, namely, that second language speech often carries traces of the first language and third language speech often carries traces of the previously learned second language. To account for interlanguage transfer in the case of the latter, it becomes necessary to explore the nature of the multilingual mental lexicon with special reference to language-specific lemma activation and its consequences in third language production. This chapter accounts for interlanguage transfer in lexical-conceptual structure, predicate-argument structure, and morphological realization patterns.

The third language data under this study were collected from two adult native speakers of Chinese (Mandarin). One has completed her graduate studies in Japan and acquired native-like Japanese proficiency as a second language and is learning English as a third language in the United States. The other has completed his graduate studies in the United States and acquired native-like English proficiency as a second language and is learning Japanese as a third language in the United States. Both of them started learning a second language in college and later a third language at an early intermediate level. The selected data for analysis reflect some most frequently occurring interlanguage transfer instances as observed in these third language learners' spoken and written performance.

5.1. Transfer in lexical-conceptual structure

Figure 1 shows that it is at the conceptual level that the speaker's preverbal messages select and activate semantic/pragmatic feature bundles. Although the conceptual structure is not language-specific (Levelt, 1989; Bierwisch and Schreuder, 1992), it is the speaker's communicative intentions that motivate the activation of language-specific lemmas in his/her multilingual mental lexicon. It has been recognized that languages differ in the way in which they lexicalize the components of a given conceptual structure (Talmy, 1985; Jackendoff, 1991; Levin and Pinker, 1991). This chapter assumes that the third language lexicon contains only those third language lexical items that the speaker has learned, and that some of these lexical items are not yet fully specified in terms of the semantic, syntactic, and phonological information that they contain. When the speaker's knowledge of the third language lexical items is incomplete or when the speaker's third language lexical items are insufficient enough to express his/her intended meaning, he/she may turn to 'equivalent' or 'similar' lexemes in his/her interlanguage at a certain point in third language production (Dewaele, 1998). If this happens, the Verbalizer must then look for a semantic form in the multilingual mental lexicon. If we assume that the preverbal message is not language-specific, then we are forced to assume that the Verbalizer mapping has to enforce a different lexicalization pattern available to the speaker (Talmy, 1985; Choi and Bowerman, 1991). As a result, language-specific lemmas for particular lexical items in the multilingual mental lexicon are selected and activated, and the consequence is interlanguage transfer (see also Jessner, this volume). Transfer in lexical-conceptual structure results in inappropriate lexical choices. This is shown in the following third language production instances.

(Target: English L3, with Japanese L2)

(1) My husband doesn't *wash* ... never *wash* the dishes.
(2) When I'm sick, when I've cold I *eat* medicine, cold medicine.
(3) In Japan all students *do* English *study* in school.
(4) In Japan students *do* many tests and exams in class.

In (1) the speaker uses 'wash' rather than 'do' based on the Japanese lemma for the verb in question. In (2) instead of saying 'take medicine', the speaker produces 'eat medicine' based on the Japanese lemma for the same concept. In (3) the speaker relies on the Japanese lemma for the lexical-conceptual structure of the lexeme 'study' which is introduced by the verb 'do' and the noun expressing the activity itself. Again, in (4) the speaker realizes the same meaning based on the Japanese lemma for the verb in question. As a result, the speaker produces 'do many tests and exams' rather than 'take many tests and exams'. These instances of inappropriate lexical choices show that activation of language-specific lemmas sends directions to the Formulator to produce the items whose lemmas are activated.

(Target: Japanese L3, with English L2)
(5) watashi wa   mai   nichi juuni ji   ni hirugohan ga   **aru**.
    I   PART/TOP every day 12   o'clock at lunch   PART/NOM have
    'I have lunch at 12 o'clock everyday.'
(6) haha   wa   shokuji no   atode shokki o   **suru**.
    mother PART/TOP meal   PART/POSS after dish   PART/OBJ do
    '(My) mother do the dishes after the meal.'
(7) kare wa   shiken o   **toru**.
    he   PART/TOP test   PART/OBJ take
    'He will take the test.'
(8) yoru   anata ni denwa o   **ageru**.
    evening   you   to phone   PART/OBJ   give
    '(I) will give you a call in the evening.'
(9) watashi wa   tenisu o   **asobu**.
    I   PART/TOP tennis PART/OBJ play
    'I play tennis.'
(PART: particle, TOP: topic, NOM: nominative, POSS: possessive, OBJ: object)

In (5) the speaker uses the English concept 'aru (have)' for 'have lunch' rather than the Japanese equivalent 'taberu (eat)'for the same concept. In (6) the speaker translates the English expression 'do the dishes' into Japanese by using 'suru (do)' rather than 'arau (wash)'. In (7) the speaker uses the verb 'toru (take)' rather than 'ukeru (receive)' for the equivalent English expression 'take the test'. In (8) the speaker translates the concept into Japanese by using the verb 'ageru (give)' rather than 'kakeru' as required in Japanese. In (9) the speaker uses the verb 'asobu (play)' based on the English expression rather than 'suru (do)' as used in combination with other nouns.

The above instances of interlanguage transfer in lexical-conceptual structure across languages provide the evidence that in third language production, although the speaker uses the target lexical items, the selections of those items may be based on the activation of language-specific lemmas in the multilingual mental lexicon. In other words, the activated language-specific lemmas for the universal concepts based on the speaker's second language may activate or retrieve the target lexical items in an inappropriate manner. Thus, 'transfer' in lexical-conceptual structure should be understood in terms of cross-linguistic transfer at the lemma level.

5.2. Transfer in predicate-argument structure

It has also been observed that in addition to transfer in lexical-conceptual structure, beginning third language learners may draw on the predicate-argument structure of their prior interlanguage. 'Predicate-argument structure' is defined as the number of arguments required by the verb and the thematic roles assigned by the verb to each of the arguments. Because of their incomplete knowledge of certain target language lexical items, although learners may choose the right target verbs, they may not know the predicate-argument structures required by those verbs and use them in an inappropriate manner (Wei, 2000a, b). The ungrammaticality is most probably caused by the activation of language-specific lemmas in the learner's prior interlanguage, which sends the directions to the Formulator for syntactic encoding. Some examples of such interlanguage transfer in predicate-argument structure are given below.

> (Target: English L3, with Japanese L2)
> (10) My brother also *graduated* New York University. Last year he *graduated* that university.
> (11) My English is not good, so I can't *help* my daughter's homework.
> (12) Will you *give* your phone number?

In (10) the speaker follows the Japanese predicate-argument structure for the verb 'graduate' where the SOURCE 'New York University/that university' is introduced without the intervention of the preposition 'from'. In (11) the PATIENT (or THEME) (my daughter's homework) is introduced without the preposition 'with' or a specific verb such as 'do' as required in the target language. The speaker employs the Japanese predicate-argument structure for the target verb 'help' where the PATIENT is directly introduced by the verb itself. Also, whereas in English the BENEFACTIVE must be introduced by the verb 'help' and the PATIENT must be introduced by 'with' or 'do', as in 'I can't help my daughter (BENEFACTIVE) with her homework (PATIENT), in Japanese the BENEFACTIVE may appear in the possessive with the PATIENT. In (12) the speaker employs the Japanese predicate-argument structure for the verb 'give' rather than the English indirect object dative or double object dative construction for the same verb. While in Japanese the verb 'give' does not require an explicit GOAL (or RECIPIENT), in English both the THEME and the GOAL/RECIPIENT must appear either in the indirect object dative construction (e.g., Will you give your phone number (THEME) to me (GOAL/RECIPIENT)?) or in the double object dative construction (e.g., Will you give me (GOAL/RECIPIENT) your phone number (THEME)?). It is apparent that the speaker's English production is influenced by the Japanese predicate-argument structures for certain equivalent verbs in the target.

(Target: Japanese L3, with English L2)
(13) ***densha o***   ***totte*** gakkoo e iku.
     train PART/OBJ take school to go
     '(I) take the train to go to school.'

In (13) the speaker uses the English predicate-argument structure for the verb 'toru/totte (take)' where the means of transportation 'densha (train)' is introduced as the THEME (the direct object). In Japanese, however, 'densha' must be introduced as the LOCATIVE in a prepositional phrase, rather than introduced as the THEME, by the verb 'noru/notte'. According to the Japanese predicate-argument structure, the same concept should be realized as below.

     densha ni notte gakkoo e iku.
     train   in take school to go
     '(I) take the train to go to school.'
(14) maiasa   watashi wa   kareno ***inu sanposaseru.***
     every morning I   PART/TOP his   dog walk
     'I walk his dog every morning.'

In (14) the speaker uses the Japanese verb 'sanposaseru (walk)' as a transitive verb whose object is the THEME (or PATIENT). However, in Japanese the direct object, or the THEME (or PATIENT) in this case, must be introduced by the particle 'o'. But the speaker uses the English structure for the same concept.

(15) haha wa   ***shoppingu iku.***
     mother PART/TOP shopping go
     '(My) mother goes shopping.'

In (15) the speaker translates the English expression 'go shopping' into Japanese, violating the Japanese predicate-argument structure for the verb 'iku (go)'. While in English 'shopping' is introduced as the GOAL by the verb 'go', in Japanese 'shoppingu (shopping)' is introduced as GOAL by the preposition 'ni'.

     haha wa   shoppingu ni iku.
     mother PART/TOP shopping for go
     '(My) mother goes shopping.'

Part of the reason for the speaker to use the English predicate-argument structure in the Japanese production is that because 'shoppingu' is a borrowed word from English the speaker may generalize the English predicate-argument structure into the target production.

(16) gozenchuu ***kare o***   ***yonda.***

in the morning him PART/OBJ called
'(I) called him in the morning.'

In (16) the speaker employs the English predicate-argument structure for the verb 'call (yoru/yonda)' where the semantic features of 'communicate with by telephone' are conflated in the verb 'call'. Thus, in English the object of 'call' is actually the RECIPIENT. Unlike in English, in Japanese the RECIPIENT must be introduced by a preposition and the phone-call itself must be introduced as the object, the THEME, by a specific verb such as 'kakeru' or 'suru'. This is shown below.

> gozenchuu kare ni denwa o   kaketa (or: denwa o   shita).
> in the morning him in phone PART/OBJ called   phone PART/OBJ did
> '(I) called him in the morning.'

It is apparent that the speaker transfers the English predicate-argument for the similar lexeme 'call' into the Japanese production.

(17) kereno uchi made *noseru o   ageta*.
     his   home to   ride   PART/OBJ gave
     '(I) gave him a ride home.'

In (17) the speaker translates the English expression 'give a ride' into Japanese, violating the target predicate-argument structure. While in English 'ride (noseru)' is introduced as the object, the THEME, by the verb 'give (ageru)', in Japanese the means of transportation must be introduced by a preposition as the INSTRUMENT rather than the THEME. This is shown below.

> kereno uchi made kuruma de okutte   ageta.
> his   home to   car   by sending gave
> '(I) gave him a ride home.' (Literally, 'I sent him to his home by car.')

The above instances of the speaker's Japanese production show transfer from English in the predicate-argument structures for certain target verbs. In other words, although the speaker produces the target verbs, the lemmas for those verbs regarding their predicate-argument structures are activated based by the learner's knowledge of his second language.

5.3. Transfer in morphological realization patterns

It has also been observed that third language learners may transfer morphological realization patterns (i.e., surface devices for word order, agreement, tense/aspect marking, etc., which are related but not the same as predicate-argument structure) from their prior interlanguage in third language production. Again, such transfer occurs before the second processing component, the Formulator, is put into action.

Since a lemma also contains information about a lexical item's morphological realization patterns, once it is activated based on the learner's knowledge of his/her prior interlanguage, the directions will be sent to the Formulator for syntactic and phonological encoding, and the result is interlanguage transfer in morphological realization patterns.

(Target: English L3, with Japanese L2)
(18) I everyday by bus go to school.
(19) Tomorrow to New York we'll go with some friends.
(20) Sorry. Only little English I know.

In (18) the speaker puts the prepositional phrase 'by bus' before the verb phrase. This is part of the typical Japanese word order where everything else goes before the verb phrase, in addition to the verb final structure. Again, in (19) the prepositional phrase 'to New York' goes before the predicate verb 'go', which is the Japanese word order. Although the speaker keeps the prepositional phrase 'with some friends' in the position as it usually appears in the English word order, the whole sentence sounds awkward because of the misplace of the prepositional phrase 'to New York'. The sentence in (20) reflects the Japanese verb final word order, where the object occurs before the predicate verb.

It has been observed that although the learner of English does not always produce sentences by following the Japanese surface word order, transfer in morphological realization patterns from the learner's second language may still appear at a certain point of target speech production.

(Target: Japanese L3, with English L2)
(21) watashitachi wa   shigoto ni iku mainichi.
     we   PART/TOP work   to go everyday
     'We go to work everyday.'
(22) watashi wa   moou   kakiowatta watashino repooto.
     I   PART/TOP already finished   my   paper
     'I already finished my paper.'

In (21) although the sentence basically keeps the Japanese verb final order, the adverbial of time 'everyday' appears in the sentence final position, which is not allowed in Japanese. The sentence in (22) is produced in the typical English word order where the object follows the predicate verb. Although the learner's violation of the target language surface word order does not frequently occur, such instances of transfer in morphological realization patterns from the learner's second language may still exist, especially in the early stage of third language learning.

6. CONCLUSION

This chapter presents a model of multilingual lemma activation in third language production. Based on this model, the nature of learner errors is defined in terms of the composite nature of the multilingual mental lexicon, and sources of learner errors are described and explained in terms of interlanguage transfer that is caused by activation of language-specific lemmas in the multilingual mental lexicon during the speech production process.

The learner's incomplete knowledge of the third language includes his/her incomplete knowledge of lemma specifications for the abstract lexical structure of the target language. This is because lemmas contain information about lexical-conceptual structure, predicate-argument structure, and morphological realization patterns of individual lexemes. The learner may overgeneralize such lemma specifications based on their previously learned second language lexical structure. Thus, third language (or multilingual) learners may activate language-specific lemmas for particular target lexemes during the speech production process. If the selection or retrieval of the target lexical items is influenced by the learner's activation of language-specific lemmas, interlanguage transfer will occur.

Language learning is driven by the lexicon. Second or further language learning is no exception. Sufficient acquisition of the target language lexical structure (i.e., lemma specifications) will eventually replace the previously learned lexical structure (cf. Jake, 1998; Wei, 2000a,b). Lexicalization and grammaticalization patterns are language-specific and must be learned as such.

Montclair State University (United States of America)

CHRISTOPHER J. HALL & PETER ECKE

PARASITISM AS A DEFAULT MECHANISM IN L3 VOCABULARY ACQUISITION

1. INTRODUCTION

The human capacity to categorise new information on the basis of similarity with existing knowledge representations is, perhaps, the most important organising principle for mental representation. It is essential for the development of conceptual relations and networks (Rosch, 1978; Smith and Medin, 1981; Schönpflug, this volume), as well as for the acquisition and organisation of the mental lexicon (Fay and Cutler, 1977; Peters, 1983). In this chapter, we discuss a model of vocabulary acquisition that has as its cornerstone the detection and exploitation of similarity between novel lexical input and prior lexical knowledge. This processing and storage mechanism has been characterised metaphorically as a "parasitic learning strategy" (Hall, 1992), and is hypothesised to constitute a default cognitive procedure, modulated in practice by other factors external to the lexicon. Earlier versions of the parasitic model were developed to explain aspects of L2 vocabulary acquisition (Hall, 1996, 2002; Hall and Schultz, 1994). In the present contribution, we extend the model to L3 (following Ecke and Hall, 1998, 2000; Ecke 2001), using evidence from a corpus of spoken lexical errors in novice learners of L3 German.

Constructing a lexicon involves the continuous, dynamic, internal mapping of patterns of external, conventional knowledge, through the cumulative experience of millions of unique sociocognitive events. At the neuropsychological level, each event begins with the reception of acoustic (or photic) energy and ends with the construction and integration, or activation and reconfiguration, of elements in lexical memory. The acquisition of novel forms will entail the construction of new representations and their initial, tentative integration into the rest of the network. For known but still relatively unfamiliar forms, existing lexical representations will be activated and subsequently reconfigured and/or strengthened. Both kinds of event inevitably entail the matching of input traces in short-term (phonological) memory (STM) with more permanent representations in long-term (lexical) memory (LTM), as in normal word recognition (see Baddeley, Gathercole and Papagno, 1998; Ellis 1997). If the initial matching process for some input is unsuccessful (i.e., if the word is not recognised), then a new lexical representation must be created. According to the Parasitic Model, new lexical representations will be

J. Cenoz, B. Hufesien & U. Jessner (eds.), The Multilingual Lexicon, 71—85.

integrated, where possible, into the rest of the network via connections with pre-existing representations ("hosts"), at points of similarity or overlap between them.

When the process occurs over representations from two or more different languages, and especially when the host item is from the L1, the literature has traditionally talked of "lexical transfer", and more recently of "cross-linguistic (or cross-lexical) influence" ("CLI") (see also Jessner, this volume). The effects of CLI from prior lexical knowledge of the first and subsequently learned languages have been documented in numerous studies of L2 learning and use (e.g., Dechert and Raupach, 1989; Gass and Selinker, 1992; Kellerman and Sharwood Smith, 1986; Ringbom, 1987; Singleton, 1999). Although many CLI studies over the last two decades have relied upon the analysis of learners' errors and processing failures, most researchers have emphasised its positive nature as an efficient learning mechanism (e.g., Færch and Kasper, 1986 a and b; Kellerman, 1983; Nation, 2001; Ringbom, 2001, 1986; Swain, 1997).

In the case of L3 vocabulary acquisition, the learner can potentially draw upon a broad base of prior lexical knowledge to aid the acquisition process (Herdina and Jessner, 2000; Jessner, this volume). Empirical studies have provided evidence for this assumption by demonstrating the frequent involvement of similar L1, L2 or L3 structures in the construction and use of the L3 lexicon (Cenoz, 2001; Dewaele, 1998; Dušková, 1969; Ecke, 2001; Ecke and Hall, 2000, 1998; Hammarberg, 2001; Hufeisen, 1993; Ringbom, 1986). It is not always clear from the literature, however, what the nature of the involvement is, since "CLI" or "transfer" are actually cover-terms for three separate but related phenomena: (a) the use of non-target lexical representations in the construction of novel target word entries ("acquisition CLI" or "ACLI"); (b) the production of non-target language items that are in competition with existing target language entries ("performance CLI" or "PCLI"); and (c) the production of non-target language items because the corresponding target language items are un- or under-represented ("competence CLI" or "CCLI").

The conditions under which such phenomena occur in tri- or multilinguals have been the object of considerable study. A number of possible (and potentially interacting) factors have been identified, and may be grouped into five domains: (a) *learner factors*, which distinguish variation between individuals; (b) *learning factors*, to do with the history and context of the acquisition process (see also Gibson & Hufeisen, this volume); (c) *language factors*, concerned with the nature of the languages involved and the formal relations between them (see also Cenoz, this volume); (d) *event factors*, involved in actual situations of use; and (e) *word factors*, i.e., relevant characteristics of the specific words involved. Table 1 lists possible factors from each domain.

Table 1. *Factors Conditioning CLI*

DOMAIN	FACTORS
Learner	• Psychotypology and metalinguistic awareness • Motivation • Attitude • Age • Learning style and strategy use • Degree of anxiety
Learning	• Order and time-course of learning • Proficiency in each language • Fluency in each language • Amount of exposure to each language • Amount of use of each language • Recency of exposure and use • "L2 status" • Learning context (instructional, natural, etc.) • Vocabulary size ("Breadth of Knowledge") • Type of bi/multilingualism (additive or subtractive)
Language	• Typological distance (on formal feature parameters) • Historical distance (from common ancestors) • Degree of contact (borrowing) • Type of writing systems
Event	• Language mode (monolingual/bilingual) • Language control • Style (formal/informal) • Task (free, test, translation, etc.) • Interlocutor • Degree of monitoring • Processing direction (comprehension/production) • Modality (written/spoken)
Word	• Degree of form similarity with competitors (phonological/orthographic) • Number of form competitors (neighbourhood density) • Degree of frame (lemma) similarity with competitors • Number of frame (lemma) competitors • Degree of concept similarity with competitors • Number of concept competitors • Degree of combined similarity (indirect and true cognates) • Content vs. function word status • Abstractness vs. concreteness • Frequency • Frequency of competitors • Recency of exposure or use • Completeness of representation ("Depth of Knowledge")

Most research has concentrated on factors in the first three domains, drawing particular attention to the role of the learner's "psychotypological" perception of similarity/differences between L3, L2, and L1 (Kellerman, 1983). Knowledge of a typologically related language provides an important advantage for the learner who can use similarities with the target language to reduce the learning burden (e.g., Ellis, 1997; Hall, 1992; Matz, Teschmer and Weise, 1988; Ringbom, 1986; Cenoz, this volume). Learners with an L1 that is typologically different from the target language tend to progress at a slower rate of acquisition, because there are fewer opportunities for ACLI (see Ringbom, 1986, 2001), although massive conceptual overlap between all speech communities will ensure generalised conceptual CLI through the assumption of translation equivalents (Hall, 1992). Other well-documented factors are the learner's proficiency (Kroll and Stewart 1994; McElree, Jia and Litvak, 2000; Ringbom, 1987; Talamas et al. 1999); his/her motivation and attitudes, e.g., desire not to appear foreign (Hammarberg, 2001); the status of interacting languages, as reflected in the "foreign language effect" (e.g., Meisel, 1983; Shanon, 1991) and the "last learned language effect" (e.g., Shanon, 1991). Recently, more attention has been paid also to the event domain, where language mode (Grosjean, 1998, 2001; Dijkstra et al. 1998; Dewaele, 2001), degree of control (Green, 1998; Kroll and Tokowicz 2001), style (Dewaele, 2001) and task (Ecke, 2001; Herwig, 2001) have been shown to determine degree of code-switching and ability to suppress CLI (see also Jessner, this volume).

These factors undoubtedly play a major role in determining variation in the overall amount of observable CLI phenomena in different circumstances of multilingual performance. They do not, however, tell us very much about what is going on inside the mental lexicons of learners, and specifically how CLI contributes to the acquisition process by affecting the ongoing development of lexical knowledge and its use through successive production (and comprehension) events. It is therefore critical to explore the cognitive processes underlying CLI in acquisition, performance and competence, and to investigate how the factors in the word domain influence the outcomes of these processes. The results of such research should help to define the limiting conditions under which lexicon-external factors (from the domains of learner, learning, language and event) can operate, resulting in the observed variety of overall patterns of multilingual lexical behaviour.

Some research has addressed the nature of these cognitive processes directly (e.g., Ellis, 1997; Ellis and Beaton, 1993; Baddeley, Gathercole, and Papagno, 1998; Jiang, 2000). There has been considerable work also on the word level factors involved, especially with regard to form similarity. An extensive body of research now exists on cognates, e.g., De Groot and Nas (1991), Sánchez Casas et al. (1992), Carroll (1992), Dijkstra et al. (1998), Talamas et al. (1999) and Hall (2002). See also Campaña Rubio and Ecke (2001), Ecke (2001) and Laufer (1991, 1988) on cross-linguistically salient form features, and Van Heuven et al. (1998) on neighbourhood density. Cross-lexical frequency effects have been studied by Grainger and Dijkstra (1992), and Murray (1986) and the effects of concreteness by Jin (1990) and De Groot (1992), among others. Semantic associations in bilingual learners have been considered by Wolter (2001) and Ecke (2001). The content vs. function word dichotomy has been touched on by Hall (1997) for bilinguals and Cenoz (2001) for trilinguals.

CLI and the interaction between the various factors at play in the word domain are best understood by viewing the lexicon in terms of an interconnected network of processing units through which activation spreads (Collins and Loftus, 1975; Rumelhart and McClelland, 1986). This approach has been applied to the bilingual and multilingual lexicon (Grosjean, 1988; Kroll and De Groot, 1997; Dijkstra and Van Heuven, 1998; Herwig, 2001) and has led to computer simulations within the connectionist framework (e.g., Meara, 1999). In the light of this work, we may associate the effects of the word factors in Table 1 with one or more of the following three properties of lexical networks: (a) representations; (b) connections; and (c) levels of activation. Lexical representations encode information about word forms (phonological and/or orthographic) and their grammatical behaviour (the "syntactic frame(s)" in which they may be deployed, including syntactic category, thematic argument structure, and other idiosyncratic information, such as gender). These lexical representations are associated with representations of meaning, which may be viewed as subsets of constellations of conceptual features stored outside the lexicon. Representations from each of the three levels (form, frame and concept) must be connected together for full wordhood, hence the use of the term "lexical triad" (Hall, 1992, cf. the similar distinction of lexeme/lemma/concept in Levelt, 1989; Levelt et al., 1999). Figure 1 illustrates the triad for Spanish *gustar* 'like', where the frame includes a thematic grid stipulating that the subject is a patient or theme (T) and the object an experiencer (E).

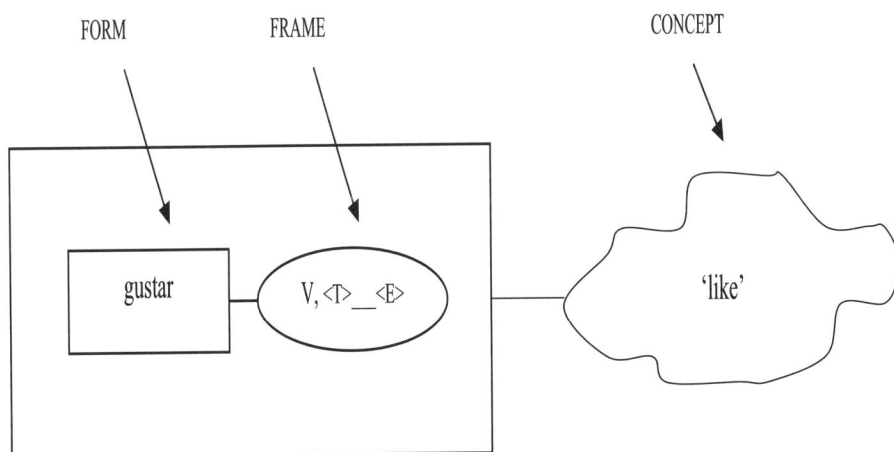

Figure 1. Example of Lexical Triad.

Within a single language, and between languages, there are also frequently "paradigmatic" connections, based on similarity. Intralinguistically, these may be at the form level (e.g., rhymes), the frame level (e.g., the class of transitive verbs) or the concept level (e.g., synonyms). The involvement of non-target language representations in the construction of a triad for a novel (L3) form (i.e., ACLI), will lead to CCLI if representations between L1/L2 and L3 are shared in distributed fashion, i.e., the new input (or part of it) is mapped onto the existing network, and to PCLI if competing L1/L2 and L3 structures coexist side-by-side, but the former become more highly activated than the latter, leading to language mixing in the output. Figure 2 illustrates a case of PCLI, where English L2 *garden* is produced instead of the intended, known, German L3 form *garten* (cf. Ecke and Hall, 2000). Figure 3 shows a case of CCLI, where the English L2 form *like* has been connected to the frame of Spanish L1 *gustar* (resulting in errors such as "It would like you" for intended "You would like it"; cf. Hall and Schultz, 1994).

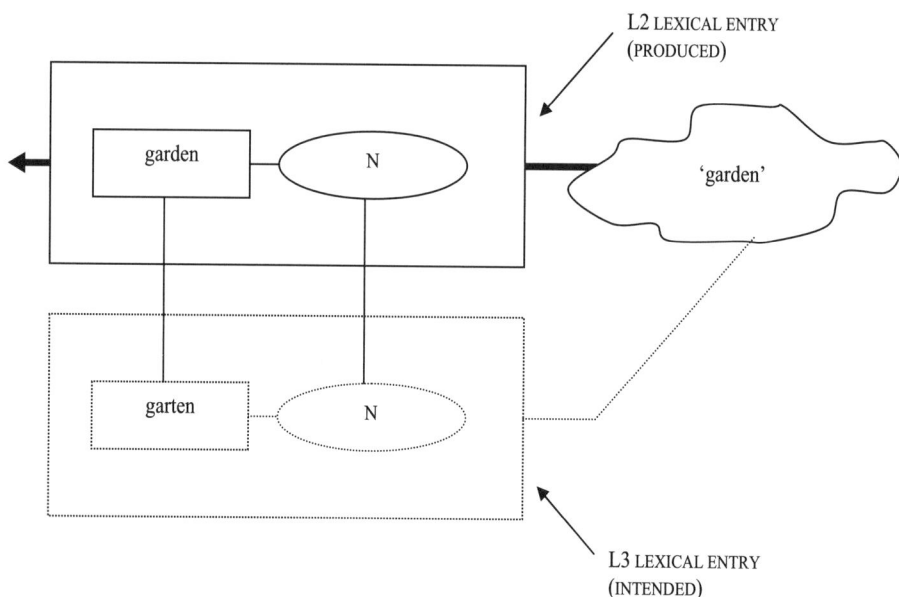

Figure 2. Example of PCLI.

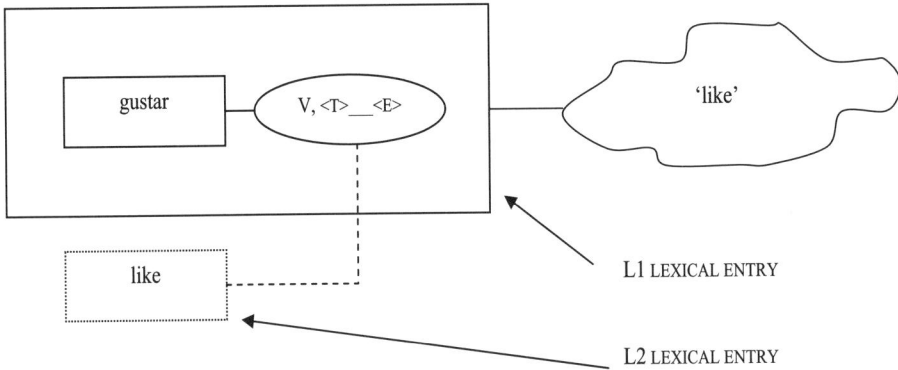

Figure 3.   Example of CCLI.

The degree of similarity and number of competitors at each representational level will be reflected in the network by the number of shared representations or connections between them. Frequency and recency of use and exposure will also be reflected in the network as degree of activation of representations and connections, and this activation will spread through the network to raise (or lower) the activation levels of related representations. In early stages of acquisition, representations will not be complete, i.e., learners will lack "depth of knowledge" (cf. Wolter 2001), because they have not received sufficient input to suppress CLI in all its manifestations and so will not be able to establish fully autonomous target language triads (also Jiang, 2000).

We now turn to a description of the processing stages that are involved in the acquisition of L3 words. The Parasitic Model presupposes that new words are integrated into the existing lexical network with the least possible redundancy and as rapidly as possible, in order to make them accessible for communication. An important characteristic of the process is that it frequently results in initially non-target representations and access routes. Non-target or incomplete representations will result in competence errors, whereas non-target access routes may result in performance errors. The most frequent type of non-target comprehension phenomena are slips of the ear, i.e., auditory misperceptions (Bond and Garnes, 1980), also called synforms or confusions (Laufer, 1991, 1988). Production failures include tip of the tongue states (e.g., Ecke and Garrett, 1998; Schwartz, 2002) and lexical "errors", more precisely, non-target productions based on interlanguage representations, connections and access routes (see Garrett, 1993; and Poulisse, 1999).

2. THE PARASITIC MODEL: STAGES OF VOCABULARY ACQUISITION

When a learner encounters a new word form in the L3, s/he is faced with the task of constructing an appropriate triad of form, frame, and their associated conceptual representation. We hypothesise that the following processes, essentially "parasitic" in nature and effect, are initially invoked by default in the development of such representations and connections:

A.   *Establishing a form representation*

   A1.   The L3 word form is registered in STM and the closest matches (if there are any) in L3, L2, or L1 are activated, based on salient form attributes (cf. Ecke, 2001).
   A2.   The L3 form is connected to a host representation (normally the most highly activated related L3, L2, or L1 form, where some threshold level of similarity between them is met) and is established in LTM in distributed fashion (activating the same nodes in the network as the host form).
   A3.   Difference(s) between L3 form and host representation are detected, new patterns are rehearsed and the representation is revised with respect to the attributes that distinguish it from the host and/or other consolidated neighbours. (This is difficult and not always achieved, leading to fossilisation of the interlanguage configuration).
   A4.   If no matching form representation is activated sufficiently, the L3 form is connected to the frame of the nearest conceptual (translation) equivalent (as in B2 below).

B.   *Building connections to frame and concept representations*

   B1.   The frame of the form-related host is adopted for deployment of the L3 form (cf. Hall and Schultz, 1994). It is retained while contextual cues confirm the inference, and is used as a link to the corresponding conceptual representation (cf. Hall, 2002).
   B2.   If subsequent context contradicts information in the frame and conceptual representation inferred from the form-related host, another perceived conceptual (translation) equivalent from L1 or L2 is activated and its frame adopted.
   B3.   If no translation equivalent can be identified, a provisional frame (based on a variety of distributional and morphological cues) is constructed and connected directly to a conceptual representation. (This, we believe, will be a very rare case at initial stages of exposure and use.)

C.   *Strengthening and automatisation of representations and access routes*

   C1.   Initially established connections with other L1, L2 or L3 representations are revised, bypassed or severed, to establish a more autonomous triad (with direct L3 form-frame-concept connections) responding to new cues in the input. (This, again, is not always achieved, leading to fossilisation, cf. Jiang, 2000)

C2. Autonomous connections between L3 form, mediating L3 frame and concept are strengthened and the representations themselves refined, with increased frequency of exposure and use.

C3. Access routes between elements of the L3 triad are automatised.

This set of strong hypotheses associated with the Parasitic Model generates a number of predictions concerning CLI in the trilingual lexicon. Most importantly, any kind of representational similarity should play a potential role in the development of L3 lexical competence and the outcomes of L3 lexical performance. Ecke and Hall (2000) refer to this as "total parasitism" in the trilingual lexicon, whereby the three languages can all serve as sources of lexical influence on each other and on themselves. Often, unconscious inter- and intralinguistic influence of this kind will become visible through the interlanguage phenomena known as errors. The Parasitic Model predicts the occurrence of PCLI-based errors (where a non-target structure is activated and produced at the expense of an existing but more weakly activated target structure, via non-target access routes), and CCLI-based errors (where non-target structures are produced because the target structures are un- or under-represented). Both kinds of errors may occur at one (or a combination) of the three levels of the lexical triad: form, frame or concept. Logically, there are therefore 18 possible error types in L3 lexical behaviour (2 transfer types x 3 levels of representation x 3 language sources). In addition, these error types can co-occur almost *ad lib*. The "magnet effect" of true cognates will result in a combination of form and concept (and normally also frame) being adopted from a non-target host (this is predicted to occur very frequently). Other examples would include: (a) identical nominal gender in L1 and L2 conspiring to override different gender cues in a novel L3 translation equivalent, resulting in the adoption of (elements of) a joint L1/L2 frame; and (b) frequent PCLI errors resulting in losses in initial L3 competence due to the strength of activation of competitors. In a large corpus, we should expect to find instances of all (or a great many) of these possible error types, since each word will have a unique history, reflecting its current point on the trajectory A1—C3, as determined by the interaction of word factors listed in Table 1.

In practice, it can prove very difficult to distinguish between the logical possibilities set out here, for a number of reasons. One is that frame representations define not individual words but whole classes of words (e.g., noncount nouns, nouns with masculine gender, verbs requiring complement prepositional phrases, etc.). This means that many words will share the same frame, and it will not always be apparent that the selection of a given frame for a new L3 form is influenced by a particular word triad from L1, L2 or L3. With the false cognate phenomenon it is especially hard to distinguish whether it is form similarity alone that is behind the error, or a combination of form and meaning (as in "indirect cognates", where there is partial conceptual overlap: cf. discussion in Hall, 2002). Finally, it is difficult to establish whether errors are a result of PCLI or CCLI (i.e., competing or shared representations).

Given these caveats, it may seem unwise to rely on only one source of evidence, namely errors, instead of triangulating with other methodologies, such as think-aloud protocols or interviews to gauge the learner intentions underlying particular CLI-associated events or compare CLI behaviours under different circumstances of L3 use (e.g., picture naming, translation or extensive word search attempts in tip of the tongue states). We believe, however, that the analysis of error patterns collected from large numbers of learners can provide a useful test of the hypothesis that this kind of automatic cognitive procedure is a universal default mechanism. Other methodologies, although better-suited to addressing the crucial role of lexicon-external factors, are often only operable with reduced numbers of participants and therefore give only a limited picture of the scope of CLI in the mental lexicon (cf. Cenoz et al. 2001c: 4) or, by focussing on lexicon-external factors, obscure the reality of the underlying internal architectural principles and procedures governing the initial configuration of the evolving lexical network.

3. EVIDENCE FOR THE PARASITIC MODEL

The speech data presented below were collected from one hundred five-minute oral proficiency interviews that were conducted by one of the researchers with his students at the end of several first semester courses of German. The subjects were native speakers of Spanish and speakers of English as an L2 at the intermediate high to advanced levels of proficiency on the ACTFL scale (ACTFL, 1986). At the time of the study, the participants had received about 60 hours of instruction in German as an L3 in a communicatively oriented program. In the interviews, learners were asked to talk about their family, study, hobbies, daily routine, eating habits, and home. The interviews were tape-recorded and transcribed, and lexical errors were identified. Each lexical error encountered in the corpus was examined to determine whether it shared attributes with other lexical items (in the L1, L2, and L3) at any level(s) of representation (form, syntactic frame, and meaning), without attempting to distinguish between CCLI and PCLI. Dual form/meaning errors were counted separately, given the high incidence of cognate effects predicted by the model. The errors were coded for locus (or loci) of CLI (i.e., the levels of representation involved) and the potential source of the influence (L1, L2, L3 or combinations thereof). An error was only coded once per subject. Repeated instances of error production by the same subject, multi-word code-switches and appeals to the teacher were not included in the analysis. Table 2 illustrates the overall distribution of CLI types with respect to representational levels (loci) and language (sources).

Learners' L3 word productions are subject to CLI at all representational levels, mostly at the combined form/meaning level (as in the case of cognates). As far as source language is concerned, the L2 appears to provide most hosts and/or mediating links for novel representations. Note, however, that also the L1 and L3 provide host representations and/or processing routes, the former especially with respect to frame representations and the latter mostly for form representations. Below, we provide examples of CLI that illustrate the different possible sources and levels of representation affected.

Table 2. Cross-lexical Influence in L3 Learners' Speech (n = 100 subjects)

Level	CLI	Source (in %)		
	n	*L1*	*L2*	*L3*
Frame	103	56.3	37.9	05.8
Meaning	185	27.0	45.4	27.6
Form/Meaning	483	24.4	65.6	09.9
Form	95	05.3	17.9	76.8
Total	866	26.7	52.8	20.5

L1 = Spanish, L2 = English, L3 = German

CLI at Meaning Level

(1)   - *ich habe neunzehn jahre alt* (target: bin)
         - [I have nineteen years old] (target: I am)
         - L1 source: yo tengo

(2)   - *ich practice fussball* (target: spiele)
         - I practice soccer (target: play)
         - L2 source: practice; L1 source: practicar

(3)   - *der tisch, da der tisch, der stuhl!* (target: stuhl)
         - [the table, there the table, the chair!] (target: chair)
         - L3 source: Tisch

Errors (1) to (3) are lexical substitutions related semantically to the target. Examples (1) and (2) clearly are permissible in the source language, but violate semantic/pragmatic constraints in the L3.

CLI at Frame Level

(4)   - *ein kaset* (target: eine kassette)
         - [a-masc. cassette] (target: a-fem. cassette)
         - L1 source: un casette (masc.)

(5)   - *fussballspielen, kino, alles sports* (target: sport)
         - [play football, cinema, all sports] (target:jeden/viel sport–non-count)
         - L2 source: sports (count noun, plural)

(6)   - *normal, milk mit cereal, ehm, hm, gemüs(e)* (target: Obst)
         - [normally, milk with cereals, ehm, hm, vegetables]
           (target: fruits, N, neuter, non-count)

        - L3 source: obst (N, neuter, non-count, also related in meaning)

Examples (4) to (6) are cases in which the syntactic frame of a source or host representation has been adapted as a mediating link between L3 lexeme and conceptual representation. In (4), the L1 equivalent's grammatical gender and corresponding article were adopted for the L3 form representation. In (5), the attribute of countable noun was matched from the L2 equivalent to the L3 representation. In (6), the target has been replaced by a semantically related L3 form along with its syntactic frame that includes specification of a non-countable noun with neuter grammatical gender.

CLI at Form and Meaning Levels

    (7)   - *das ist a <u>skribentisch</u>* (target: schreib-)
              - this is a writing desk (target: write- in compound)
              - L1 source: escribir, Scribe (common paper brand), perhaps also L2: script

    (8)   - *ich arbeite semesterarbeit und <u>exams</u>* (target: examen)
              - I work final paper and exams (target: examination - plural)
              - L2 source: exams

    (9)   - *sie ist <u>sechzig</u> jahre alt (sechzig?) no sechs sechzehn.*
             (target: sechzehn)
              - she is sixty years old (sixty?) no six sixteen (target: sixteen)
              - L3 source: sechzig

Errors at the combined form/meaning levels are cognates, i.e., substitutions related in form and meaning to the target. Most of the intrusions from L1 and L2 are translation equivalents. Other meaning relation types, however, are possible as well, as evident in the intralingual error (9).

CLI at Form Level

    (10)   - *ein stuhl, <u>cómod(o/a)</u>, comodor(o), kom'ode (target: kom'ode)*
              - a chair, comfortable/chest of drawers, commodore (target: chest of drawers)
              - L1 source(s): cómodo/a, comodoro

    (11)   - *essen, ah <u>soap</u>, ein soap, rindersteak* (target: suppe)
              - [food, ah, soap, a soap, beef steak] (target: soup)
              - L2 source: soap

    (12)   - *der <u>kuchen</u>schreiber* (target: kugelschreiber)
              - [the cake pen] (target: ball point pen / lit. writer)
              - L3 source: Kuchen

Examples (11) and (12) illustrate the error type known as malapropisms, which have received relatively little attention by vocabulary researchers (see however, Laufer, 1991, 1988). The substitutions in these examples are related exclusively in form to the target word without displaying any meaning relation. Again, lexical information from any of the learner's languages can potentially serve as the source of form transfer. In our data, the L3 exercises a particularly strong influence in this respect.

4. CONCLUSIONS

The data reported above demonstrate clearly that the architecture of the multilingual mental lexicon admits CLI from all possible source languages and at all representational levels (see also Jessner and Gibson & Hufeisen, this volume). Some of the errors clearly are due to PCLI (see examples (3), (9) and (10)) since the learner is able to self-repair the erroneous utterance by retrieving the target word. Which particular cases of ACLI emerge as CCLI is, however, more difficult to tell since many errors remain undetected and uncorrected by the speaker. Probing the substituted targets in subjects' productions for comprehension could help identifying instances of CCLI. Such follow up testing, however, was not possible in the present study. General patterns of CLI over the contents of an individual learner's lexicon will not only depend on *general* word factors like frequency and recency of exposure, but also on *specific* word factors within and between the learner's languages, such as degree of meaning similarity (perhaps conditioned by concreteness/abstractness and content/function word status), closeness on the cognate continuum, neighbourhood effects, etc. Learner and event factors would seem to determine aspects of PCLI by influencing the learner's general tendency to code-switch (i.e., select a non-target alternative to target representations), and language factors almost certainly determine the availability of criterially similar knowledge to induce CCLI. Learning factors, on the other hand, should play a role in determining both kinds of CLI, since the overall dynamics of individual multicompetence will affect both what is learned and how it is deployed. Reconciling this tangle of interrelated variables into a coherent set of predictions about the nature of the multilingual lexicon would appear to be an almost hopeless task. Selective appeals to one or more of the full range of factors conditioning CLI may appear to plausibly account for individual data sets, but if such a large array of factors may be invoked without restraint, then their explanatory power is clearly attenuated.

For example, the distribution of data reported here may apparently be accounted for by a number of lexicon-external factors. We note that most CLI at the form level comes from L3, most CLI at the conceptual level is from L2, most CLI at the frame level is from L1, but that L2 has the greatest effect overall. It is tempting to speculate that for our population, the parasitic mechanism has been modulated by: (a) the recency effect, perhaps together with a proficiency effect reflected in beginning learners' focus on form (cf. Ecke, 1997; Henning, 1973; Meara, 1983;

Talamas et al., 1999), explaining the role of L3 in providing form CLI; (b) the psychotypology effect (Kellerman, 1983), resulting in higher meaning and form/meaning (cognate) influence, and highest overall CLI, from the typologically closer L2 (e.g., Ringbom, 2001, see also Cenoz; Gibson & Hufeisen and Müller-Lancé, this volume); (c) language effects, accounting for the high instance of L1 frame influence by appealing to the presence of grammatical gender in Spanish and German, but not in English.

Although it is likely that part or all of this explanatory package is correct, it is difficult to see ways of moving it beyond the level of informed speculation. Asking participants why they produced such errors (either immediately afterwards or at longer intervals) might give us some insights into how learners reflect on and monitor (or fail to monitor) their performance, but will reveal little of the nature of the cognitive events involved. Conducting error analysis (or measuring CLI in some other way) with the same set of participants but across different circumstances of use (formal or informal, translating, free-writing, etc.), will certainly help to account for differences in the conscious deployment or unconscious occurrence of PCLI, but will tell us little of CCLI and therefore little about the scope of ACLI in general. What we can do, certainly, is extend the work on lexicon-internal factors of CLI and in so doing help to provide a more substantial foundation for work on external determinants of CLI deployment (or avoidance). Probably the most promising methodologies for this purpose are controlled acquisition-recognition tasks, and acquisition-production experiments (e.g., Campaña and Ecke, 2001; Gathercole, et al., 1999) as well as primed translation and picture naming tasks (e.g., Forster and Jiang, 2001). If these tasks are combined with measures of word characteristics (e.g., Murray, 1986), such as ratings of word familiarity, word and phonotactic frequencies, typicality of word pair relations, and cross-lexical similarity in judgment or word association tasks (Chaffin, 1997; Söderman, 1993), it may become possible to sketch out a more detailed description of the CLI mechanism in vocabulary acquisition.

What we have attempted to do in this chapter is unpack the complex notion of CLI, arguing that the phenomenon is a major determinant of the acquisition and organisation of the multilingual lexicon and therefore deserves closer scrutiny than it has thus far been afforded in the literature. We have proposed that CLI operates in the lexicon via a default mechanism which integrates new input into the existing network in parasitic fashion, affecting the initial representations and connections established (ACLI), their evolving configuration (CCLI), and access to them on specific occasions of use (PCLI). The data presented confirm the model's prediction of "total parasitism," and illustrate the difficulties involved in pinpointing overall patterns of CLI. We argue, nevertheless, that trying to establish the baseline conditions of CLI is not only crucial to an understanding of multilexical architecture, but should also be kept clearly separate from (and serve as a prerequisite for) attempts to explain how CLI may be modulated in practice by lexicon-external factors. While our understanding of the baseline conditions may be fine-tuned with further research on word factors using different methodologies, we suggest that studies of the external conditions under which CCLI and PCLI may be favoured will continue to resist detailed analysis, due to the methodological challenge posed by the interaction of so many different factors, played out as they are over vast numbers of individual sociocognitive events.

Universidad de las Américas (Mexico)
Univeristy of Arizona (United States of America)

MARTHA GIBSON & BRITTA HUFEISEN

INVESTIGATING THE ROLE OF PRIOR FOREIGN LANGUAGE KNOWLEDGE: TRANSLATING FROM AN UNKNOWN INTO A KNOWN FOREIGN LANGUAGE

1. INTRODUCTION

The motivation for our study is the assumption that foreign language learners browse through the lexicon/s of their different languages when reading, listening to, writing or speaking a specific target language, not only searching the mental lexicon/s of their L1(s) but also – to an even higher degree - their other foreign and second languages (see Jessner and Wei, this volume). As part of a larger project, the present study aims to highlight different stages and aspects of the foreign and second language production process. While some researchers believe (and find support for in their respective theoretical and methodological frameworks) that there is no salient or noticable difference between bilingual and multilingual learners with regard to the production of target language lexical elements (see for instance Dijkstra, this volume) others have found evidence that the L2 learner differs substantially from the L3 or Lx (x > 3) learner when perceiving and producing a second/foreign language (see for instance articles in Cenoz & Genesee, 1998a, Cenoz & Jessner, 2000, Cenoz, Hufeisen & Jessner, 2001a and 2001b).

In earlier parts of this larger project (see e.g. Gibson & Hufeisen (2001)) we have found evidence that knowing more foreign languages, especially similar ones like English and German, facilitates the learning, especially the reception and perception, of yet further languages in general, because learners tend to use – among other conscious and subconscious strategies - transfer techniques which make use of their different (foreign) languages in order to understand or produce the target language item(s) (for the concept(s) of the term *transfer* see Dechert & Raupach, 1989a, x-xii). These findings have been verified by interview studies (see for instance Missler, 1999 and Hufeisen, 2001b). However, when producing a target language that is similar to another language a learner already knows, this previous language can be the source of many lexical traps, facilitating the production of interference errors, and hindering access to the correct lexical item, a process which Juhasz (1970) has called 'homogeneous inhibition' (see also Gibson & Hufeisen,

87

J. Cenoz, B. Hufeisen & U. Jessner (eds.), The Multilingual Lexicon, 87—102.
© 2003 *Kluwer Academic Publishers. Printed in the Netherlands.*

2001; Gibson & Hufeisen, 2002; Gibson, Hufeisen & Libben, 2001). As well, Targonska recently found that her learners of German as a second foreign language who had English as a first foreign language and who had already learned some German (one school year of instruction with approximately three to four sessions weekly, or A2 in the *Common European Frame of Reference*) were able to make much more use of their previously learned languages than the total beginners learning German as a second foreign language (Targonska, forthcoming).

In the present study we wanted to find out how well multilingual foreign language learners are able to translate text from an unknown language into a foreign language such that the languages investigated are very similar, especially with respect to lexical items (see also Malakoff 1992, Thomas 1988 and 1992, Klein 1995, Zobl 1991, Nation & McLaughlin 1986, McLaughlin & Nayak 1989 for studies investigating differences between learning a second and a third language). We also wanted to check whether the learners were aware post-task of any transfer strategies, whether lexical, syntactic or at the discourse level, that they used while trying to decipher the unknown text, and which ones these were.

We based our investigation on foreign language learning/acquisition models and hypotheses which assume:

1. that the foreign language learner tends to be a polyglot, i.e., monolingual speakers are not the norm, but instead a speaker who uses more than one means of communication (be it language, dialect, or sociolect). We therefore assume that multilingualism is the generic umbrella, and bilingualism or trilingualism, and therefore second language learning or third language learning are specific subtypes of multilingualism and multiple language acquisition respectively,

2. that the learning process is dynamic and unique to each individual speaker (including – among other factors the acquisition, the maintenance effort, and the possibility of loss of parts of a language) (see Herdina & Jessner, 2002; Jessner, this volume),

3. that foreign language learning is defined by various diachronic and situational factors which change along a continuum of language acquisition from language to language and which make the acquisiton/learning of an L2 significantly different to that of an L3 or L4 (for details see Hufeisen, 2000a).

2. METHOD

2.1. Participants

In the EFL (English as a Foreign language) group there were ten learners, all participating in a university translation course (German to English). The five men and five women's ages ranged from 20-34, with a mean age of 24.

In the GFL (German as a Foreign Language) participant group there were 26 participants, all students in three different intensive language courses, Upper-Intermediate German, German for Special Purposes (Technical German), and Advanced Grammar. This group consisted of eight males and 18 females with an age range of 19-55 and a mean age of 25. All were students studying and living in and around Darmstadt, Germany. We use the term 'Foreign Language' here and not

GSL, or German as a Second Language, even though the target language is being learned in Germany because Germany has a tradition of heterogeneous polyglot learner groups who come from various corners of Europe and the Middle East in particular, and it therefore seems misleading, if not simply wrong, to suggest that German is truly these learners' first foreign language.

2.1.1. Language Backgrounds of Participants

In this study we define the terms L2, L3 and L4 using chronological criteria. An L2 is equivalent to the first foreign language that a learner had learned, an L3 is the second foreign language, L4 the third, and so on.

Every participant had previously studied or acquired more than one foreign language. Fourteen of the 26 GFL learners had three previous foreign languages. Specifically, ten of the GFL participants were studying German as their second foreign language, i.e. L3. Seven listed German as their first foreign language, (L2) and nine as their third foreign language, i.e. their L4. As for English knowledge, 24 of 26 participants included English as one of their foreign languages, nine listing it as their first foreign language (L2), 12 as their L3, and three as their L4. These 24 participants had studied English for an average of 7 years, ranging from 3 months to 16 years. As a whole, the 26 participants had studied German, both at home and in Germany, for an average of 4 years, ranging from 1 year to 20 years, with a mode of 2 years.

All of the EFL participants had previous knowledge of English and German, the majority of the ten having German as their L1. One each listed German as their L2 and L4 respectively. Six of the ten EFL participants listed knowledge of three foreign languages. The EFL participants had studied English in school/university for an average of 13 years, ranging from 8 to 22 years in total.

The GFL participants came from a great variety of L1 backgrounds, including: Ukrainian, Bulgarian, Polish, Lithuanian, Chinese (Mandarin), Spanish, Armenian, Russian, Chinese, Czech, Romanian, Persian, Slovak, Hungarian, Vietnamese, Mongolian, Portuguese, and French.

2.2. Stimuli

The first part of the task was to translate a short text from its original Swedish into the foreign language the participants were currently studying, i.e., either German or English. This task was based on work by Müller-Lancé (2000b), who had his learners translate a text from a foreign language of the Romance family that they knew into a related Romance foreign language that they were currently learning. Our participants' task was somewhat more difficult, as our learners had never encountered Swedish before. We took the text from the beginner's Swedish textbook *Svenska för nybörjare*/'Swedish for New beginenrs' (Engbrant-Heider, Rising Hintz & Wohlert 1986). It featured a short text describing three children, their ages and their accomplishments (e.g., reading books and riding bicycles). The syntax consisted of basic subject (either proper names or pronouns), verb, object/prepositional phrase constructions. To lessen the cognitive load and ease the way into this potentially daunting task we included the accompanying picture and changed the name of the town where the children live from Kise to Stockholm. The text and picture are reproduced below.

Lasse och Pelle
Det här är Lasse och Pelle. De är bröder.
Lasse är fem år.
De bor i Stockholm.
De har en liten syster, som heter Åsa.
Hon är tre år.
De har en hund, som heter Tusse.
Lasse har en cykel. Han kan cykla.
Pelle kan läsa. Han har många böcker.
Lasse kan inte läsa. Åsa cyklar inte.
Hon läser inte. Hon leker med Tusse.

English Translation:

This is Lasse and Pelle. They are brothers.
Lasse is five years old.
They live in Stockholm.
They have a little sister whose name is Åsa.
She is three years old.
They have a dog whose name is Tusse.
Lasse has (got) a bicycle. He knows how to ride a bike.
Lasse can read. He has (got) many books.
Lasse cannot read. Åsa cannot ride a bike.
She cannot read. She is playing with Tusse.

German Translation:
Das sind Lasse und Pelle. Sie sind Brüder.
Lasse ist fünf Jahre alt.
Sie leben/wohnen in Stockholm.
Sie haben eine kleine Schwester, die Åsa heißt.
Sie ist drei Jahre alt.
Sie haben einen Hund, der Tusse heißt.
Lasse hat ein Fahrrad. Er kann Rad fahren.
Pelle kann lesen. Er hat viele Bücher.
Lasse kann nicht lesen. Åsa kann nicht Rad fahren.
Sie kann nicht lesen/Sie liest nicht. Sie spielt mit Tusse.

In the second part of the task participants answered a questionnaire on the process of translating the given text. We were interested in how participants described the types of influence, both linguistic and metalinguistic, on their attempts to translate the text. They were asked to describe how their a) L1, b) previous foreign languages and c) the context of the text itself influenced them either positively or negatively while completing the translation.

We were interested in both the objective outcome of the task and the subjective impressions of the participants themselves of how this metalinguistic processing took place. We therefore divided the study into two parts. The first part was an objective measurement of accuracy, in terms of success in completing the translation, and in terms of non-success, that is, errors made in the task. The second part took the form of a questionnaire that asked participants specific questions about the translation process and the types of hindrance and facilitation they experienced from their L1 and foreign languages. Our overall goal then, was to investigate using both quantitative and qualitative measures how these multilingual learners handled a task deliberately designed to require a fairly high amount of cognitive, metalinguistic manipulation.

We therefore broke down the investigation into the following research questions:

1.   What is the degree of influence, either positive or negative in nature, provided by a) the participant's L1 , b) previous foreign languages and c) the context of the text itself in completing the translation?

2.   How does the accuracy level of the GFL group compare to the EFL group in the task? As Germanic languages with about the same genetic

distance from Swedish, does either language group show an accuracy advantage?

3.   Within the text itself, which part of speech will be the most difficult or easy for the two groups to translate? In which part of the text do the most errors occur? Are most of the errors lexical, or are there any syntactic errors?

3. RESULTS AND DISCUSSION

In the following section we first discuss the results of the post-task questionnaire, with illustrative examples from individual participants (4.1). In order to avoid a repetitive listing of examples we also comment on trends apparent from these data. The second part of this section evaluates the quantitative results of the task, including task accuracy (4.2 and 4.3) and errors (4.4).

3.1. Research question 1: What is the degree of influence, positive or negative, provided by the participant's a) L1, b) previous foreign languages, and c) the text itself (i.e. the context, lexical content, and syntactic structure).

3.1.1. How did your first language (L1) help you in translating? With which specific words or phrases?
The participants, especially the GFL learners, were surprisingly emphatic about the degree of help their L1 gave them in the task. And the most emphatic comments came from those who stated that their L1 was of no help in the translation task. From their comments on the helpfulness of their L1, it was clear that most participants were thinking in terms of lexical similarities between Swedish and their L1 (see also Hall & Ecke; Cenoz; Müller-Lancé, this volume). They seemed to take for granted any syntactic structure similarities between the two languages. Below are a representative sample of both negative and positive answers from the GFL and EFL participants. Translations of German comments are provided in square brackets and task accuracy scores in round brackets. Mistakes in language have been left in the original unless comprehension is at issue.

GFL learners (N=26):

      #3 [L1 Bulgarian L2 Russian L3 English L4 German] *Meine Muttersprache hat mir nur bei den Wörtern 'bröder' und 'syster' geholfen.* [My mother tongue only helped me with *bröder* and *syster*.] (97%)
      #5 [L1 Polish L2 English L3 French L4 German] *Meine Muttersprache hat mir leider überhaupt nicht geholfen, weil sie zu der slawischen nicht zu der germanischen Sprachgruppe gehört.* [My mother tongue didn't help me at all unfortunately because it belongs to the Slavic, not the Germanic family.] (81%)
      #11 [L1 Armenian L2 Russian L3 English L4 German] *Meine Muttersprache hat gar nicht geholfen. Armenische Sprache ist ganz andere Sprache, es sind keine bekannte Wörter vorgekommen.* [My mother tongue didn't

help at all. Armenian is a completely different language. No words looked familiar to me.] (82%)

#16 [L1 Portuguese L2 English L3 German L4 Spanish] *Fast nichts. (cykel = biciclets) Ich glaube meine Muttersprache hat nichts zu tun mit dieser Sprache.* [I don't think my mother tongue has anything to do with this language.] (51%)

#18 [L1 Romanian L2 English L3 German L4 French] *Meine Muttersprache hat mir nicht so viel geholfen (vielleicht 5%)* [My mother tongue didn't help me very much. Maybe 5%.] (88%)

#21 [L1 Slovak L2 German L3 English] *Überhaupt nicht.* [Not in the least.] (94%)

#22 [L1 Hungarian L2 German L3 English] *Gar nicht, meine Muttersprache ist ganz anders.* [Not at all, my mother tongue is completely different.] (33%)

#24 [L1 Lithuanian L2 German L3 Russian] *Die Muttersprache hat absolut nicht geholfen* [My mother tongue did not help whatsoever.] (50%)

EFL learners (N=10):
The EFL participants (most of them having German as their L1) listed all the cognate words that were familiar to them from similarity to German. A typical comment comes from #1:

#1 [L1 German L2 English L3 French L4 Latin] *Some words were familiar/similar to German/English ones. That helped to understand it a little better.* (85%)

Another detailed positive comment came from EFL student #19 who had L1 French, who correctly inferred "cykel, cykla – cycle (bicyclette)".

These types of comments reveal a distinct cross-linguistic awareness on the part of certain participants. This awareness admits a potential for using this metalinguistic knowledge in the foreign language learning classroom to the benefit of students and teachers alike (see also Jessner 1999 and 2001). This notion will be further discussed in the conclusion.

3.1.2. How did your previous foreign languages help you in translating? With which specific words or phrases?

GFL learners
Again, it was mainly lexicon that learners concentrated on, the majority simply listing Swedish/German/English cognates. Syntactic cues, such as the relative pronoun occurring after a comma in a subordinate clause, were not picked up on. In this case then, the participants made equal, if non-use of their German and English as part of their inferencing strategy. Some selected participant comments follow:

#1 [L1 Ukrainian L2 Russian L3 English L4 German L5 Polish] –(listed English and German cognates to Swedish) *Weil Ukrainische Sprache eine slawische Sprache ist, gibt es im Text keine Wörter, die ähnlich sind. Deshalb ohne Deutsch und Englisch Kenntnisse würde ich der Text nicht übersetzen.* [Because Ukrainian is a Slavic language, there weren't any similar words in the text. So I wouldn't be able to translate the text without knowledge of German and English.] (90%)

#11 [L1 Armenian L2 Russian L3 English L4 German]- *Russisch, Englisch und Deutsch haben mir bei der Übersetzung geholfen (bröder, bor, liten syster, hund, cykla, kann, läsa).* [Russian, English and German helped me with the translation.] (82%)

#12 [L1 Croatian L2 German L3 French L4 English] *Deutsch – bröder, hund, manga, böcker, läs; Englisch – liten syster.* (76%)

#14 [L1 Chinese L2 English L3 German] *Deutsch hilft mir etwas, z.B. bröder, *bor* (translated incorrectly as **ist geboren [is born].) Englisch auch ein Bisschen, z.B. syster, cykel.* [German helps me somewhat, for example, with *bröder, bor*. English also a bit, for example, *syster, cykel*.] (32%)

#16 [L1 Portuguese L2 English L3 German L4 Spanish] *Englisch hat viel geholfen. (syster, bröder, bor, böcker)* [English helped a lot.] (51%)

#19 [L1 French L2 English L3 German L4 Latin] (listed nine cognates to German and four to English) *Sie (Englisch und Deutsch) waren beiden ganz hilfsvoll.* [Both English and German were fairly helpful.] (92%)

#20 [L1 Persian L2 English L3 German] *syster* (Schwester; von Eng), *bor*, (Participant translated this incorrectly as **ist geboren [is born]*), *Hund* (Hund; Deutsch.), *liten* (klein; English) *cykel* (Fahrrad; English), *kan* (kann; Deutsch), *heter* (heißt; Deutsch), *har* (hat; Deutsch), *med* (mit; Deutsch) (57%)

#21 [L1 Slovakian L2 German L3 English] (Participant listed words): *bröder, bor, tre, hund, kann, cykla, inte.* (This participant was one of the very few who translated *bor* correctly as the verb 'live') (94%)

It is likely that the very common error of translating bor as 'born/ist geboren' probably results from the phonological similarity between the Swedish *bor,* the English *born* and the German *geboren*. Historically these words belong to the same semantic family.

EFL learners:
The EFL learners not only listed the various words that could be detected by transfering from English but also gave explanations, and the learner who had also learned French saw possible parallels:

#4 [L1 Bulgarian/Russian L2 German L3 English L4 French] *The text is mixed of words which are similar to German, English and French.* (82%)

The following EFL learner, #3, states that Latin was no help at all to him. The fact that he sees the common origin of German and English as Germanic languages shows that he has some metalinguistic knowledge that often comes with the acquisition of Latin. The other EFL comments also showed a fairly high degree of cognate knowledge.

> #3 [L1 German L2 English L3 Latin] - *English was quite a help because of its Germanic origin. Another helping fact was that English was also influenced by Scandinavian languages. Helpful phrases were: syster, böcker. Latin was no help at all.* (94%)
>
> #5 [L1 Portuguese L2 English L3 Spanish L4 German] *I used associations with English but most of the situations with German. E.g. böcker, läsa, kan, de, liten…*(87%)
>
> #6 [L1 German L2 Spanish L3 English L4 French L5 Latin L6 Vietnamese] *English: är, fem, *bor, de liten syster, har, cykel, han.* (92%)
>
> #7 [L1 German L2 English L3 French L4 Italian] *French and Italian couldn't help me at all. But English did help me with – little sister, bicycle.* (82%)

3.1.3. With which words or phrases in the translation did your <u>mother tongue</u> interfere during the translation process? With which words/phrases in the translation did your <u>other foreign languages</u> interfere during the translation process?
This question was more often than not left blank, or answered with a simple *'Ich weiß es nicht.'* [I do not know], especially by GFL participants. The number or nature of the questions may have become too taxing for many participants by this point in the questionnaire. As well, for this question the comments often overlapped in category, with many comments on helpful transfer as well as the non-helpful type.

GFL learners:

> #3 [L1 Bulgarian L2 Russian L3 English L4 German] *English hat mir sehr geholfen. Bei den Wörtern det, är, år, syster, liten, cykla, en = a. Deutsch hat auch geholfen: kan, har, en= ein, många, böcker, läsa, med.* [English helped me lot. With the words *det, är, år, syster, liten, cykla, en = a.* German also helped, *kan, har, en =ein, många, böcker, läsa, med.*] (97%)
>
> #10 [L1 Polish L2 Russian L3 English L4 German] *Meine Muttersprache hat keinen störenden Einfluss auf die Übersetzung gehabt.* [My mother tongue didn't have any negative influence on the translation.] (74%)
>
> #12 [L1 Croatian L2 German L3 French L4 English] – This participant simply mentioned the word *leker* in his/her answer, obviously aware that s/he had translated it incorrectly as 'good contacts'. (76%)
>
> #14 [L1 Chinese L2 English L3 German]–[Muttersprache] *Chinesisch ist ganz anderes, es wird nicht geholfen und auch nicht gestört.* [Fremdsprachen] *Ich glaube, mein Deutsch ist nicht gut genug. Am letzten Teil habe ich nicht ehrlich wie Deutsch gesehen, dann ich kann nicht weiter übersetzen.* [[ ] Chinese is completely different. It didn't help and it didn't hurt. [Foreign languages] I

don't think my German is good enough. In the last part I didn't see any [similarity to] German, so I couldn't translate anymore.] (32%)

#16 [L1 Portuguese L2 English L3 German L4 Spanish]–*Ich weiß es nicht. Ich glaube es hatte keinen störenden Einfluss auf die Übersetzung. Es war nur raten.* [I don't know. I don't think it had any disturbing influence on the translation. I was only guessing.] (51%)

#17 [L1 Czech L2 Russian L3 German L4 English L5 Hungarian] *Man weiß nicht, ob sich nicht zufällig hinter den Wörtern etwas anderes verbringt, als dass, was man auf Grund der anderen Fremdsprachen vermutet.* [You don't know if the words mean something else than what you guess from your other foreign languages.] (72%)

EFL learners:

#1 [L1 German L2 English L3 French L4 Latin] *böker* → *similar to German 'Bäcker' but wrong translation. Fem år* → *thought it means 'älter', heter* → *'haben', but wrong. English: inte* → *'into', han, heter* (85%)

#2 [L1 German L2 English L3 French L4 Italian L5 Spanish] *'bor' leaded me to 'born' but I decided 'live' instead of it.* (Unfortunately this participant did not explain why he decided against 'born'.) (100%)

3.1.4. How did the <u>context</u> of the paragraph help you in translating the text when you weren't sure of the translation for a word or phrase? With which specific words or phrases did this help?

Participants who mentioned not just cognate similarities but metalinguistic and/or world knowledge strategies in interpreting the context (which may or may not have included the picture, and the discourse and overall syntactic structure of text) tended to do very well on the task. While the overall accuracy rate for the 26 GFL learners was 72%, the mean accuracy of the eight participants in this subgroup (listed below) who documented the positive effect of the context and meta-context on their translation attempts was 86%. This result emphasizes what previous interview studies combined with or backed by proficiency tests (e.g., see Köberle, 1997) have revealed. The more learners think *about* the languages and how they might work, how they might be interconnected, how the learning process might work well for them, the better they score in the texts (see for instance Missler, 1999 and Hufeisen, 2000b). Positive results in turn work to encourage and enhance the use by participants of conscious transfer and inferencing strategies in such tasks.

GFL learners:

#1 [L1 Ukrainian L2 Russian L3 English L4 German L5 Polish]– *Vornamen, das Bild hilft* [First names, the picture helps.] (90%)

#2 [L1 Bulgarian L2 Russian L3 English L4 German]-mentioned strategies of comparing English and German cognates (100%)

#3 [L1 Bulgarian L2 Russian L3 English L4 German]– *Ich konnte raten, worum es ungefähr geht.* [I could guess what the text was talking about more or less.] (97%)

#8 [L1 Spanish L2 English L3 German] – *Ich habe immer wieder vorne und hinten im Text zugekuk und wieder Wörter veränder auf Grund von die 'Neuer' Wort die ich entdekt hatte.* [I went back and forth over and over and checked again at the beginning whenever I discovered a new word.](76%)

#11 [L1 Armenian L2 Russian L3 English L4 German]– *Durch die Wörter zB. År, är, här, de, hon, wusste ich xxxxx, dass es um Alter, um Pronomen...geht.* [I knew through the words e.g. År, är, här, de, hon, that it had something to do with age and pronouns.] (82%)

#13 [L1 Russian L2 English L3 German]– *Der Kontext spielt eine wichtige Rolle. Wiederholende Wörter.* [Context plays an important role. Repeated words.] (76%)

#19 [L1 French L2 English L3 German L4 Latin] – *Åsa ist zu klein, um rad zu fahren.* [Åsa is too young to ride a bike.] (92%)

26 [L1 Hungarian L2 Russian L3 English L4 German] – *Wörter sich wiederholen, Namen.* [Words are repeated, names.] (76%)

One case where the lexical repetitiveness didn't help at all was GFL #22 who said the context helped *Ganz wenig, die zurückehrende(?) Wörter habe ich nicht verstanden.* This participant scored very low at 33%.

EFL learners (positive comments):

#1 [L1 German L2 English L3 French L4 Latin] *It helped me (picture) to look who is who and what the person's like most. Also showed me who is younger than the other.* (85%)

#2 [L1 German L2 English L3 French L4 Italian L5 Spanish] *The context helped me sometimes when new words appeared. E.g. the third sentence, Lasse är fem år.* (88%)

#5 –[L1 Portuguese L2 English L3 French L4 Latin] *I read the sentence again and when I didn't understand a word or a particle, I tried comparing with the same in other contexts. Eg. De, har, inte,...* (87%)

#6 [L1 German L2 Spanish L3 English L4 French L5 Latin L6 Vietnamese] *Didn't know the word leker → picture: playing* (92%)

#7 [L1 German L2 English L3 French L4 Italian] *The picture helped me in translating the text. It helped me with the book, the bicycle, the dog, the little sister and the two boys. The text itself couldn't help much.* (82%)

#9 [L1 German L2 English L3 French L4 Latin] *Words which are repeated in different contexts like: fem, tre, år, är, inte, som hete, han...* (89%)

#10 [L1 German L2 English L3 French] – *Picture: two boys, one girl –the structure of the text: subject, verb, object. [inte] could be 'too' or something like 'not.' I decided [against] 'too' because Åsa is to (sic) young for biking/reading.* (89%) (This participant also gave a detailed account of how he came to recognize that *hon* and *han* was 'he' or 'she' with examination of prior sentences via word order and antecendents, i.e., that something is three years old and that it was not a name, because all the people in the picture had names. Later in the text there were names of a person plus a verb and their ability, so that *han/hon* in the next sentence had to be a pronoun.)

EFL Learners (negative comments):

#3 [L1 German L2 English L3 Latin] *I didn't need the context of the paragraph because I thought that I knew most of the words in the text. The rest of the words in the sentence I guessed except for the word 'fem'.* (94%)
#8 [L1 German L2 Croatian L3 English L4 French] *The context of the paragraph didn't help me much.* (27%)

3.2. Research question 2: How does task accuracy of the GFL group compare to the EFL group? As Germanic languages about the same genetic distance from Swedish, does either language group show an accuracy advantage?

Task accuracy was calculated based on the number of correct words that would go to make up either a correct English (from 66 to 69 words, depending on slight lexical variations) or a correct German translation (a slightly longer version, from 69 to 72 words) of the Swedish text. Overall accuracy by both learner groups on the task was 76%. The EFL learner group reached 82% accuracy and the GFL learner group, 72%.

The results of one participant with a score of 22% were discarded from the analysis because this particular participant appeared to have extremely low motivation for the task and it is suspected that s/he made only a bare effort to complete it. The number of participants in the EFL group was therefore nine, making non-parametric analysis the choice for analysis. A chi-square comparing participants with below and better than average scores resulted in a significant result at $\chi 2(2, N=35) =12.4, p=.002$.

Thus, there is a distinct trend for the EFL group to be better at the task. There are also two other potential factors which play a role in these results. The first has to do with the length of time that each group had studied/learned their current foreign language. That is, although the GFL learners were in an intensive academic language setting, and learning the language of the country they were currently living in, this group on average had only been studying German for 3.84 years. The EFL group, on the other hand, were in a much less intensive, albeit academic, English program but had studied English on average for 12.5 years, all having had English instruction in high school. Thus, even though both the German and English learner groups were judged to be upper-intermediate in German and English proficiency respectively at the time of the study, proficiency level may still have played a role.

The second factor that may have given the EFL group the edge is the differing amount of motivation brought to the task by the two groups. In our opinion, the EFL group seemed to take the task more to heart than the GFL group did, who seemed to view the task as yet one more in a series of grammatical tasks that they were required to perform in their intensive program.

3.3. Post-hoc questions

We were interested in a current issue in multilingualism research as to whether learning a new foreign language as a second or later foreign language provides any benefit over those learning the same language as their first foreign language (see also Wei, this volume). We therefore broke down the GFL learner group into those who were studying German as their first, second or third foreign language, (L2, L3 and L4 respectively) to see whether the number of previous foreign languages made a difference to accuracy. Those seven learners who were learning German as their L2 had either 2 or 3 foreign languages in their repertoire. Of those learning German as their L3, five had two previous foreign languages, four had three foreign languages and one participant had four foreign languages. Finally, seven of the nine participants who were learning German as their L4 had three foreign languages and one had four previous languages. We formulated this experimental question as follows:

Is there any accuracy difference among the GFL learners comparing those who have German as an L2 (N=7), L3 (N=10) or L4 (N=9)?

Those learners with German as an L4 outperformed those with German as an L2 at 81% and 59% respectively. The means and standard deviations for the three groups are reported below in Table 1. A Chi-square comparing those GFL participants with below versus above average scores indicated a significant difference at $\chi 2(1, N=25) = 4.8$, $p=.028$. Thus, it appears that the more foreign language experience that learners have, the better able they were to both overcome the lexical and syntactic traps in the task, as well as to apply their metalinguistic strategies to figure out the correct translation.

Table 1. Accuracy by GFL sub-groups

German as FL	Mean Accuracy	Standard Deviation
L2 (N=7)	59%	23.4
L3 (N=10)	74%	12.5
L4 (N=9)	81%	14.6
Total	72%	

Another cause for the difference in accuracy among these sub-groups could be the so-called recency effect, a factor discussed by Williams & Hammarberg (1998) and Hammarberg (2001), such that one might expect that GFL participants who have learned English more recently may be able to draw on this knowledge more easily during the translation process as part of their inferencing strategies. The assumption was that those who learned English later in their repertoire of foreign languages might have fewer competing languages between their English and German, also providing a facilitatory effect for the purposes of transfer of cognates. We looked at this variable by comparing scores of those GFL learners who learned English as their L2 (N=9) versus those who learned English as their L3 (N=12). This result was not significant in a 2-tailed independent samples t-test, t(19)=.306, p=.763. It appears then that when they learned English is not contributing to the difference in accuracy on the task.

3.4. Research question 3: Which part of speech was the most difficult or easy for participants to translate? In which part of the text do these errors tend to occur?

Errors were scored according to how many of the Swedish words the participant missed out of a total of 34 total words that were different (since many words were repeated in the text).

     EFL group – average number of words missed – 4.6
     GFL group – average number of words missed – 6.0

     Table 2 below shows the top five errors made by each learner group. It turned out that the two learner groups very often had difficulties with the same lexical items.

Table 2. Words missed by GFL versus EFL learners

Words missed by GFL group	Error rate	Words missed by EFL group	Error rate
som 'die/der/whose' (relative pronoun)	69 %	*som*	80 %
fem 'fünf/five ' (quantifier)	69 %	*fem*	60 %
bor 'leben/live' (main verb)	58 %	*bor, inte*	40 %
har 'haben/have' (main verb)	46 %	*Många* 'a lot/viele/eine Menge'	30 %
inte 'not' (negative particle) *de* 'they' (subject pronoun)	both 42 %	*är* 'is/are/ist/sind'	20 %

     The most common error by far was the relative pronoun *som*, made by both learner groups. The predominant substitute was a simple subject pronoun, *she/he* or *die/der*. This substitution occurred even when the subject pronouns *hon* and *han*, *she/sie* and *he/er*, which occur later in the text, were correctly interpreted. Participants did not seem to realize the syntactic inconsistency. Some participants got around this inconsistency in both German and English by translating the relative clause with 'her/his/its name is Åsa/Tusse', avoiding the necessity of putting a pronoun of some sort with the verb *heter* i.e., the construction 's/he is called'. These latter participants may be using this avoidance as part of a general translation strategy. Another possibility is that since Swedish relative clauses do not shift the verb to postposition as German does, there is therefore no salient syntactic signal for the presence of a relative clause. Thus, the GFL group got this item wrong most of the time. In fact, however, the EFL group performed even worse with regard to this pronoun, again maybe because their L1 was predominantly German.

Another interesting syntactic/semantic error occurred in the last sentence in the text, *Hon leker med Tusse* ('She is playing with Tusse/sie spielt mit Tusse'). The picture shows (semi)clearly that Åsa is playing with the dog on the ground. There were a few interpretations of this sentence that included either the word *gern* (with pleasure) or *lieber* (rather) or *mag* ('likes' -3rd person singular) with *spielen* suggesting that *leker* is a partial false-friend with both *lieber* (rather) or *lecker* (yummy) both of which imply something enjoyable. These choices were made by participants even though only one word, *leker*, was available in the text to convey both the meaning of 'playing' and of 'liking'. This is an example of participants' perception of overall textual or contextual clues competing with and taking precedence over the bottom-up lexical-semantic level.

When participants missed *inte* 'not', it was to translate it as 'also', instead of 'not'. At the structural and the grammatical level, there is no reason to suppose it should be the latter and not the former, as both fit syntactically. But in terms of the lexical or cognate level, *inte* resembles 'not' or 'nicht' phonologically much more than it does 'also' or 'auch'. As well, at the contextual level or world-knowledge level, it is unlikely that a 3 year old could ride a bike and read. Here the top-down world knowledge information is being ignored by participants in favour of bottom-up evidence.

Mistranslating *fem* or 'five' i.e. *Lasse är fem år* (Lasse is 5 years old/ist 5 Jahre alt.) was the second most common mistake made by EFL learners and tied for first place with *som* for the GFL participants. 18 of the 26 GFL learners and six of the ten EFL learners got this wrong. The most common substitution for *fem* was leaving it out altogether. Four of the GFL participants decided this sentence was *Lasse ist älter* or 'Lasse is older'. And three participants thought that *fem* was somehow related to 'feminine' and put down *Lasse ist weiblich.* (Lasse is female.) or *Lasse ist eine Frau.* (Lasse is a woman).

The EFL learners did not use the 'feminine' partial false-friend strategy for *fem*. Instead they tried a wider range of numbers than the GFL group's guesses of 6 and 9, speculating that Lasse was 7, 10 or 9 years old. Both groups also suggested that *Lasse ist älter/is older* was the correct translation. Here world knowledge is superseding evidence of phonological similarity provided by the /f/ phoneme being common to all of *fem, fünf* and *five*.

4. CONCLUSION

Overall, the 'unknown new language' translation task has brought to light several interesting features of how language learners approach a translation task, as revealed both by the strategies that learners used to translate the Swedish text as accurately as possible, and by their perceptions of how they went about the translating process. We deliberately constructed a task that was rich not just linguistically, i.e. lexically, syntactically and textually, but one that also provided an opportunity for learners to optimize use of their previous (foreign) languages, especially German or English. There were several robust indications that not only are learners able to exploit their foreign language knowledge when approaching a 'new' foreign language, but that this exploitation is facilitated by the sheer number of previous languages. Furthermore, there is encouraging evidence from these results that it is those multilingual learners who have more than one foreign language who are more skilled at making use of their metalinguistic knowledge, that is of how languages work and are constructed, and who are consequently more accurate overall in their dealings with a task which requires a synthesis of several types of language and meta-language learning strategies. Additional language skills put to use in this task include knowledge of text cohesion and coherence and their relationship to general world knowledge.

As mentioned in the results section, the fact that at least some of the learners have a clear metalinguistic awareness not only of how languages tend to be structured as a whole, but also of the intersecting lexical branches among languages, strongly indicates the potential usefulness of metalinguistic awareness or knowledge as a tool in the foreign language classroom. Learners could systematically be made aware of the fact that it is not only words, but sentence structure and semantic concepts which can function similarly or differently in different languages. Furthermore, learners could be trained in the use of or to further develop transfer and inferencing strategies such as 'going back over the text and checking against new words', as mentioned by one of the GFL learners.

In conclusion then, an acquired synthesis of overall language awareness, combined with specific knowledge of the lexical, syntactic and semantic systems of other languages, allows the metalinguistically aware learner to evaluate, extrapolate and even 'guess' intelligently to process even a new and unknown foreign language.

Technical University of Darmstadt (Germany)

JASONE CENOZ

THE ROLE OF TYPOLOGY IN THE ORGANIZATION
OF THE MULTILINGUAL LEXICON

1. INTRODUCTION

The study of the multilingual lexicon has been approached from different perspectives including theoretical proposals and empirical studies of speech production and speech perception. In the case of speech production, most research studies have focused on cross-linguistic influence in the acquisition of third or additional languages (see Cenoz, Hufeisen & Jessner, 2001a and b). This chapter reports a research study on cross-linguistic influence and examines the effect of language typology on the activation of languages in the multilingual lexicon.

2. CROSS-LINGUISTIC INFLUENCE AND LANGUAGE TYPOLOGY

Most models of speech production have not devoted specific attention to the multilingual lexicon. Even though the study of trilingualism and multilingualism is still in its early stages and more research is needed to identify the specific characteristics of processing several languages, it is obvious that the presence of more than two languages implies more complex patterns in the activation of languages in language perception and production (see also Jessner, this volume). Speech production in the different languages a multilingual uses can potentially share most of the general characteristics of speech production in monolinguals and bilinguals but necessarily presents more complexity and implies some specific characteristics derived from the interaction between different linguistic systems. Some models of bilingual speech production such as De Bot (1992), Poulisse (1997a) and Pienemann (1998) are adaptations of Levelt's speech production model (1989) to bilingual processing.

Other models (see for example De Bot, in press; Hall & Ecke, this volume) have made specific proposals for multilingual processing. One of the most important issues in the study of the multilingual lexicon is the selection of languages and cross-linguistic influence. According to De Bot (in press) there is a 'language node' that is responsible for language selection in multilingual processing. Hall & Ecke (this volume) consider different factors to explain cross-linguistic influence at the

J. Cenoz, B. Hufesien & U. Jessner (eds.), The Multilingual Lexicon, 103—116.

meaning, frame and form levels. Cross-linguistic influence in speech production has attracted more attention than other areas of study in the multilingual lexicon because only multilinguals have the possibility of activating several languages at the same time and the interactions between these languages can give us important information not only about the multilingual lexicon but about the mental lexicon in general.

The study of cross-linguistic influence has focused on the identification of the specific conditions that can explain the use of one or more languages (for example L1, L2) when speaking in another language (for example, L3). Two types of influential factors have been identified:

i.   Individual and contextual factors such as age, anxiety, metalinguistic awareness, characteristics of the task, characteristics of the interlocutors, etc

ii.   Characteristics of the languages involved such as typology or proficiency.

In the case of individual and contextual factors we can mention the effect of age in the study conducted by Cenoz (2001) who found that older learners of English used Spanish (rather than Basque) more often than younger learners as the source language of transfer in oral production in English. When comparing formal and informal communicative situations, Dewaele (2001) reported that trilinguals (Dutch-French-English) presented a higher percentage of mixed utterances in informal situations.

When the characteristics of the languages involved are considered the most common factors identified by researchers are typological distance, proficiency in the different languages and factors related to the use of the language such as frequency and recency (see, however, Franceschini et al., this volume). The main focus of this chapter is typology but other individual, contextual and language-related factors will also be taken into account.

The role of typology has already been considered in the case of bilingual processing. For example, De Bot (1992) suggests that the separate storage for different languages is linked to typological distance so that the same procedural or lexical knowledge is used when two closely related languages are involved. Paradis (1987:16) also highlights the role of typological distance:

> According to such view cerebral representation of bilingualism would be on a language pair-specific continuum, ranging from a bi-or multiregister unilingualism to a bilingualism involving two unrelated languages

Although Paradis is only referring to two languages, the idea of a continuum is useful in the case of typology because languages are relatively distant or relatively close, not distant or close in absolute terms. For example, Spanish can be considered distant from English as compared to Dutch but closer to English as compared to Japanese. In terms of language processing, it seems that the idea   'the less two languages have in common, the more they are represented separately' (Paradis, 1987: 16) is borne out by data on cross-linguistic influence. Studies involving L3 speakers of different languages have consistently reported that they use a second language which is typologically closer to the L3 as the source language of transfer or default supplier rather than the typologically distant first language. For example, learners of French and English who are native speakers of a non-Indoeuropean language tend to transfer vocabulary and structures from other Indoeuropean languages they know rather than from their first language (Ahukanna, Lund & Gentile, 1981; Bartelt, 1989; Stedje, 1977; Ringbom, 1987; Singh & Carroll, 1979). Studies conducted with Indoeuropean languages also confirm these findings (Ecke, 2001; De Angelis & Selinker, 2001; Singleton, 1987; Möhle, 1989). In fact, typology has been considered one of the main predictors of cross-linguistic influence in third language production along with recency, proficiency and L2 status (see Williams & Hammarberg, 1997, 1998; Hammarberg, 2001).

Why is typology important in cross-linguistic influence? There are at least two mutually non-exclusive possible explanations. The first is commonly referred to as 'psychotypology', that is the individual's perception of language distance and has been considered an important factor to explain cross-linguistic influence from the L1 in second language acquisition (Kellerman, 1983). Research studies have shown that learners tend to transfer more elements from the first language when it is typologically close than when it is a distant language (Kellerman, 1978, 1983, 1986) and interview studies based on self-reports confirm this trend (Missler, 2000; Hufeisen 2000b). The second explanation is related to the differences between linguistically distant languages mainly at lexeme (form) and lemma (frame) levels. Typological distance is often reflected in lexems and lemmas as in the following example:

(1)   Mirenek sagarra jan zuen (Basque)
        [Miren+ergative + apple + the+ eat + aux past]
(2)   Miren ate the apple (English)
(3)   Miren comió la manzana (Spanish)
        [Miren ate the apple]

These examples involve three languages. Basque is a non-Indoeuropean language of unknown origin, English is an Indoeuropean Germanic language and Spanish an Indoeuropean Romance language. Therefore, Spanish and English are relatively closer than Basque and English or Basque and Spanish. The examples show that the lexemes are different for the three languages but if we look at the morphosyntactic level (word order, ergative declension, verb form) we can see that the language that it is different from the other two is Basque.

Language typology has a historical origin and cannot be studied without considering the history of the language and the language contact situations. Language contact is more likely to be more influential at the lexeme than at the lemma level. Let's see the following examples:

(4)   Peter is responsible for that (English)
(5)   Peter es responsable de eso (Spanish)
(6)   Me gusta esa moto (Spanish)
(7)   Moto hori gustatzen zait (Basque)

Examples 4 and 5 show that 'responsible' and 'responsable' are very close in English and Spanish because this word comes from Latin. Examples 6 and 7 show that 'moto' has the same form in Basque and Spanish and 'gusta' 'gustatzen' have the same root because of the long lasting contact between these two languages. If typology is an important predictor of cross-linguistic influence, languages which are relatively close to each other are more likely to be activated at the same time, not because of their historical origin but because of their similarities at the lexeme and lemma levels, that is because they are neighbours in the multilingual lexicon. In some cases neighbours can belong to typologically distant languages which have been in direct or indirect contact (see also Hall & Ecke, this volume).

Some studies have also reported that learners tend to transfer from the second language rather than from the first language in spontaneous oral production in the third (or additional) language. These results have been related to a 'foreign language effect' (Meisel, 1983; Hufeisen 2000b; De Angelis and Selinker, 2001) or 'L2 status' (Hammarberg, 2001) and have important implications for the study of language processing in multilinguals because multilinguals could use different processing and acquisition mechanisms for second languages as compared to first languages (see Hammarberg, 2001). It seems that in the case of L3 production, the second language and not the first is activated while the third language is selected. The simultaneous activation of two languages is also consistent with the findings reported by Clyne (1997) and Dewaele (1998), who found that learners use one of the languages in their linguistic repertoire as the support to learn the target language. Simultaneous activation is also compatible with the Competition Model proposed by MacWhinney (1997: 119) for second language acquisition:

> The model claims that the second language learner begins learning with a parasitic lexicon, a parasitic phonology, and a parasitic set of grammatical constructs. Over time, the second language grows out of this parasitic status and becomes a full language in its own right.

Hall and Ecke (this volume) have developed this idea of parasitic learning as related to the multilingual lexicon and propose the parasitic model for vocabulary acquisition. There is a need for longitudinal studies of the multilingual lexicon in order to provide enough empirical evidence to support this model but the dependence on another language can explain the higher number of transferred items in the first stages of second and third language acquisition (Poulisse & Bongaerts, 1994; Hammarberg, 2001). In the case of third language acquisition we could hypothesize that learners use parasitic phonology, lexis and syntax from one of the languages they know until they develop a third language system.

Even though most studies on third language acquisition production highlight the role of the second language as the source language of transfer or default supplier they do not isolate this effect from the effect of typology, either because the L2 language is typologically closer to the L3 than the L1 or because the three languages are close to each other or have experimented extensive contact (Williams & Hammarberg 1997, 1998; Hammarberg, 2001; Dewaele, 1998; Ahukanna, Lund & Gentile, 1981; Bartelt, 1989; Stedje, 1977; Ringbom, 1987; Singh & Carroll, 1979 Ecke, 2001; De Angelis & Selinker, 2001; Singleton, 1987; Möhle, 1989). As De

Bot (in press) points out, it is necessary to isolate the effect of these two factors, typology and L2 status, so as to know their relative influence in language activation. Another important point to consider is that different languages can interact in different ways at the conceptual, lexeme or lemma levels. Hall and Ecke (this volume) found that Spanish and English had a different influence on German at the lexeme (frame) and conceptual (meaning) levels.

Cross-linguistic influence has been related to several functions (Williams & Hammarberg, 1997; Hammarberg, 2001), different levels of intentionality and automaticity (Poulisse & Bongaerts, 1994) and different language modes (Grosjean, 1998). According to Hammarberg (2001) switches can be classified into seven categories: edit, meta comment, meta frame, explicit elicit, implicit elicit, non-elicit and wipp. The first six categories have a specific pragmatic purpose and the speaker does not attempt to use the L3 while 'Wipp' switches occur when the speaker is formulating an utterance in the L3. Poulisse & Bongaerts (1994) distinguish intentional from non-intentional or automatic switches. Non-intentional switches are performance switches that take place when another language has erroneously been accessed. Non-intentional switches can be identified because they "were not preceded by any signs of hesitation and did not stand out from the rest of the utterance by a marked intonation" (Poulisse & Bongaerts, 1994: 43). Grosjean (1998) considers that cross-linguistic influence is related to the specific context in which communication takes place including the interlocutors (bilingual or monolingual), the setting and the topic of the conversation. These factors determine the relative position of conversation as close to the bilingual or the monolingual mode so that if the speaker adopts a bilingual mode his/her production is more likely to present more cross-linguistic influence.

Taking into account these different dimensions of cross-linguistic influence we propose a continuum which presents two extreme positions: interactional strategies and transfer lapses:

$$\longleftarrow \hspace{6cm} \longrightarrow$$

Interactional   Transfer
Strategies   Lapses

Interactional strategies are intentional switches into languages other than the target language and their presence will depend on language mode so that their frequency is related to the bilingual or monolingual mode adopted by the speaker (see also Grosjean 1995). Following Levelt's model (1989) and De Bot's adaptation (1992) we can say that in the case of interactional strategies the language choice takes place in the conceptualizer. If we consider the 'multilingual processing model' (De Bot, in press) the choice to use a language other than the target takes place at the conceptual/communicative intention level. In the case of interactional strategies, the multilingual speaker makes the decision to use a language other than the target language when s/he is asking help from her/his interlocutor or making comments about her/his own production.

Transfer lapses are non-intentional switches which are not preceded by a pause or false start and can be regarded as automatic (see Poulisse & Bongaerts, 1994).

They are to a greater degree independent of language mode or at least of those elements related to language mode that exist in the specific context in which the production is taking place. When transfer lapses occur the other languages the multilingual speaker knows are activated in parallel to the target language and some elements from these languages are accidentaly fed into the articulator.

It is possible to find intermediate situations in which the learner uses a term from other languages s/he knows as a communication strategy which is intentional but can have different levels of explicitness.

The study of cross-linguistic influence presents special interest because multilinguals could potentially use two or more different languages for interactional and transfer lapses and this choice could be related to factors such as L2 status, typology, recency, proficiency and language mode. For example, Hammarberg (2001) reported that his subject, a native speaker of English, used English as an interactional strategy, that is in word elicitation units in which the learner asked her interlocutor for help. On the other hand she used German as the default supplier for transfer lapses with no specific pragmatic function.

This research study aims at comparing the relative weight of typology and foreign language effect or L2 status as predictors of language activation in oral production in a third language. A previous study involving the same languages (Cenoz, 2001) indicated that both Basque L1 speakers and Spanish L1 speakers used Spanish as the main source language of transfer in oral production in English as a third language. This study aims at comparing the relative influence of two competing languages as activated languages in L3 production by isolating the effect typology vs. the effect of L2 status. Specifically it tries to answer the following research questions:

1) Do learners of English as a third language activate their second language to a higher level than their first language in oral production in English?
2) Do the L1 and the L2 have different roles as supplier languages in L3 production?

3.   THE PRESENT STUDY

3.1. Participants

Participants were 18 primary schoolchildren (50% male; 50% female) who were studying English as a third language in the Basque Country. All the participants, who had a mean age of 9.11 were in their fourth year of Primary School. They all had Spanish as their first language and used Spanish at home but had attended a Basque-medium school since the age of three. Basque is the school language and the only language of instruction for all the subjects except English and Spanish. The children had received instruction in English since the age of four and started to study Spanish at school in the third year of primary school, that is one year before the data presented here were obtained. Their proficiency in English was low as compared to Basque and Spanish.

Basque and Spanish are used in the community but Basque speakers are bilingual in Basque and Spanish while most Spanish speakers are monolingual. English is not used in the community and can be considered a foreign language.

3.2. Instruments

All the participants were asked to tell two stories in English. The first story was the wordless picture story 'Frog, where are you? (Mayer, 1969). This story consists of 24 pictures and has been used in a large number of contexts with different languages both with children and adults (Berman & Slobin, 1994; Kellerman, 2001; Griessler, 2001). The second story was a picture story the children already knew because they had worked with it in their English classes.

Participants completed a background questionnaire which included questions on the knowledge and use of Basque in their social networks. The stories were told individually to a trilingual speaker and the questionnaries were completed in groups in one of the class sessions.

3.3. Procedure

All the stories were audio and videotaped. The stories were also transcribed and all cases of cross-linguistic influence at the lexical level were identified. For the present research two types of cross-linguistic influence were considered:

i. Interactional strategies. This category refers to direct or indirect appeals to the interlocutor in order to get help to produce a specific term in English. It includes four of the categories included in the seven types of switches identified by Hammarberg (2001): 'metaframe' 'insert: explicit elicit', 'insert: implicit elicit' and 'insert: non elicit'. Interactional strategies are considered intentional and present a marked interrogative intonation pattern.

ii. Transfer lapses. This category refers to the use of one or more terms (but not whole sentences) in Basque or Spanish as part of an utterance produced in English. This category includes borrowings and foreignizings. Borrowings refer to 'the use of an L1 (or Ln) word without any phonological and/or morphological adaptation' (Poulisse 1990, 111). Foreignizing refers to 'the use of an L1 (or Ln) word with phonological and morphological adaptation' (Poulisse 1990, 111). These switches are considered non-intentional and they did not present any special formal characteristic such as marked intonation or hesitations (Poulisse & Bongaerts, 1994).

Other strategies such as code switching understood as the production of whole sentences in Basque or Spanish when the speaker is not appealing to the interlocutor for help were not frequent in the data and are not considered in this chapter.

3.4. Results

In order to answer our research questions a first step was to analyse the frequency of cross-linguistic influence in the data. The total number of utterances produced by the 18 participants and the number of utterances that presented elements transferred from either the L1 or the L2 are presented in table 1.

Table 1. Total number of utterances and cross-linguistic influence

	STORY 1		STORY 2	
	UTTERANCES	*CROSS-LINGUISTIC*	*UTTERANCES*	*CROSS-LINGUISTIC*
1	22	10	47	7
2	22	1	15	-
3	36	2	51	-
4	26	1	25	1
5	42	10	16	-
6	25	-	12	-
7	16	2	15	-
8	29	3	16	2
9	40	4	23	1
10	34	1	24	-
11	38	3	22	1
12	42	8	25	1
13	50	27	25	9
14	35	1	14	1
15	35	2	19	1
16	40	12	15	2
17	34	3	25	-
18	60	33	25	12
TOTAL	626	123 19.6%	414	38 9.2%

The data indicate that most of the utterances are produced in the L3 and only 19.6% of the utterances in story 1 and 9.2% of the utterances in story 2 include elements transferred from the L1 or the L2 (total 161 utterances). It can be observed that there is more cross-linguistic influence when learners produce a story that has not been included in their classroom activities.

In the following table we present the instances of cross-linguistic influence for the two stories and the source language of transfer or supplier language used in the case of interactional strategies.

Table 2. Interactional strategies and source languages

	BASQUE	SPANISH	BASQUE/SPANISH	TOTAL
1	13	1	1	15
2	-	-	-	-
3	1	-	-	1
4	2	-	-	2
5	6	-	-	6
6	-	-	-	-
7	-	-	-	-
8	1	-	1	2
9	1	-	-	1
10	-	-	-	-
11	-	-	-	-
12	6	-	-	6
13	26	1	1	28
14	1	-	-	1
15	-	-	-	-
16	11	-	-	11
17	2	-	-	2
18	34	1	9	44
TOTAL	104 89%	3 2.6%	10 8.4%	119

Results in table 2 indicate that Basque is the source language or default supplier when learners use interactional strategies. In fact, 89% of the transferred units have been taken from Basque. Some examples of utterances containing Basque elements are the following:

(8)   .... nola da erakutsi? (how is 'show'?)
(9)   …the dog and the boy was # aurkitzen? (the dog and the boy was # 'find'?)

We can observe that these are word elicitation units in which the learners ask their interlocutor for help to go on with the stories. There are only three examples of interactional strategies in Spanish and ten in Basque and Spanish.

Spanish seems to be more accessible than Basque for some specific words and learners tend to formulate the question in Basque and to include a Spanish word as it can be seen in the following examples:

Basque question or utterances including a Spanish word:

(10)   ... then Alex # <u>bosque nola da</u>? (how is 'forest'?)
(11)   ...<u>ez dakit zer da ladrar</u> (I don't know what 'bark' is)
(12)   ... <u>nola esaten da botellan</u>? (how do you say in the 'bottle'?)

In examples 10-12 we see that the speakers have decided to use Basque to ask the interlocutor for help to go on with the story but they include words in Spanish when telling their interlocutor that they need help in Basque. In examples 10 and 11, the speakers produce 'bosque' and 'ladrar' instead of their Basque equivalents 'basoa' and 'zaunka egin'. In example 12 'botellan' is a Spanish word (the Basque equivalent is botila) with a Basque ending 'n'. These examples show that the speakers' intention was to use Basque when asking their interlocutor for help to go on with their oral production in English but Spanish seems to be more easily accessed in some cases.

Spanish word

(13)   … at the end # <u>riachuelo</u>? (stream)
(14)   …in the boy the # her her <u>árbol árbol</u>? (tree tree)
(15)   …# <u>encontrar</u>? (find)

In examples 13-15 speakers ask their interlocutor for help to go on with the story but in these specific examples they use Spanish and not Basque although all speakers use Basque in the case of interactional strategies elsewhere in their oral productions. It is interesting to see that speakers do not use interrogative pronouns to formulate these questions and that when they do as in examples 10 and 12 these pronouns and the verb are always in Basque. Once again we can see that Spanish is more easily accessed in spite of not being the language that the speakers had intended to use.

The data also indicate that individual differences are important as 60.5% of the switches were produced by two subjects while 6 subjects did not use interactional strategies at all.

Table 3 includes the data corresponding to transfer lapses. The data indicate that the total number of transfer lapses in non-intentional automatic switches is not as high as in the case of interactional strategies but they also indicate that individual differences are not as important. It is even more interesting to observe that Spanish and not Basque is the source language of cross-linguistic influence or default supplier for 78.6% of the transfer lapses. Transfer from Spanish can be found in the L3 production of 16 subjects in examples such as the following:

From Spanish

(16)   …Alex <u>y</u> on the xxx (and)
(17)   …saw <u>a</u> another frogs (-) (to)
(18)   …### and # in the door middle <u>hay</u> the crocodiles (there are)

(19)   …aaah rock the # the <u>chark</u> (pond; Spanish= charca)

Some examples of transfer lapses from Basque are the following:

From Basque

(20)   …and she's <u>deit</u> to the frog but she is not happen (call; Basque= deitu)
(21)   … # boy <u>behean</u> look frog two frog (below)
(22)   … <u>eta</u> # Peggy and this a Peggy and Sarah this (and)

Table 3. Transfer and source languages

	BASQUE	*SPANISH*	*BASQUE/SPANISH*	*TOTAL*
1	-	2	-	2
2	-	1	-	1
3	1	-	-	1
4	-	-	-	-
5	-	4	-	4
6	-	-	-	-
7	-	2	-	2
8	-	3	-	3
9	1	3	-	4
10	-	1	-	1
11	-	4	-	4
12	2	1	-	3
13	3	5	-	8
14	-	1	-	1
15	-	3	-	3
16	-	3	-	3
17	-	-	1	1
18	1	-	-	1
TOTAL	8 19%	33 78.6%	1 3.3%	42

We can observe that Spanish is used both for content and function words but it is not very common to transfer function words from Basque (see also Cenoz, 2001). It is interesting to observe that some learners tend to include a redundant preposition in front of animate direct objects ('a' in example 17) because this preposition is necessary in Spanish and in fact according to the Competition Model (MacWhinney, 1997) it is the strongest cue to identify the subject and the object in Spanish when both are animate. Learners seem to use parasitic lemmas from Spanish in oral production in the third language. Foreigneizing such as in 'chark' or 'deit' is not very common but it is more common when the terms are taken from Spanish than from Basque. In fact 'deit' is the only term foreignized from Basque in the corpus.

4. DISCUSSION

Our results indicate that learners use both the L1 and the L2 as the source languages of transfer or suppliers and as in Hammarberg (2001) the two source languages play different roles. Nevertheless, and contrary to Hammarberg's results the L2 (Basque) is the default supplier in the case of interactional strategies and the L1 (Spanish) in the case of transfer lapses. Why do the L1 and the L2 have the opposite roles as compared to those identified in Hammarberg's study?

The use of the L2 (Basque) as the default supplier in interactional strategies can be explained by the specific social context in which the L3 productions took place. The L2 is the school language and participants attend a Basque-medium school and always use Basque with their teachers. They know that their interlocutor is fluent in Basque and following Grosjean (1995) we can say that the productions take place in a bilingual mode. We can also say following Poulisse and Bongaerts (1994) that these intentional switches contain the specification +L2 in the pre-verbal message. This explanation also accounts for Hammarberg's reported use of the L1 in interactional strategies as he explains that the subject's L1 (English) was frequently used between the interlocutors.

It is more difficult to explain the use of the L1 (Spanish) and not the L2 (Basque) in the case of transfer lapses taking into account that most research studies on cross-linguistic influence highlight the important role of L2 status (see for example Hammarberg, 2001; Dewaele, 1998; Ringbom, 1987).

The most obvious explanation is related to typology or linguistic distance (see also Gibson & Hufeisen; Müller-Lancé and Hall & Ecke, this volume). The L1 (Spanish) is a Romance language and the L3 (English) a Germanic language but they are both Indoeuropean while the L2 (Basque) is not an Indoeuropean language. The different origin is mainly reflected at the morphosyntactic level as Basque is a fully inflected language with a complex verbal morphology. The differences at the lexical level are also important although long years of contact between Basque and Romance languages can explain the high number of loanwords from Spanish into Basque. Following De Bot (1992) and Paradis (1987) it could be hypothesized that the representation of the Basque linguistic system is more independent or distant from the representation of the Spanish and English linguistic systems, that is, Basque is represented relatively more separatedly because it is typologically distant and presents a different syntactic structure. Therefore our results indicate that when the languages involved are typologically distant and present important differences at the lexeme and lemma levels, the effect of typology would be stronger than the effect of L2 status.

It is difficult to establish the perception of typology that subjects present. Subjects in this sample are only 9.1 years old, have acquired the L2 (Basque) in a full immersion program and have only been introduced to the study of Spanish at school one year before the data were collected. In a previous study in which cross-linguistic influence at different ages was analysed, we found that learners with Basque or Spanish as their L1 used more Spanish than Basque as the source language but older students even used more Spanish than younger learners (Cenoz, 2001). These results suggest that older learners are more aware of linguistic distance than younger learners (see also Franceschini et al., this volume). Our data indicate that even though the degree of awareness of linguistic distance is probably low the different typology of the languages involved favours the use of the L1 as the default supplier in the case of non-intentional transfer lapses.

An alternative explanation that is compatible with the effect of typology is related to the specific social context in which the learning process is taking place. Even though our learners are proficient in the L2 and use both the L1 and the L2 in everyday life the specific minority status of Basque and the fact that all Basque speakers are bilingual could trigger a higher level of activation of Spanish relative to Basque in all situations unless the speaker intentionally uses Basque when interacting with Basque-Spanish bilinguals in a context in which Basque is the required language. The examples of interactional strategies including terms in Spanish indicate that Spanish is highly activated at all times, even when the speaker has decided to use Basque as the language to address his/her interlocutor. The L1, Spanish, is continuously co-activated and when a learner lacks a specific word in English or Basque, the Spanish word is more available than the Basque word. This explanation integrates the social and psycholinguistic factors that can affect L3 production both in the case of interactional strategies and transfer lapses.

The results presented here also raise other issues which are relevant for L3 research. Learners present important individual differences in cross-linguistic behaviour and mainly when this behaviour is intentional. Another interesting point is the relationship between cross-linguistic influence and proficiency in the target language. According to Poulisse and Bongaerts (1994) and Hammarberg (2001) cross-linguistic influence is more common in the first stages of acquisition. Nevertheless, the relatively low number of transferred items found in this study and the positive correlation between cross-linguistic influence and proficiency in the first stages of L3 acquisition (see Cenoz, 2001) point out to the existence of a threshold level of proficiency as suggested by De Angelis and Selinker (2001) and De Bot (in press).

5. CONCLUSION

The study of cross-linguistic influence in third language acquisition is complex and presents more diversity than the study of cross-linguistic influence in second language acquisition (Cenoz & Genesee, 1998; Cenoz, 2000). Cross-linguistic influence in third language acquisition can be affected by a large number of individual, contextual and linguistic factors. More research that explores the relationships between the L1, L2 and L3 can provide useful insights so as to get to know the characteristics of multilingual processing and the multilingual mind.

JASONE CENOZ

ACKNOWLEDGEMENTS

The research study described in this chapter was supported by the Spanish Ministry of Science and Technology grant BFF 2000-0101 and the Basque Government grant PI 98/961999.

University of The Basque Country (Spain)

JOHANNES MÜLLER- LANCÉ

A STRATEGY MODEL OF MULTILINGUAL LEARNING

1. CHARACTERISTIC FEATURES OF MULTILINGUAL LANGUAGE PROCESSING

In this chapter, a collection of characteristic features of multilingual language processing, based on empirical studies, will be presented first. Afterwards there will be a short overview of some well-known models, regarding their capacities of representing these features. Finally, a new model of language production and comprehension, adjusted specifically to the conditions of third language acquisition, will be proposed.

Many researchers agree on the following characteristics of multilingual language processing:

a) An individual's competences in various languages will normally not be at equal levels (Marx, 2001, summarizing models of multilingualism); L2-knowledge is usually not complete (Poulisse, 1999: 54).

b) "L2 speech tends to be less fluent than L1 speech" (Poulisse, 1999: 55).

c) Between the various languages of an individual, there is always some kind of interlanguage transference (Marx, 2001; Poulisse, 1999: 55).

d) L2 learning experiences and strategies affect learning of an L3 (Hufeisen, 2000).

The observations a) - d) are generally accepted as a fact. But to what extent they are valid is not clear at all. This is, above all, the case for points c) and d). In order to examine this question more closely, I developed two studies which should help qualify and quantify the dimensions of interlanguage transference, and the learner's strategic influence on multilingual processing.

It would take up too much space to describe in detail the two empirical studies which form the database of the following elaborations. Aside from that, abstracts of these studies are either already published (Müller-Lancé, 2000, 2001) or forthcoming (Müller-Lancé, 2003 for the complete studies). I will confine myself to briefly describing the samples and the methods of data elicitation:

The first study was based on an anonymous questionnaire distributed among 174 language learners of different target languages and educational institutions (high

J. Cenoz, B. Hufeisen & U. Jessner (eds.), The Multilingual Lexicon, 117—132.
© 2003 *Kluwer Academic Publishers. Printed in the Netherlands.*

school, university, adult evening classes). We tested which strategies these learners used for inferencing (Carton, 1971) the meaning of distinct words in Spanish and Italian texts. Aside from this test of reading comprehension, one group of the participants was included in a test which analyzed the capacities and conditions of foreign-language verbal memory in both comprehension and production.

The second study worked with a smaller sample, but a wider range of questions and methods: 21 students of Romance Philology were tested in the domains of written and aural comprehension (partially of languages they didn't know), and of written and oral production. Their individual processing in these tests was analyzed by means of "Think aloud" protocols. As well, the participants were submitted to a test of "learner types" and to a multilingual word-association test.

In all these tests, special focus was given to the use of formerly acquired foreign language competences and on the effect of the individual learner biographies. The target languages in the tests were Spanish, Italian and Catalan (+ German and French in the word-association test). Most subjects had competences in German, English and French, some also in Latin or other Romance or European languages.

In the following I'd like to present results of these studies, concerning the characteristic features of multilingual language processing. The different features are sorted into the categories I mentioned earlier in regard to psycholinguistic models.

1.1. Language Production and Comprehension

Every subject used inferencing strategies, but individual variety was enormous regarding quantity and quality of strategies employed. This variety depended less on individual language competence than on temperament, motivation and learning experiences of the individual. The following results were of general validity:

- Interlingual strategies (e.g. unknown Cat. *abandonar* => Fr. *abandonner*) were used much more often than intralingual strategies (e.g. unknown Sp. *delantero* => Sp. *delante*), or strategies based on context, or on knowledge of the world.

- Foreign language comprehension tests elicited more inferencing strategies than production tests.

- In foreign language production (Spanish, Italian), the mother tongue as a source of transference bases was avoided by native German speakers, but intensely used by native speakers of Romance languages. In comprehension, the avoidance of L1 was not as strong - so, the degree of typological relationship between source and target language seems to play a certain role, but language proficiency seems more important (see below).

- In foreign language production there was more *intra*lingual inferencing than in foreign language comprehension.

1.2. Structure of the Multilingual Mental Lexicon

The following results were valid for the supposed structure of the mental lexicon:

- Most inferencing strategies were based on formerly acquired lexical competences in other foreign languages - the mother tongue was less important.
- Subjects memorized words most easily which they could infer by means of better-known words from other languages.
- The decisive point for the choice of a lexical transference base at the sight of an unknown word was the similarity of the first syllables; less attention was given to the end of the word (e.g. unknown It. *arcivescovo* 'archbishop' => Ger. *Archiv* 'archives').
- L1 stimuli mostly provoked semantic associations (antonyms, synonyms, collocations etc.) in the same language (e.g. the stimulus Ger. *links* 'left' provoked the reactions Ger. *rechts* 'right' and Ger. *geradeaus* 'straight on'). Reaction to foreign language stimuli was more difficult to predict: The better the language was mastered by the participant, the more we found semantic associations. The less the language was mastered, the more we found phonetic associations (e.g. stimulus Cat. *feblesa* 'weakness' > Ger. *Fabel* 'fable'). Switching between different languages was more frequent with foreign-language stimuli.
- Interlingual cognates were extremely frequent as transference bases or associations (e.g. stimulus Cat. *primerament* > Fr. *premièrement* > Sp. *primeramente*).
- Subjects who had acquired their foreign language competences abroad preferred semantic target language associations regarding this stimulus language; subjects who had learned the respective language only at school tended towards translating the stimulus into their L1 and/or into other foreign languages (e.g. stimulus It. *porta* > Ger. *die Tür* > Fr. *la porte* > Eng. *the door*).
- Subjects who used their competence in different languages frequently and consistently in the framework of inferencing strategies did the same in the association test (see also Cenoz 2001 and this volume; Gibson & Hufeisen; and Hall & Ecke, this volume). The analogous regularity was to be observed in subjects who preferred using only one of their foreign languages or who primarily restricted themselves to the use of their L1. This observation was valid independently of the foreign language number and competence of all these polyglots.

1.3. Language Acquisition and Learning

The manner of language acquisition influenced multilingual language processing in the following way:

- For the degree of proficiency, time and order of foreign language learning were less important than motivation and visits abroad.
- The individual degree of proficiency in a foreign language and its degree of activation were more important than its typological similarity with the target language in choosing this as a source language in the framework of inferencing strategies.
- The effect of attrition was stronger in active than in passive vocabulary.

The next section will show to what degree all these features are represented in some popular models of multilingualism.

2. MODELS OF MULTILINGUALISM/MULTILINGUAL PROCESSING: AN OVERVIEW

It needs to be said that the international market for models of multilingualism is still dominated by models which are, strictly speaking, designed for bilinguals - namely for balanced bilinguals. A great number of these models is even derived from the famous *monolingual* Speaking Model designed by Levelt (1989). Since (asymmetrical) multilingualism is the worldwide norm, and monolingualism the exception, we can state that, in the domain of multilingual research until today, the ordinary case is mostly described by means of exception, which in our case means by monolingual or bilingual models.

Before designing a new model, it seems certainly useful to review the features of the existing models, and to analyze to what degree they correspond to the requirements of asymmetrical multilingualism.

The models I would like to take into consideration can be classified according to their focus of description (production/comprehension, structure of mental lexicon, acquisition/learning/attrition) and to their linguistic extent, meaning, to the number of considered languages. Here we can distinguish between bilingual and multilingual models - bilingualism figuring as a special subgroup of multilingualism. For the classification see Table 1 - the models influenced by Levelt's monolingual Speaking Model are underlined.

For reasons of space, it is not possible to go into all the details describing these models, nor is it necessary, since some of them have already been compared (Poulisse, 1999; Marx, 2001; Müller-Lancé, 2003). So, in the following, I will only point out a few particularities.

Table 1. Classification of models of multilingualism

	bilingual	multilingual
production/ comprehension	De Bot 1992 De Bot/Schreuder 1993 Poulisse/Bongaerts 1994	Meißner 1998 Williams/Hammarberg 1998
structure of mental lexicon	De Groot 1993 Kroll/Stewart 1994 Albert 1998	Green 1986/1998
acquisition/learning/ attrition		Hufeisen 2000 Herdina/Jessner 2001

2.1. Models of production/comprehension (language processing models)

De Bot (1992) is the Levelt modification which is closest to the original. Different languages are taken into account by means of a language-separated *microplanning* in the *conceptualizer* and the assumption of one *formulator* for each language. De Bot/Schreuder (1993) add the *verbalizer* function to distinguish which conceptual primitives (e.g. MOTION, FIGURE, CAUSE) go together for a particular language. For successful separating of languages, they suppose a *monitoring system* for language switching, Paradis' *subset hypothesis* and Green's conception of three different *levels of activation* (see below). Poulisse/Bongaerts (1994), too, start from the point that language selection is done in the *conceptualizer*. They further assume that both languages are stored in one mental lexicon and that language separation is guaranteed by language *tagging*. The selection of lemmas is achieved by *spreading activation*. Meißner (1998: 63) is a Levelt modification that represents production and comprehension (conceived as an inverted production process) at the same time. The question of language selection and language separation, however, has been excluded. This is the domain of Williams/Hammarberg (1998): They assume that in L3 production L1 and L2 are equally activated, but with different functions, one language acting as a *default supplier* (e.g. generally used as transference base), the other one as an *instrumental supplier* (limited to more specific tasks).

2.2. Models focusing on the structure of mental lexicon

De Groot (1993) argues that, due to a particular kind of storage, concrete words and cognates are more easily translated from one language to the other than abstract words and non-cognates. She also sets an end to the discussion about compound vs. coordinate bilinguals. Kroll/Stewart (1994) propose a hierarchical model which takes account of the asymmetrical relations between the lexical representations of L1 and L2 in the case of non-balanced bilinguals. Albert (1998) assumes different stores for the lexical representations of L1 and L2, but common stores for the graphemic and phonological representations of both languages. Green's Inhibitory

Control Model (1986) starts from the hypothesis that language production needs energy, and that resources are limited. So, all languages cannot be equally activated all the time: the most activated language inhibits the others. Therefore Green distinguishes three levels of activation: selected, active and dormant language. Language separation is guaranteed by means of tagging. Green (1998) adds multiple levels of language control, e.g. for routine behaviour or well learned actions. Where automatic control is insufficient, as in creative language tasks, Green assumes a Supervisory Attentional System (SAS).

2.3. Models focusing on language acquisition/learning and attrition

Hufeisen's Factor Model (2000) lists factors that distinguish Third Language Learning from Second Language Learning - e.g. foreign language learning experiences (metalinguistic awareness included), knowledge about one's own learner type, and L2 (-interlanguage) itself. The Dynamic Model of Multilingualism (Herdina/Jessner, 2000; 2002) takes account of some features of multilingual development, such as non-linearity of acquisition, learner variation, language attrition, interdependence of language systems, and the development of specific skills tied to language learning.

I need to warn that empirical verification of psycholinguistic models is a delicate subject: Monolingual and bilingual models are usually based on data such as reaction times, reading spans, artificial languages and "pseudo words". In this approach of "laboratory conditions", problematic factors such as different foreign language competences, different individual vocabularies etc. can easily be excluded. In turn, my own studies are based on everyday language practice and can be re-enacted anytime in different language-learning institutions - yet not identically reproduced: every change of verbal material or test subjects may somehow influence the results of my tests. Another methodological difference regards the problem of lexical access: In my studies, the processing of unknown words plays an important role. Yet, monolingual and bilingual models assume that the vocabulary being processed is already completely represented in the mental lexicon. Therefore these tests focus on automated processes of lexical access; whereas my tests focus on cognitive strategies of problem solving.

Therefore, the following is not about empirical verification of hypotheses, but about the question: Which of the models presented is most compatible with our everyday practice of multilingualism (compare the features in 1)?

The following table shows which features of multilingual language processing are represented in the models already mentioned: An X in the table stands for the complete representation of the respective feature, an (x) stands for partial or implicit representation. Of course, it has to be said that the number of x marks should not be regarded as an evaluation – their number just gives an impression of the variety of topics considered in the respective model.

Table 1. *Representation of various features of multilingual language processing*

models	considered features of multilingual language processing												
	more than 2 languages	inferencing strategies	distinction of product-ion and comprehension	different levels of language proficiency	role of typological similarity (L1-L2-L3...)	organisation of language separation	role of word beginnings	role of cognates	learning conditions	learning experiences	monitoring	role of motivation / temperament	development / attrition
De Bot 1992			(x)	(x)		X					(x)		
De Bot/ Schreuder 1993			(x)	(x)	(x)	X		X			X		
Poulisse/ Bongaerts 1994				X		X					(x)		
Meißner 1998	X	X	X	(x)	X	(x)		(x)					
Williams/ Hammar-berg 1998	X	X		X	X	X			X	X			X
De Groot 1993						X		X					
Kroll/Ste-wart 1994			(x)	X	(x)	X		X					X
Albert 1998				X		X		X					
Green 1986	X			(x)	(x)	X		(x)	(x)				(x)
Green 1998	(x)		X	(x)		X							
Hufeisen 2000	X	X		X	X				X	X	(x)	(x)	(x)
Herdina/ Jessner 2000	X	X		X	(x)			(x)	X	X	(x)	X	X

Models focusing on automatical language processing, as e.g. the Levelt Speaking Model or its bilingual modifications, can hardly represent the particularities of multilingual language processing - which, to some extent, was not intended anyway. But the more languages people know, the more occasions of cognitive influencing control they have on their foreign language processing, especially in the framework of inferencing strategies. Since they do not all seize these occasions in the same manner, the result is enormous individual variation regarding the utilization of other foreign language competences when producing or receiving target language utterances.

Accordingly, a language processing model designed for multilingual subjects has to take into account the influence of cognitive strategies and the conditions of inferencing as e.g. formal similarities of lexical items. Such a model will be presented in the following section.

3. STRATEGY MODEL

A model trying to include many features will inevitably be quite complex. Yet, to keep clarity in this model, I have decided to divide it into three different aspects: mental lexicon, language comprehension, and language production. My model is purely synchronic; the processes of foreign language acquisition and attrition had to be left aside for reasons of clarity.

Since the specific structure of the multilingual mental lexicon figures at the same time as condition and nucleus of such a model, I will start with this aspect:

The frequency of switching between various languages, including L1, makes it plausible that the languages of an individual are not separated in different "compartments of the mind". In the mental network the connections between the elements of different foreign languages are not necessarily weaker than those between foreign language elements and L1 elements. This evidence is compatible with an organisation structure along the lines of the *subset hypothesis* (Paradis, 1981). It remains difficult however to explain how the affiliation of lexical elements to a certain language is mentally represented. Since connections between L1 elements and L2 elements can be even stronger than between two L1 elements, it is not sufficient to suppose that elements of the same language are only marked by the strength of their mutual connection, as it is done in the *subset hypothesis*. So, in addition, we have to suppose a kind of *language tagging*. This tagging not only marks individual languages, but allows at the same time the distinction of L1 from the totality of the foreign languages. Otherwise it would be difficult to explain how it is possible that the L1 is often systematically avoided as a transference base in foreign language production.

Another essential aspect of the multilingual mental lexicon is the different "strength" of mental connections: extremely strong are those between *cognates*, i.e. phonetically and semantically related words of different languages. For this reason, cognates often serve as *trigger words* in the framework of bilingual code switching (Clyne, 1980). In the case of experienced foreign language learners, cognates of different languages seem to be connected even stronger mutually than to the respective L1 element, or to the other elements of the respective foreign language. Interlingual connections can therefore be stronger than intralingual connections. In addition, the multitude of spontaneous translations in the word-association test shows that there have to be very strong connections between certain foreign language forms, their L1 equivalents, and respective concepts. The fact that foreign language stimuli were often first translated into L1, and then into other foreign languages (above all in the case of concrete words), makes it plausible that the respective forms of L1, L2, L3 etc. are grouped around (metaphorically spoken) one common concept. The strength of the connection between two of these elements depends, among other things (e.g. frequency), on their formal similarity. The better a language is mastered, the stronger are the connections between elements of semantic similarity or contiguity. Finally, cross-linguistic connections can be built up quickly - but they can also be affected by attrition. So instability is a characteristic feature of the multilingual mental lexicon.

All these considerations lead to the connective model of the multilingual mental lexicon shown in Figure 1. It needs to be said that the distance between the nodes is merely metaphorical. For my example, I chose the concept of 'water' because the connections between Germanic and Romance cognates are easy to demonstrate in this case. It is also evident that we have to distinguish between the lexical signification in a certain language on the one hand, and the visual concept on the other hand: For instance, German *Wasser* is connotated with 'abundance', while Spanish *agua* is connotated with 'shortage'.

The subject represented in this model is an average germanophone student of Romance languages with competences in English, Latin, French, Spanish and Italian - according to individual competence in any of these languages, the respective connections have to be imagined as stronger or weaker (graphically represented by line width).

Of course, lexical significations can also be tagged. In the model, however, this tagging is already evident from the language indication inside the circles. An additional tag would be redundant in the model, and reduce clarity. Another point is the fact that this tagging is the most likely to be missing: Many learners are not at all aware of the differences in the significance of Ger. *Wasser* and Sp. *agua*. Since typological similarity plays a certain role in the choice of transference languages, we can also suppose the existence of a tag which distinguishes language families (e.g. Germanic vs. Romance languages). Of course, the network structure is different in every learner: Students of Romance Linguistics with etymological interests would even connect Fr. *eau* with Lat. *aqua*. In the case of students with particular semantic interests, we would also have to suppose connections between all language-bound significations. But representation of all eventualities would make the model less clear.

Let us now approach the question of how the elements of the multilingual mental lexicon are used in the process of L3 production or comprehension. The following essentials need to be taken into account:

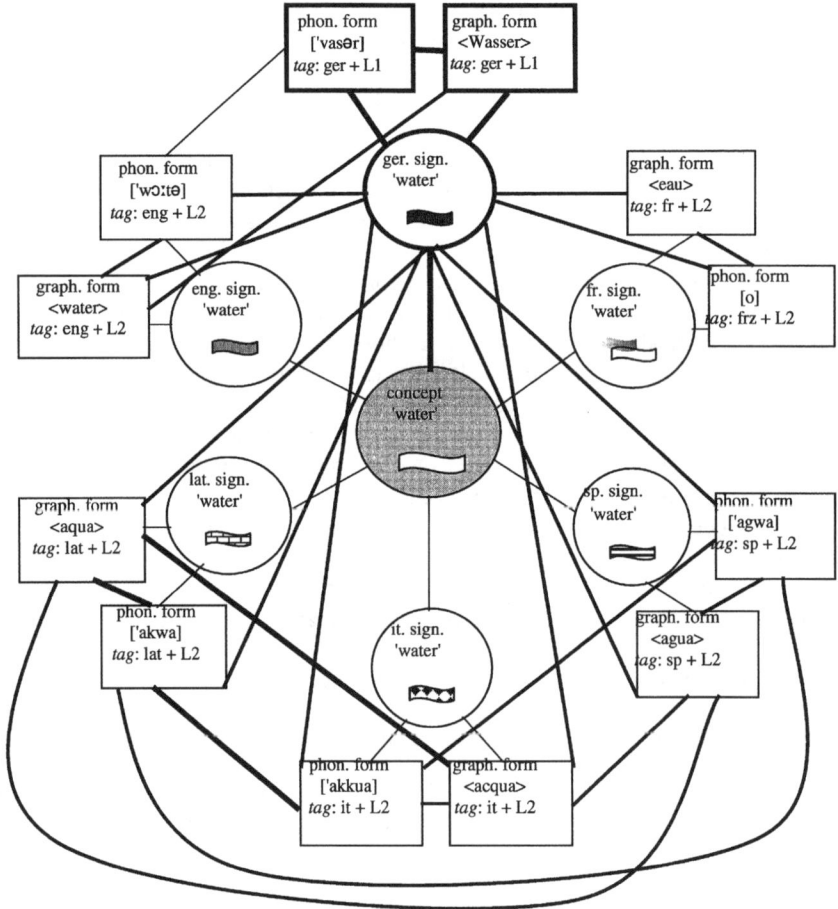

Figure 1 Connective model of multilingual mental lexicon

- The decisive point for the processing of unknown words is the formal similarity of a word's beginning (first and second syllable) to the beginning of a better-known word. This is a good argument for assuming a separate syllabary, as it was in Levelt/Roelofs/Meyer (1999).

- My association tests have shown that, if a subject has the choice of semantic *and* phonetic connecting, he usually opts for the semantic possibility. If there is no semantic access to a word form, he will opt for phonetic associations.

- Different languages can be activated in different ways (Green, 1986, 1993 and 1998). If a concrete language is *selected* as a transference base in the framework of inferencing strategies, it will probably be selected for the next lexical problem as well.

- In the context of selection, language activation and proficiency are more important than learning time or learning order.

- Learning experiences are not only decisive for the organisation of mental lexicon (tendency: language acquisition leads to intralingual semantic associations, language learning to translation associations), but also for the choice of inferencing strategies: We can suppose a kind of access filter for comprehension and production whose setting depends on individual language combination and proficiency, learning experiences and temperament. This explains, for instance, why experienced *germanophone* language learners (in contrast to *romanophones*) avoid transferences from their L1 in foreign language production when the target language is Romance - they have often had the experience that the risk of interferences is extremely high for this constellation; and on the other hand they have often seen that other Romance languages or English can be extremely useful in this context. According to Green's (1986) terminology we can formulate for this case that the Romance target language figures as *selected* language, the foreign transference language as *active* language, and the L1 as *dormant* language.

- The setting of the comprehension/production filter is also responsible for the search width when a subject is looking for transference bases: The higher the target language proficiency is developed, the smaller or more precise is the lexical field in which the transference base is searched. Subjects who have no competences for a target language normally search the whole net (i.e. mental lexicon) - provided that they are motivated.

- The result of a transference base search is controlled by a monitor in the sense of Krashen (1981). The monitor setting depends above all on target language proficiency and temperament.

- Regarding the choice of inferencing strategies, it seems that the world knowledge store can be inhibited by the mental lexicon. This assumption would explain the small number of inferences based on context, learning episodes (e.g. "Yesterday I still knew this word!") or world knowledge.

- There are differences between L3 production and comprehension regarding the principles of processing and the inferencing strategies: In L3 production for instance context, world knowledge and L1 are often ignored as sources of inferencing. A forced switch of language is first of all problematic in language production, and language production is also more affected by attrition.

These essentials are the basis of a new model of multilingual comprehension and production which I call the "strategy model". As it is the case in the model presented by Wei (this volume), both versions (comprehension and production) follow the monolingual Speaking Model of Levelt (1989) and Levelt/Roelofs/Meyer (1999), but they integrate the problem of identifying foreign language items and the use of inferencing strategies, and they distinguish between graphic and phonetic input and output. The processing steps in both versions are represented by colourless boxes; their order is symbolized by arrows. Storage-media are round and grey, accesses to these storages are marked by dashed lines. The structure of the mental lexicon in the model's heart should be imagined similar to our connective model (Figure 1), but with morphological and syntactical information in addition. The inferencing processes on the right side of the model are only triggered off if the "standard"-processing on the left side comes to nothing.

The starting point of my models is the scenario that a certain linguistic item has to be received or produced (designing a model for *complex* utterances is too difficult because foreign language utterances can contain known and unknown items. In these two cases however, processing is completely different). Regarding inferencing strategies, it needs to be said that they strongly differ between individuals. Beside this, individual influence is clearest in the motivation filter and in the comprehension/production filter, both marked by grey boxes. The motivation filter setting decides whether the intention of comprehension/production is maintained in spite of an initial failure. The comprehension/production filter is responsible for extending the width of search for every repeated attempt of comprehension/ production.

Since, in multilingual processing, comprehension normally precedes production, the comprehension version is presented first (see Figures 2 and 3).

Both models neither integrate problems of misunderstanding nor communication strategies as "demanding lexical help from the interlocutor", "change of subject" or "looking up in a dictionary". Monitoring in inferencing processes corresponds to the question: "Can the result of this strategy really be correct?" Each comprehension not only requires access to world knowledge, but it also confirms and completes world knowledge. The question of which language is selected as a transference base was left aside for reasons of clarity. Regarding inferencing strategies, we can suppose that after every renewed attempt of inferencing a certain unknown word, the search width is extended in the comprehension/production filter.

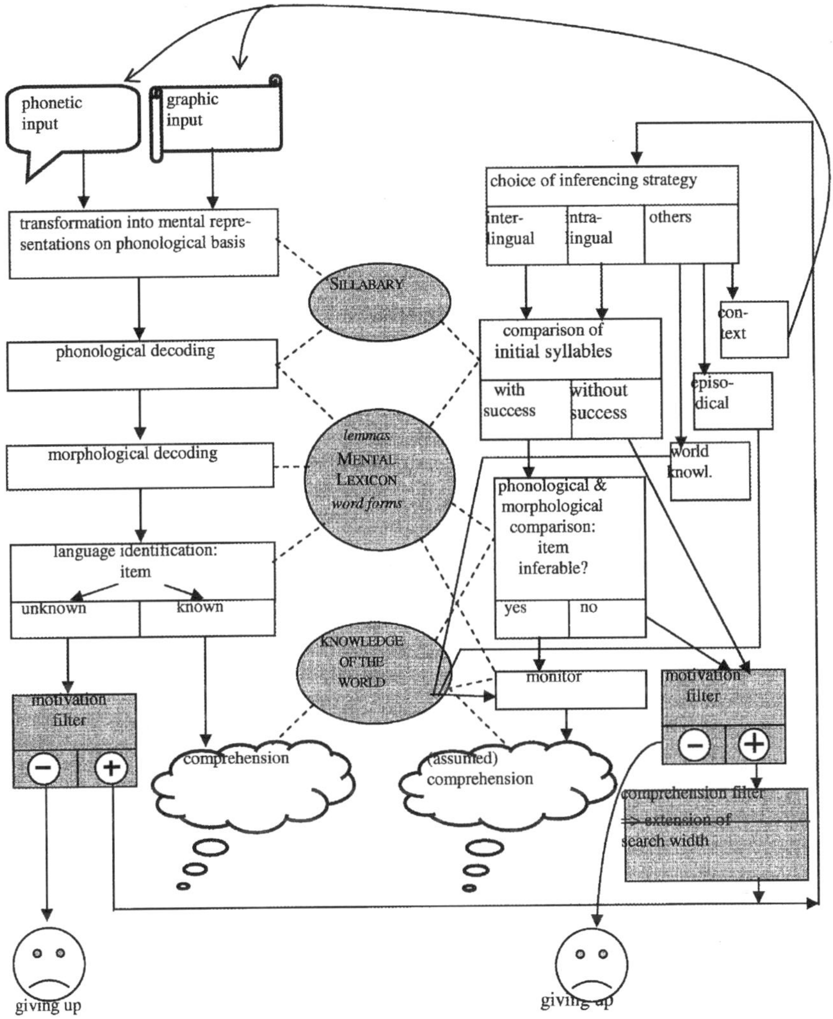

Figure 2 Model of multilingual comprehension (strategy model)

conceptual mes-
sage (intention)

KNOWLEDGE
OF THE
WORLD

choice of inferencing strategy

| inter-lingual | intra-lingual | others |

message generation
L1

episo-
dical

selection of lexical items
target language

lemmas
MENTAL
LEXICON
word forms

selection of
transfer base
=> successful?

re-phra-sing

| with success | without success |

| yes | no |

syntactical/morphological
encoding

motivation
filter

⊖ ⊕

analogous
target language
construction
possible?

retrieval of
target
language
equivalent
successful?

| with success | without success |

| no | yes |

| no | yes |

self-moni-toring

SILLABARY

monitor

phonological encoding,
generation of syllable structure

production filter
=> extension of
search width

phonetic
encoding

graphic
encoding

phonetic
output

graphic
output

giving up

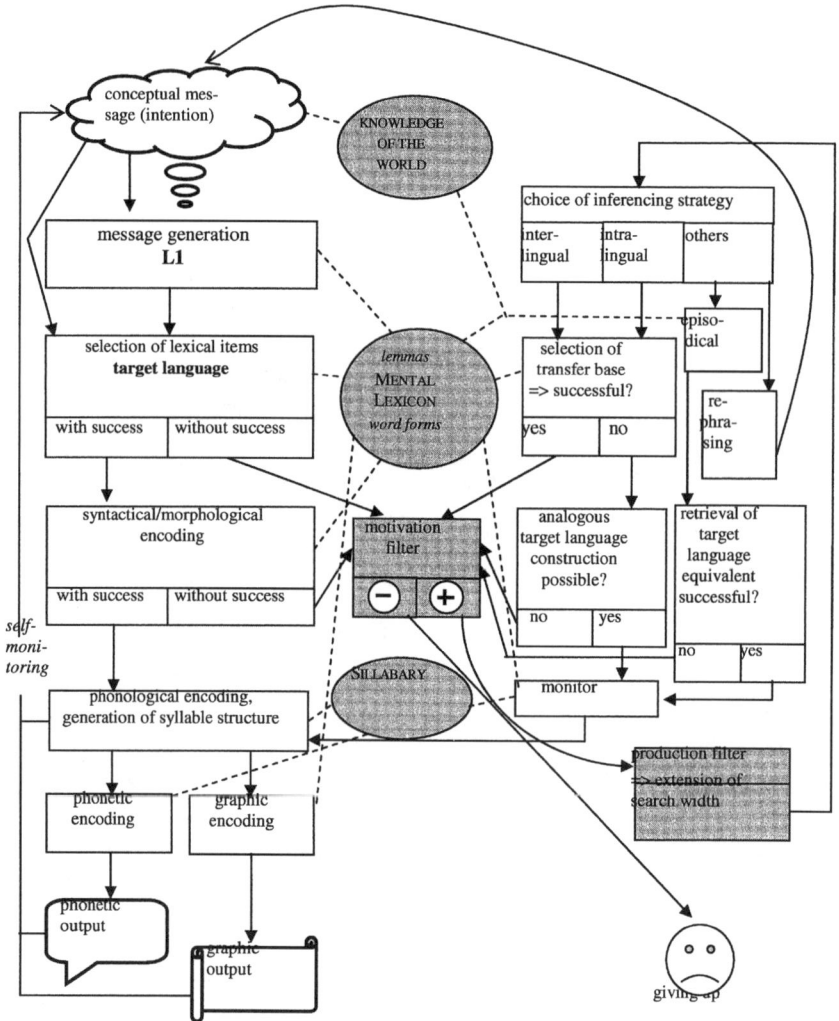

Figure 3 Model of multilingual production (strategy model)

With regard to the processes of L3 production, the difference of competences in the various languages is difficult to take into account - in bilingual models, this problem can be left aside. A speaker with high L3 proficiency, for instance, will normally abstain from generating a preceding L1 message plan. Such a speaker will directly encode the conceptual message into the target language (Albert, 1998: 94). The more frequent case of a speaker who first encodes his conceptual message into a verbal L1 message before translating this into the target language is also represented in my model. For reasons of clarity, I left aside the case of a learner who knows a target word approximately, but doesn't know exactly how to produce it phonetically - or graphically - correctly.

I have already mentioned that the individual willingness of making use of cross-linguistic relations differed widely from subject to subject. Some participants liked switching vividly between their different languages; others clearly preferred two of their languages; others were focussed on their L1. This not only affected the conscious inferencing strategies, but also the unconscious word associations and, what is more, it was independent from foreign language combination and proficiency (Müller-Lancé, 2000 and 2001). Therefore I assume that this behaviour is a result of individual temperament, monitor setting and structure of the mental lexicon (see Figure 1). Concerning the organisation of the mental lexicon, I propose three different types of multilinguals I call *monolinguoid – bilinguoid – multilinguoid*. In the case of multilinguoids, "strong" cross-linguistic connections exist between the mental representations of all languages; in the case of bilinguoids such connections are limited to two languages. The language biographical data of my participants led to the conclusion that this organisation of the mental lexicon is mainly a result of language learning conditions: Multilingual participants who learned a certain foreign language for the most part abroad clearly preferred this language over their other foreign languages. The processing by these bilinguoids could almost be explained by a bilingual model. Participants, however, who learned foreign languages mainly in the classroom, and were used to learning various languages at the same time and with cognitive methods, tended more to cross-linguistic connections which concerned *all* their languages (=> multilinguoids). This was particularly valid for participants who started their foreign language career with Latin. By the way, multilinguoid participants were also characterized by a particularly high degree of metalinguistic awareness, and are therefore best represented by the strategy model.

Now what about monolinguoid subjects, i.e. about individuals who are multilingual "on paper" only but who act like monolinguals when inferencing or associating? According to my data, these learners are the result of an unhappy combination of reserved temperament, monitor overuse, and a misguided foreign language education in the classroom. As long as teachers' explanations and textbooks continue ignoring common features between L1, L2, L3 etc. instead of stressing them, and as long as they continue offending in this way the nature processes of language learning (Jessner, 1999), we will continue having to deal with a depressingly large number of learners to whom "real" multilingualism remains an unfulfillable dream.

4. CONCLUSION

Research on the neurophysiological particularities of multilingualism is actually
booming, but it has not yet progressed to a degree that would allow us to
physiologically explain every step of multilingual language processing. And even if
this were possible one day, we would still have the problem of explaining the great
individual varieties in the manner of processing. Therefore, our knowledge about the
structure of the multilingual mental lexicon will keep being based on
psycholinguistic research for some further time. This research has shown e.g. the
specific role of interlingual cognates, of word beginnings and the evidence of
different degrees of activation in every multilingual mental lexicon. Furthermore, it
seems important to take into account some kinds of filters processing in the mental
lexicon and finally the distinction of different types of structures in the mental
lexicon: those of monolinguoids, bilinguoids, and multilinguoids.

University of Freiburg (Germany)

CAROL SPÖTTL & MICHAEL MCCARTHY

FORMULAIC UTTERANCES IN THE MULTILINGUAL CONTEXT

1. INTRODUCTION

In this paper we attempt to gain insight into how formulaic sequences in a multilingual context are accessed and utilised in the solving of comprehension tasks. We hope to show from the evidence presented that the processing of formulaic utterances would appear to differ from that of single-word vocabulary items and that this processing is more problematic in general for the (multilingual) learner. We consider the use of phonological cues to access meaning, the use of holistic and avoidance strategies and cross-linguistic interaction to gain direct or indirect access to shared meaning stores in L1, L2, L3 and L4.

2. VOCABULARY LEARNING TO DATE

The main body of vocabulary studies in SLA to date, whether interests have been on organisation, storage, retrieval or creative use, have centred on data gathered in the context of the processing of single words (Ringbom 1978/1983; Kellerman 1978; Meara 1984).

Recently De Carrico (1998) has questioned what the relevant unit of analysis for L2 vocabulary studies should be: the single word unit or the multi-word unit. She refers to Krashen and Scarcella (1978) as dismissing prefabricated lexical units as incidental and peripheral to the main body of language and their view, which to her knowledge remains unchanged, that such units play only a minor role in language acquisition. However, research into idiomaticity has long recognized that many everyday linguistic phenomena cannot be explained simply in terms of an open syntax into which single lexical items are inserted. Bolinger's (1976) seminal paper on the 'atomization' of meaning, in which he criticized the componential analysis of words, made the case for looking at semantic 'wholes', which may consist of stretches of frozen, unanalysable strings of words. Meanwhile, the neo-Firthian tradition in Britain, also from the 1960s onwards, has consistently argued for a view of meaning based on syntagmatic combinations (especially collocations, see Firth, 1951/1957; Halliday, 1966; Sinclair, 1966). Additionally, Pawley and Syder (1983) put forward convincing arguments that lexicalised sentence stems and other types of

J. Cenoz, B. Hufeisen & U. Jessner (eds.), The Multilingual Lexicon, 133—151.

fixed idiomatic strings play an important role in languages. They suggest that "the stock of (these units) known to the ordinary mature speaker of English amount to hundreds of thousands" (1983:192).

Sinclair's work is important in relation to the present paper. Engaged in writing the pioneering COBUILD learners' dictionary in the early 1980s, he became increasingly aware that certain long-held principles of linguistics (the primacy of syntax, the unpredictability and 'irregularity' of lexis) were no longer tenable in the face of corpus evidence. Lexis seemed to be far from irregular; patterns appeared everywhere in the lexical concordances generated from the corpus. Idiomaticity, far from being a marginal aspect of language, seemed to be ubiquitous and at least as significant as syntax in the construction of meaning (Sinclair, 1991: 112). Fixed, repeated strings abounded in Sinclair's data, and especially in combinations of the most frequent, everyday words (as opposed to the whimsical, low-frequency idioms often associated with foreign language teaching). This led Sinclair to assert the existence of a tight bond between sense and structure, and to the conclusion that collocations and idiomatic (in the sense of individual) but very frequently occurring combinations were the real glue that held texts together. Syntax was more, in Sinclair's view, a toolbox for repairing the occasional gaps and cracks amid the fluency of formulaic language. Others have followed on from Sinclair and focused their attention on formulaic sequences, and argued for giving them a more core position in descriptive and pedagogical linguistic concerns. (Weinert 1995; Nattinger and de Carrico 1992; Moon 1998, Howarth 1998; Wray 2000; Wray 2002). Additionally, Kellerman (1986) has offered important insights into how language learners perceive the transferability (or otherwise) of idiomatic and extended metaphorical meanings from their L1 to a target L2 which underline the need for greater investigation into the area of idiomaticity and beyond-word phenomena in SLA. Singleton (1999: 144) also comments on idiom avoidance among learners.

The majority of lexical acquisition studies have, furthermore, examined lexical operations between the learner's L1 and L2 (Meara 1984/1996, Ringbom 1978; Laufer 1989, de Bot and Schreuder 1993, Nation 2001). Although carefully stating that L2 can mean any number of other languages, the studies seldom present data of lexical processing involving a third language or more, notable exceptions being studies in Dutch and Scandinavian countries and bilingual communities in Spain where English is L3 (Bouvy 2000, Cenoz 1998, Lasagabaster 2000, Genesee 1998, Hammerberg 1998; 2001, Ringbom 1982; 2001).

The present paper examines formulaic language in a multilingual context. It presents part of ongoing research into the processing of formulaic utterances by the multilingual learner, based on high-frequency fixed expressions extracted from a corpus of present-day informal spoken British English.

3. PROCESS AND PRODUCTION AT WORD-LEVEL

3.1. L1-L2 Process

Research into lexical development in SLA in its early stages modelled its responses on psycholinguistic research into the construction and development of the L1 lexicon. What native speakers did, how children used and expanded their vocabulary formed the basis for theories on the construction of an L2 lexicon. Initial beliefs that the L2 lexicon and the L1 lexicon were similar were understandably logical. Issues such as the relationship between input and output, or that between form and meaning or even processing written and spoken forms of the target language all play a central role in these studies. Later research focused round the premise that unlike the L1 lexicon, L2 processing is not semantically focused but phonologically driven (Laufer 1989:17, Gass and Selinker 1994, Harley 1995: 7). Once again, though, conclusions that the second language lexicon is more form driven rest on results from single word studies such as the Birkbeck Vocabulary Project (Meara 1984) which worked with word association tests. Some of these results have since been questioned (Singleton 1997) on frequency grounds of the stimulus words in French and the possible semantic interpretation of the responses. The present paper tries to address this problem of low frequency stimuli in studies by confining its data to automatically retrieved high-frequency items.

3.2. L2 production

Ellis' essentially empiricist account of phonological memory in SLA states that "language learning is the learning and analysis of sequences. The learner must acquire sound sequences in words. The learner must acquire sequences in phrases. These sequences form the data base for the abstraction of grammar." The interests of the present study lie in how the multilingual learner perceives these sequences in formulaic strings. Ellis further argues that "individuals differ in their ability to repeat phonological sequences" (1996: 92). It is also interesting to note claims that the relative efficiency of phonological working memory is as important in determining the rate of L2 lexical development as it is in determining the rate of L1 lexical development. (Baddeley et al 1988). Both Levenston (1979) and Laufer (1991b) have shown that learners avoid words they cannot pronounce. This was found to be true also of the multilingual learner processing single word items (Hinger and Spöttl 2001). Just as children struggle with the sounds of new words in their L1 so do learners with their L2, L3 or L4. Many of these sounds are not present in their L1 and as such present an almost L1-like learning situation. However, the key issue is that the paradigm for single-word studies may not be applicable to multi-word items, where processing clearly cannot be based primarily on phonological cues at word level; if phonology is important it is likely to include supra-segmental features and possibly inter-word associations of sound and pattern. Furthermore, while Söderman's idea (1993) that each lexical item has its own processing history passing from a more phonological profile to a more semantic profile as it becomes more integrated into the internalized system may well hold true for single word items, there is no reason to suppose that the same conditions apply to multi-word items.

Wray (2000) puts forward powerful arguments concerning the non-analytical nature of formulaic language in native speaker competence. Attempts to encourage the analysis of formulaic strings in second language pedagogy are, in effect, "pursuing native-like linguistic usage by promoting entirely *un*native-like processing behaviour" (p.463, her emphasis). This is undoubtedly true; however, it needs to be balanced by two factors: (1) the psycholinguistic evidence that, even among native speakers, at least some degree of literalness or at least metaphoric awareness is retained in the processing of figurative expressions (Gibbs, 1986; Gibbs and O'Brien, 1990), and (2) the fact that language classrooms are loci of conscious analysis, unlike the real world. Additionally, one must distinguish between receptive knowledge and productive knowledge. Although productive knowledge of formulaic utterances might not be enabled by conscious analysis (insomuch as their syntactic or lexical variability may be very subtly restricted), receptive knowledge may well gain from analysis and, above all for our present purposes, from cross-linguistic comparison.

4. FORMULAIC SEQUENCES IN SLA AND TLA

To approach the role of formulaic utterances in a SLA and TLA contexts requires three things; clarification of how they are to be defined, consideration of their function in these contexts and the possible research approaches into how to access the learner's knowledge of this phenomenon.

Raupach (1984), investigating the interruption in the flow of spontaneous speech productions of German students of French, identified the number of words or syllables per "chunk" as one of the most reliable variables in the description of systematic differences between first and second language production. His definition is not primarily linguistic but more a psycholinguistic interpretation, seeing formulae as planning units in language processing. De Carrico describes lexical phrases as differing from other phrasal units in that they are form/function composites with more or less idiomatic meanings but with a further associated discourse function (1998:130); this builds on Nattinger and de Carrico's earlier work, which sees lexical phrases as important in the learner's grasp of pragmatic functioning (insomuch as lexical phrases tend to develop pragmatic specialisations) as well as being a useful set of items for cohesive production (Nattinger and de Carrico, 1992).

Wray defines the formulaic sequence as, "A sequence, continuous or discontinuous of words or other meaning elements, which is, or appears to be, prefabricated: that is stored and retrieved whole from the memory at the time of use, rather than being subject to generation or analysis by the language grammar," (Wray 2000:465). Retrieval, and the pathways taken by learners who have access to an L3 or L4, is one of the main interests of the present paper. Wray's concerns include how multi-word units function in L1 acquisition and how they function in the language of adult speakers. Corpus linguistics has yet to provide reliable statistics for the distribution of multi-word items in adult native speaker usage, partly because of the difficulty of automatically retrieving such units. Computers cannot reliably distinguish between strings which simply recur but which have no psychological status as units of meaning (e.g. the syntactically dependent string *to me and* occurs over 100 times in the corpus used in the present study) and those units which have a semantic unity and syntactic integrity, even though they may be less frequent (e.g. the unitary discourse-marker phrase *as far as I know* occurs less than half as often as *to me and* in the corpus). This has led some linguists to broaden the scope of chunking to incorporate syntactically incomplete strings (e.g. Altenberg, 1998; De Cock, 2000) simply on the basis of recurrent word combinations, which might include phrasal and clausal fragments (e.g. De Cock gives the examples of *in the* and *that the*) as well as intuitively meaningful but syntactically incomplete stems such as *it is true that*. In the present paper we have confined ourselves to those items in automatically extracted strings which display syntactic and semantic integrity, which has necessarily involved manual sifting of the automatically generated data (see below).

Research and debate on the structure of the trilingual lexicon centres round theories of independence or interdependence. For instance, Abunuwara (1992) looked at the relationship among different language systems which were on different levels of proficiency. The data from a trilingual Stroop colour naming test with Arab native speakers learning Hebrew and English led him to propose the developmental interdependence independence hypothesis. Herdina and Jessner's Dynamic Model of Multilingualism (2002) argues that as within the psycholinguistic model, language systems are seen as interdependent and not as autonomous systems, and that the behaviour of each individual language system in a multilingual system largely depends on the behaviour of previous and subsequent systems. It would therefore not make sense to look at the systems in terms of isolated development. They argue further that the acquisition of several language systems results in a qualitative change in the speaker's psycholinguistic system which adapts its own nature to meet new social and psychological challenges. The present research raises the possibility of ascertaining whether formulaic language presents such a challenge to the multilingual learner.

Krashen and Scarcella (1978: 183) acknowledge Filmore's claim that patterns are useful in establishing and maintaining relations but argue that routines and patterns do not serve a key role in acquisition and performance. This view too must be questioned in view of more recent studies. The fact that many first attempts in successful production of any second language frequently involve prefabricated language may lead to the belief that the task is a simple one for learners. This can be shown to be untrue. Secondly, many pedagogical approaches recommend making the learners aware of the existence of formulaic sequences, arguing that this enables them to recognise and use such strings with ease and thus improve their grasp of idiomaticity. In the long term this may be true. But both accurate use of multiword strings and particularly the ability to detect them are two difficult tasks for the learner. This study looks at the ease or difficulty subjects had in detecting multiword sequences in L1 -L4.

Formulaic language, when mastered, is argued to have processing advantages in real time language production. Raupach classified formulae according to their function as either 'fillers' or 'modifiers' and 'organisers'. Storing the 'big word' (Ellis, 1996:111) with a holistic meaning has been suggested as a means to by-pass the normal processing route (Wray 1992). This in turn has been shown to have associated discourse functions as it aids the learner's ability to hold the turn while constructing the new real message (Bygate 1988; Tannen 1989). One might further add that the very notion of 'fluency' must, to some extent be premised on the existence of ready-made, off-the-peg language being available to the speaker in real time.

Granger's data (1998) on EFL writing and Howarth's (1998) work on academic writing both point out that little has been done to attempt a description of the learner's phraseological performance. However, De Cock (2000) has produced interesting results which demonstrate that designing and including such descriptors in the speaking component in the large international exams might raise awareness, and produce data which would provide the beginnings of an understanding of how phraseological competence develops.

5. THE PRESENT RESEARCH

If we accept the recent powerful arguments for the more central position of formulaic sequences in language studies in general then the question must similarly be put as to their position in second and third language acquisition and pedagogy. The goals of this study were to establish learner ability in detecting these sequences and to gain insights into their phraseological competence in L2, L3 and L4. The specific research questions set were:

• Is there evidence that processing of formulaic utterances involves any significant use of phonological cues?

• Do particular types of word within formulaic utterances trigger searches? and if so how is this reflected in cross-lexical consultation in all four lexicons?

• Is there evidence of the use of holistic strategies and/or avoidance strategies in processing?

• Does proficiency level play a role?

5.1. Corpus and Analytical Procedures for the Present Study

The present study uses the five-million word CANCODE spoken corpus of British English. CANCODE stands for 'Cambridge and Nottingham Corpus of Discourse in English'. The corpus was established at the Department of English Studies, University of Nottingham, UK, and is funded by Cambridge University Press. The corpus consists of five million words of transcribed conversations. The corpus recordings were made non-surreptitiously in a variety of settings including private homes, shops, offices and other public places, and educational institutions in non-formal settings across the islands of Britain and Ireland, with a wide demographic spread. The CANCODE corpus forms part of the much larger Cambridge

International Corpus. For further details of the CANCODE corpus and its construction, see McCarthy (1998).

The procedure for extracting the data samples used in the present study was the following:

1 A rank-order frequency list was generated for the entire five-million word corpus. The list consisted of word-forms (non-lemmatised; i.e. *get* and *got*, for example, are two separate entries). Non-lemmatisation was purposeful: Sinclair (1991) argues convincingly that inflected and derived forms of words may enter into different syntactic patterns with different semantic/pragmatic meanings.

2 Working through the list of the 100 most frequent tokens, and ignoring articles, pronouns and other high-frequency non-lexical tokens such as *yes* and *and*, but including prepositions, other conjunctions, and basic adverbs such as *here/now*, concordances were generated for 20 high-frequency tokens ranging across the word-classes. These were:

know, got, think, get, go, when, had, now, said, see, sort, say, good, time, want, back, more, here, down, thing

3 Using software able to produce all recurring strings of variable lengths based on each key word, lists of all 4-word strings with a frequency greater than 10 were generated for each item. This produced clusters such as *you know when you* (for *when*), which were rejected (see the discussion in section 4 above), but also more integrated sentence-stem clusters such as *do you remember when [x]?*, which are certainly useful, frequent chunks in terms of fluent production. For the present purposes, and given our research questions, we were more interested in opaque or semi-opaque chunks which might present a processing challenge to the learner and which might or might not have accessible equivalents in L1 or L3, such as *when it comes to [x]* 'in the sense of 'when it is a question of [x]'), i.e. strings displaying at least a degree of semantic opacity).

4 The next step, therefore, was to identify and agree upon the most frequent non-transparent 4-word string in each list. In the case of *when*, this was indeed *when it comes to [x]*. The list of the ten chunks selected for use in the experimental part of this study is:

Know: as far as I know
Got: haven't got a clue
Think: had a think about it
Get: get rid of
Go: have a go
When: when it comes to
Had: had a word with
Now: every now and again
Said: turned round and said
See: to wait and see

5 The final step was to extract from the concordances a typical context for each selected string, which could either be used verbatim or edited to provide a suitable stimulus for the experimental learner context. The first ten items were finally chosen for the experiment, and these are reproduced as edited for the test contexts in Appendix A. Editing was necessary because unedited concordance lines often do not provide enough context to enable an item to be used fairly in a test. Learners are most likely to meet multi-word items in the real world in adequate contexts, not out of context or in impoverished or (to the outside observer) impenetrable contexts.

5.2. The Classroom Study

5.2.1. Project Description

A team teaching project was designed to try out various pedagogical/methodological approaches to instructed vocabulary acquisition for full time undergraduate students studying for a general degree in English and/or Spanish and/or French at the University of Innsbruck, Austria. The students were taught in English, Spanish and French simultaneously in five four-hour block sessions Classes were conducted in French, Spanish and English, with student contributions restricted to oral production in these three languages. Topics were chosen from the communication themes, task and purposes outlined in the Council of Europe's Common European Framework (CEF), 2001. Each lesson was designed around a common theme and semantic field; CEF theme 1. personal identification, CEF theme 10. food and drink and CEF theme 14. weather were chosen to provide enough vocabulary in the three target languages to build up towards the target goal of managing "small talk". Multi word strings were not explicitly taught. Teaching input was designed to strengthen metalinguistic awareness and develop oral competence in moving between the three languages.

The subjects who took part in the trilingual teaching were seventeen full time undergraduate students, three male and fourteen female, studying English as their first subject and Spanish or French as their second at the University of Innsbruck. As the course was a voluntary extra course open to all students, the group was understandably extremely heterogeneous. The range of proficiency levels was wide in English but largely more homogenous in Spanish and French. Scores on the Oxford QPT (Quick Placement Test) revealed that proficiency levels in English varied from band 2 (PET) to 5 (CPE). In Spanish, eight of the group were complete novice beginners and three were complete beginners in French.

Students were given two questionnaires; one to establish the number and chronology of languages learned and the other to illicit the student perspective on the dynamic nature of their abilities in the individual skills in each of their languages, both learned and acquired. The second questionnaire was designed to accommodate a more dynamic acquisition model (Herdina and Jessner, 2002) acknowledging that competencies in the various languages may shift over time (Hufeisen 1998, 169/170). Hufeisen's idea was developed further to include fluctuations in competence levels within the individual skills and respective languages. It was hoped this would provide more accurate information into the true multilingual nature of the group and insight into associated metalinguistic awareness.

The course ended with an associated introspection activity (think aloud protocols). Students were first trained in the procedure using a multiple choice activity on the mini domain of food, then given ten short dialogues containing the selected formulaic sequences in English and asked to translate them into German, Spanish and French. Thus for the keyword *know*, the chunked contexts were:

Know

> A <$1> How's Audrey then? How is she keeping?
> <$2> Fine **as far as I know**. I haven't really heard from her since the last time
> B <$1> So is George seeing someone else?
> <$2> Not **as far as I know**. And to be perfectly honest I'm not interested.

The think aloud protocols were taped on mini disc and subsequently transcribed. Permission to use the responses was obtained. It is the data from this activity that will be presented.

5.3. Results and Discussion

5.3.1. Questionnaires
Seventeen questionnaires were returned. All seventeen subjects had at least three languages in various combinations, fourteen had a fourth language and six had a fifth. Sixteen gave German as their dominant language and one Dutch. Twelve of the group gave English as their L2 and five as their L3. Italian (3), French (3) and Spanish (5) were the other most common L3s, reflecting the present Austrian foreign language practice in schools and Innsbruck's geographical proximity to South Tirol. Italian (4), French (5) and Spanish (3) were the most frequent L4s. L5 and L6 saw the addition of individual cases of Russian, Portuguese, Croatian, and Thai, evidence enough that the group was indeed multilingual. For the teaching context this does deserve mention as only too often the individual teacher sees the student as a native speaker of that country, learning whatever language the teacher is teaching, whereas quite complex interrelationships with other languages known to the learner may well influence the learning context. Such attitudes leave the teacher in the dark about potential metacognitive and metalinguistic awareness. The individual skills proficiency self-reports saw the receptive skills generally rated one grade higher that the productive skills with each additional language being rated one grade lower. This data was found useful for triangulation purposes with the introspective data. The task was a production task and students frequently voiced the fact that they understood (or thought they understood) the particular string but couldn't find suitable solutions in the L3 or L4.

142 CAROL SPÖTTL & MICHAEL MCCARTHY

5.3.2. Think-aloud Protocols

As a close link between the general level of language proficiency and phraseological competence may be hypothesised and further that the level of this competence would be highest in the L1, the starting point was to look at how the sample performed in the L1 responses to all the L2 English chunks.

Formulaic Utterances English L2- German L1

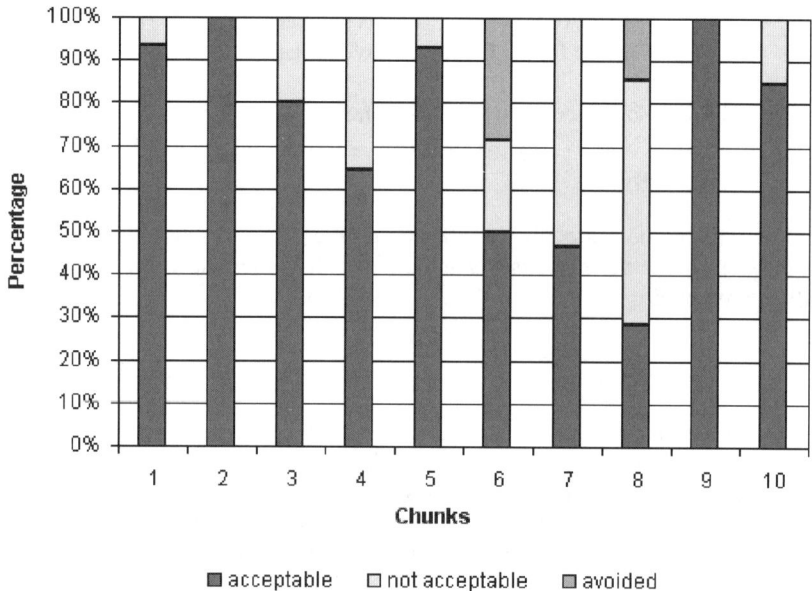

Figure 1. Formulaic utterances English L2 - German L1

Although in L1 these sequences in general did not pose a great problem, avoidance was still recorded in two strings (6 and 8) and on three strings (6, 7, & 8) more than 50 % gave an inappropriate response. Our next step was to see if this had any effect on the response in L3 and L4. Given that student mistakes can offer insights into how the multilingual mental lexicon is organised, the study divided the responses given to the formulaic word strings into three categories:

1. searches in the multilingual lexicon that produce an appropriate result
2. searches that produce a partial response (i.e. L1 but no L3 or L4) or inappropriate result
3. searches that produce no result

Transcript extracts: [**English**] [Spanish] *[German]* ***[French]***.
No alterations of any sort have been made.

Searches in the Multilingual Lexicon That Produced an Appropriate Result

[Corpus extract 2]

A. <$2> But I **haven't got a clue** how they work or anything.

This string produced the most homogeneous response with a large number of the sample producing the following search results:

[Student 2:Wolfgang]

[ich habe keine Ahnung], **I have no idea**
je ne sais comment I don't know
[Pero yo no sé cómo] I don't know

It would seem that the concepts clue: *Ahnung* (idea); *sais* (know); sé (know) are stored in close proximity with easy access in all four lexicons. This example suggests that the string search was not initiated by phonological features. Rather there seems to be a strong noun or verb around which the search has begun.

[Corpus extract 1]
B. <$2> Fine **as far as I know**. I haven't really heard from her since the last time.

[Student 3:Michaela]

In Spanisch: ¿Qué tal Audrey? ¿Qué *hace? Oder, ja, was macht sie? Und die Antwort. Gut.* Bien, que lo, no, que yo - *ich weiß* - saber *ist wissen - und ich* sabo?

Seventy three per cent produced the L1 response **so weit ich weiß** rather than the more appropriate **so viel ich weiß** which only 13% chose, suggesting cross-linguistic influence from L2 to L1: **far**/*weit* rather than *viel*/**many**. Bouvy's study of French L1 business students learning English L2 and German L3 or Dutch L3 produced similar data. She further argues that L2/L3 transfer is a feature of language use and not of language structure (Bouvy 2000:143). She states: *"L3/L2 transfer cannot be a by-product of learning but must be a performance process, attributable to the discrepancy between learner's linguistic competence and their communicative needs." (Bouvy 2000:152)*

Data from searches that produced an appropriate response also provided an insight into the learners' phraseological competence. Subjects' phraseology production ability in this study proved to be restricted to producing synonyms only from the stimulus L2 formulaic sequence to their L1.

144 CAROL SPÖTTL & MICHAEL MCCARTHY

[Student 6:Edith]

wait and see *Wir müssen warten und schauen und Däumchen drehen*

[Student 1:Kim]

Have a go *versuch es halt einfach mal* und äh *probier's aus*

[Student 3:Michaela]

get rid of *warum willst du es los werden*? Also, *warum gibst du es weg. probier's nur...* **have a go***...wie übersetzt man* **have a go with it***? ähm.. Ja eben so - probier's halt!*
wait and see *Wir werden warten müssen... also... und schauen müssen... also... ähm ...warten wir mal ab*

Widest range of responses: Chunk 6 "when it comes to"

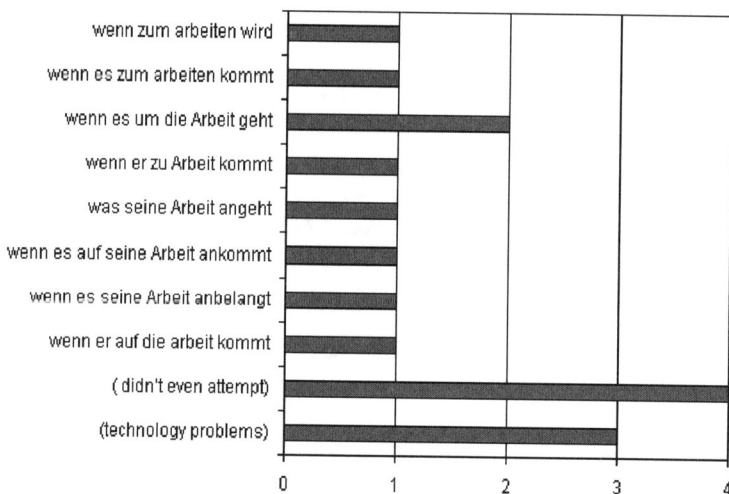

Figure 2. Widest range of responses

The data indicate that:

"The learner is searching for sequential patterns with reliable reference, and throughout this process, they are acquiring knowledge of the sequential aspects of language. From this perspective, language acquisition is essentially a sequence learning problem." (Ellis 2001:41)

The learners certainly demonstrate Ellis's reliable reference. They run through various L1 sequential patterns and check with the L2 stimulus string. The strings in L3 or L4 however do not appear to have established sequential patterns or connections. The data produced no evidence of synonyms or alternative phraseology being available for either L2 to L3, or L2 to L4, or L3 to L4.

The widest range of responses was generated by Chunk 6, "when it comes to" (see Figure 2).

Searches That Produced an Inappropriate Result

A. <$2> So why are you **getting rid of** it then?

Over 30% of the responses to this string in German were inappropriate. Students produced a wide range of seven different German chunks for this item with a higher rate of mismatch. Data suggested that the low frequency predicative adjective/adverb cue *rid* was so specific that it produced no connections in any lexical search L1/L3 or L4. Yet a search for the high frequency verb "get" was equally unproductive possibly suggesting that storage or retrieval of meaning with such delexicalised verbs is problematic and as such can offer little help as a starting point for lexical operations.

B. <$1> That's a good wine. That's one of my favourites. I keep buying it **every now and again**.

This chunk best illustrates Wray's (2000) claim that these formulaic sequences are difficult for the learner. Approached analytically this string is not difficult. Its component parts are covered in the first fifty hours of teaching. Yet as a formulaic sequence its meaning proves to be illusive. The total responses here produced the narrowest range of alternatives: three in German, two in Spanish and one in French

Table 1. Responses in German, Spanish and French

German	Spanish	French
ab und zu (now and again)	siempre (always)	tous le temps (every time)
hin und wieder (now and again)	Cada semana (each week)	
immer wieder (always)		

Just over 70% of the German responses were the inappropriate *immer wieder*. This in turn appears to have influenced the lexical search in the L3 and L4, even among those subjects who chose the appropriate German chunk.

[Student 3:Michaela]
now and...every now and again...*also hin und wieder...ähm...was heißt „immer" jetzt auf Spanisch?*

Searches That Produced No Result

Phonology and Avoidance. In the present study the ability to pronounce individual words in the multi word string was shown to have no effect on success in the task. Evidence of avoidance however was strong. Even after voicing and repeating the multiword strings, learners ignored chunks that produced no search results. The following is typical of the approach taken by many of the subjects.

[Corpus extract 3]
<$2> And that's gonna be 498 pounds including your tax.
<$1> Four nine eight.
<$2> Including your tax and everything.
<$1> Right. Okay. That's lovely. Thank you very much for your help Trevor. I'll get back to you erm when I've **had a think about it** yeah?

[Student 2:Wolfgang]: L1 G, L2 E, L3 S, L4 F.
German
Und das macht 498 Pfund inklusive Steuer. 498. Inklusive Steuer und alles. Richtig. Ok. Das ist schön. Danke für deine Hilfe, Trevor. ähm... Ich komme darauf zu..., ich komme auf dich zurück, *wenn ich darüber nachgedacht habe.* Ok, kein Problem. Danke. Ok dann. Bye. Bye.

The response showed no hesitation in real time production into the L1 and no reliance on repetition of the stimulus phrase to gain processing time. Yet this changed to avoidance and code-switching at the boundaries of the formulaic strings in L3/French and L4/Spanish.

[Student 2:Wolfgang]: L1 G, L2 E, L3 S, L4 F.
French
Je sais 498 avec le tax. 498. avec tax. Right. *C'est bon. C'est bon* (laughs). *Merci pour ..., merci, Trevor, ja...* I'll get back to you when I've had a think about it...Ok, no problem, *merci*, ok, *salut, salut.*

[Student 2:Wolfgang]: L1 G, L2 E, L3 S, L4 F.
Spanish

Y son (ja, das Wort da) ciento, cuatro ciento, noventa ocho con la tax, no sé...ähm...cuatro, neun, nove, ocho, con la tax y todo. Ok, es bueno. Muchas gracias para tu ayuda, Trevor ...ähm...Yo **get back to you when I've had a think about it**... yo te di, dice, dico ...Sé yo sé (laughs). Bueno, no problema, muchas gracias, bueno, ciao, ciao.

A multilingual view of task performance: All chunks L2 to L1,L3, L4

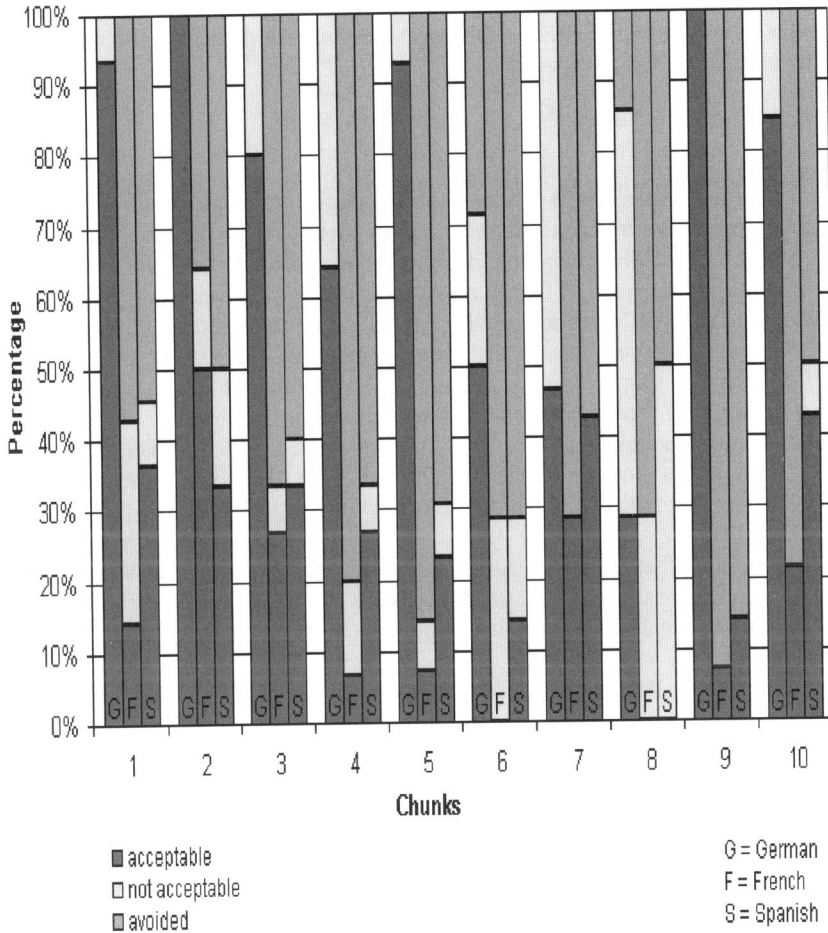

Figure 3. A multilingual view of task performance: L2 to L1,L3, L4.

Detection. Although some searches produced no result, the data produced evidence of learner ability to detect the parameters of the formulaic sequence. Code-switching in this study frequently took place at the boundaries of formulaic sequences, as also reported in Backus' studies with bilinguals (1999).

[Student 1:Kim]
[Je ne sais pas] [how they work]
[Merci] [for your help] Trevor

Receptive knowledge would appear to be evidenced but productive phraseological competence to end the task is not sufficiently developed. Yet this also seems to lend support to Raupach's psycholinguistic argument that formulae are planning units in lexical processing.

6. CONCLUSION

This study broadly questioned whether the paradigm for single-word studies was applicable to multi-word items. The results show this not to be the case. Söderman's idea of the learner building a phonological profile for each word which develops to a more semantic profile was not found to be evidenced in the processing of formulaic utterances. Futhermore, word knowledge of individual items in the string was not found to have influenced success in search responses. The learner must acquire phrasal sequences: sequencing in L3 and L4 was found to be a more highly developed skill with fewer commonalities to fall back on, with fewer shared words or similar sound structures that are closely interconnected. The data has shown such processing to be in the main difficult from L2 to L1 and considerably more problematic for the multilingual learner, thus lending support to Wray's (2000) claim discussed earlier.

Word searches focus simultaneously on form and meaning. The search takes place in a meaning based lexicon; word entries are stored as double entries linked to words that share similar characteristics, either sound, form, meaning or lexical field. This seems to be the accepted stage of understanding of the organisation the second language lexicon. Formulaic utterances would seem to require a further developmental stage to organise meaning associated with strings in various languages. The search does not appear to begin with sound for reasons related to the compositional nature of fixed expressions. Our subjects appear to have to followed two types of path. Either the meaning of the phrase in the L2 or L3 has been learned and clearly stored as such or the search begins with a grammatically-biased search for a strong verb or noun in or near the formulaic sequences. In the present data the de-lexicalised verb forms led to a higher degree of inappropriate choice of meaning. The more idiomatic the use in the L2, the more difficult the task in finding a suitable search result in the L3 or L4.

Wray (2002: 5) further asserts: "It is proposed that formulaic language is more than a static corpus of words and phrases which we have to learn in order to be fully linguistically competent. Rather, it is a dynamic response to the demands of language use, and as such will manifest differently as those demands vary from moment to moment and speaker to speaker"

For the multilingual learner and user of formulaic sequences, on the basis of the evidence here, it might appear that the four or more lexicons function independently in regard to formulaic sequences. Relatively little evidence was found of cross-formulaic consultation. Yet if these strings have not been taught with a unitary meaning and are only likely to be acquired through developmental sequencing with reliable reference, it is difficult to see how they can be stored in relation to one another in the several lexicons of the multilingual learner. Moreover if the formulaic phrase is not known then there may be nothing to consult. That no data was found in this study, however, cannot be interpreted as evidence for the independence of the various lexicons. As always, absence of evidence does not necessarily constitute evidence of absence, and a considerable amount of further research in different contexts of multilingual learning and with a wider range of lexical chunks is desirable.

University of Innsbruck (Austria)
Univesity of Nottingham (United Kingdom)

7. APPENDICES

Chunks in their contexts

1. Know
<$1> How's Audrey then? How is she keeping?
<$2> Fine **as far as I know**. I haven't really heard from her since the last time.
<$1> So is George seeing someone else?
<$2> **Not as far as I know**. And to be perfectly honest I'm not interested.

2. Got
<$2> I was thinking of buying a camcorder.
<$1> Mhm.
<$2> But I **haven't got a clue** how they work or anything.

3. Think
<$2> And that's gonna be 498 pounds including your tax.
<$1> Four nine eight.
<$2> Including your tax and everything.
<$1> Right. Okay. That's lovely. Thank you very much for your help Trevor. I'll get back to you erm when I've **had a think about it** yeah?
<$2> Okay. No problem.
<$1> Thank you.
<$2> Okay then.
<$1> Bye.
<$2> Bye.

4. Get

\<$2\> See, that looks nice on you actually.
\<$3\> That suits you. It does it suits you.
\<$1\> It's a lovely, lovely blouse.
\<$3\> It suits you.
\<$2\> So why are you **getting rid of** it then?
\<$1\> Because it's too short for me.

5. Go

\<$2\> I can use a computer reasonably well.
\<$1\> You can?
\<$2\> Except that's not how we normally log on.
\<$1\> I know it might look a bit different. This is just the log-in thing.
\<$2\> Oh, right, okay.
\<$1\> Well, just try it out and **have a go** at it.
\<$2\> So, I just follow the instructions
\<$1\> Yeah.
\<$2\> Right, okay, that's brilliant.

6. When

\<$2\> You know what Ted's like.
\<$3\> Mhm.
\<$1\> He's very, very intense **when it comes to** his work. I suppose you have to be with doing a P H D. But I mean I've got a friend who's doing it who just isn't as intense as Ted.

7. Had

\<$1\> Did he explain what he had done when he looked into it?
\<$2\> Well he just said he'd looked into it and **had a word with** Mr Bowen.

8. Now

\<$1\> That's a good wine. That's one of my favourites. I keep buying it **every now and again**.
\<$3\> You buy a bottle a week.
\<$1\> We've had some good Australian wines too.

9. Said

\<$2\> Gloria says to him, "Oh, you know, somebody's got to come in and fill the tanks up," she says. And she **turned round and said** "What are you telling me for? I'm away."
\<$1\> What tanks?
\<$2\> Acid tanks.

10. See

<$1> I don't know whether or not we're going to have anyone free to go to that meeting. We'll have **to wait and see**.

RITA FRANCESCHINI, DANIELA ZAPPATORE & CORDULA NITSCH

LEXICON IN THE BRAIN: WHAT NEUROBIOLOGY HAS TO SAY ABOUT LANGUAGES

1. INTRODUCTION

Linguists look with high expectancy towards the neurosciences and their findings on the neuronal basis of language(s). New functional neuroimaging techniques such as Positron Emission Tomography (PET) or functional Magnetic Resonance Imaging (fMRI), but also EEG and MEG[i], have raised an enormous interest in the scientific community (as well as in the general public) and led to enthusiastic exclamations such as "finally, we can have a look at the brain while it is at work". However, these techniques, just as any other technique, have their specific limitations (cf. Posner and Raichle 1996; see Fabbro 2001 for a summary). The view on the brain with neuroimaging techniques (fMRI and PET) is not yet as fine-grained in spatial resolution as one may wish (see also De Bot, in press). We do not see single neurons at work, but only areas of a variable extension (from about 1.5 to 3 mm, with a 1.5 tesla-tomograph). In the dimension of time, we cannot follow the brain's activities step by step in the order of milliseconds. Electrophysiological techniques, on the other hand, provide a good time-resolution, but are even less precise in the localisation. Compromises between a better time or spatial resolution have always to be made[ii].

The goal of this paper is to present a state of the art on issues concerning language(s) and the brain. The field is too wide to be fully embraced within this limited space. We therefore decided to concentrate on studies using neuroimaging techniques, as these investigations have made major new contributions. The reader, however, should not expect definite answers. We are only at the beginning of a vigorously developing branch among disciplines.

This chapter looks at neurolinguistic studies from a linguist's perspective seeking answers to crucial questions in multilingualism research. Section 2 first briefly reviews some studies addressing the issue of the neurobiological reality of linguistic components such as phonology, morphology, syntax, and semantics and the lexicon, and then, secondly, dwells, in more detail, on studies on bilingualism. Thirdly, it offers generalizable outcomes based on the review. Section 3 places the

J. Cenoz, B. Hufeisen & U. Jessner (eds.), The Multilingual Lexicon, 153—166.

generalizable results in a wider theoretical framework. Before this, section 1 situates the present effort between the questions asked in the research fields of multilingualism and of the neurobiology of language.

1.1. Multilingualism: Main Questions

In multilingualism research – we prefer *multilingualism* (and not *bilingualism)* as the more generic term – the main questions concern the shared or separate handling of the multilingual competencies of individuals. A body of evidence from surface data such as interferences, code switching, code shifting behaviour, interpreters activities, etc. suggests common, shared or overlapping activated features of two (or more) languages as well as their independent or competing activation. Are languages in a multilingual individual closely related or only, in a peripheral sense, inter-related? Is selective access possible by suppressing the other competencies? To date, linguistics – both from behavioural and experimental data collected in different theoretical settings – has not given a clear picture[iii] and insights into the brain's functioning are hoped to elucidate the above mentioned questions. Two principal aims can be distinguished:

On the grammatical side, there is an enormous interest in knowing whether there is a common ground for grammatical distinctions of two and more languages. Is each language represented separately in the brain or do we have evidence for totally or partially shared modules or features and additional, language-specific parts? Are all levels or modules shareable between two and more languages? Does the brain differentiate among languages according to typological distance (see Cenoz, this volume)?

On more extra-grammatical levels, the main questions concern the representations of multilingual abilities and competencies depending on the age of exposure and acquisition, the explicit and implicit knowledge, the motivational and emotional involvement, the biographical circumstances of acquisition (e.g. tutored or untutored), and the learner profile. Are languages learned early, in the family (mostly with great emotional impact), represented in a different way than languages learned later, e.g. as a foreign language at school? Do languages best known and highly automatized at the moment of testing show similar patterns? Are languages acquired exclusively orally and nowadays usually not written (see regional dialectal varieties in Romance languages or Southern German Dialects) represented in a different way? Do different reading traditions (e.g. Latin alphabet vs. Chinese characters, reading from left to right or vice versa) influence the organisation of a language in the brain?

1.2. Main Directions in the Neurobiology of Language

For the purposes of empirical testing, these questions are too general. They need to be curtailed, because only specific abilities or single features can be observed in neurobiological/-psychological experiments. Within the various tendencies we may recognise two extreme poles:

a) One major tendency can be characterised as pursuing an atomistic and very detailed programme, with small units being tested, measured and localised. The advantages are the high level of control, the decontextualisation, and the level of abstractness of the linguistic categories tested. The disadvantages concern the difficulty to relate the different and often highly specific results to each other, and to find the exact correlate to a realistic language ability. Two examples: Persons may have to learn a nonsense language for a test or to produce rhyme-words under time pressure. Are these central linguistic abilities? And, to what extent do test-situation abilities interfere with the original question to be tested (such as the syntax-semantic independence)?

b) The second tendency can be characterised as a holistic, global, or a systemic approach. More general abilities are tested, such as 'narrating or listening to a story', 'recognising words pertaining to language A or B'. Thus, instead of small, reductive categories as in a), the interplay between different systems comes into focus. This implies that knowledge about the functioning of other systems (such as memory, attention, co-ordination of specific activities) is needed. Although, at first glance, we may have the impression that more realistic abilities are under observation, the disadvantages of this approach become evident when interpreting the data: a concert of brain activities is visible and its exact interpretation is yet unclear. Moreover, individual differences may become more apparent in investigations using a holistic task. The cultural shape of activities may also play a greater role in this approach. As for a), generalisations are hard to make, and interferences of the test-situation cannot be excluded.

Proponents of both approaches agree on the fact that a simple localisation in the brain of (sub-)components of language(s) is not sufficient to explain the functioning of language abilities. The very heuristic question is, however, how to reach results for such complex activities such as language production and perception: inferencing from single, reduced parts to the whole, or by means of analysing directly a complex system of activity?

2. THE STUDY OF LANGUAGES IN THE BRAIN: A REVIEW

2.1. Classical Language Areas

About 140 years ago Paul Broca and Carl Wernicke first described the classical cortical language areas. They are localised in the left hemisphere, which has been established as the dominant hemisphere for language processing in right-handed persons[iv]. Broca's area is situated in the frontal lobe and encompasses Brodmann's area[v] (BA) 44 and BA 45. It is said to subserve mainly motor processes of language production and syntactic computing. Wernicke's area is localised in the temporal lobe, in the posterior part of BA 22 and is involved in the processing of language comprehension. It is also supposed to be part of the lexical and semantic knowledge system. These areas are located at the two ends of the Sylvian fissure (Fig. 1). Not only Broca's and Wernicke's areas, but also all other cortical structures around the Sylvian fissure (the so-called perisylvian areas) are involved in language processing.

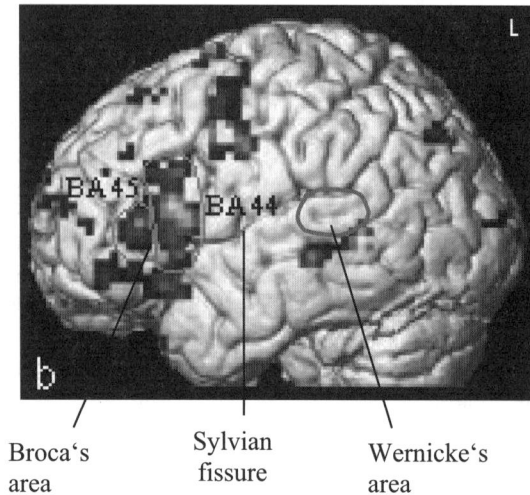

Broca's area   Sylvian fissure   Wernicke's area

Figure 1 Reconstruction of a normalised human brain

Areas activated during speech production (see Wattendorf et al. 2001) are marked in red to yellow shading. The classical language areas Broca and Wernicke are surrounded by a green line.

2.2. Studies with (Presumed) Monolinguals

In the following description of imaging studies we describe only the task condition. It should be borne in mind, however, that the activation found is always the activation in relation to a reference task. Evidently, the type of reference task will influence the outcome of the study.

2.2.1. Dissociating Semantic and Syntactic Processing, and Broca's Area

Numerous imaging studies have investigated the cortical structures processing (morpho-) syntactic and semantic information. Moro et al. (2000), e.g., tried to disentangle the representation of morphology, syntax and phonology in the brain. To "neutralize the access to any semantic component" (Moro et al. 2000: 111), the investigators used Italian sentences consisting of non-words with functional words and morphemes being fully preserved. The results showed a partly shared activation pattern for all three levels of processing, but also revealed additional specific neural networks in cortical and subcortical structures, for phonological, morphological and syntactic computation.

One of the debates in this field deals with the question of whether Broca's area is specialised for syntactic processing only or whether part of that region is involved in semantic processing as well. Friederici et al. (2000a, b) found that BA 44 was selectively activated by syntactic aspects, whereas activity in BA 45 was elicited by task demands focusing on semantic aspects. Similarly, a previous study (Dapretto and Bookheimer 1999) revealed engagement of BA 44 when computing syntactic structure and a neighbouring region to Broca's area, i.e. BA 47, for processing of lexical-semantic information. Evidence is accumulating suggesting that the two prefrontal areas BA 45 and BA 47 may be involved in "retrieving, maintaining, monitoring and manipulating semantic representations stored elsewhere" (Martin and Chao 2001: 198).

2.2.2. Processing Lexical Semantic Aspects
Several other studies investigated the representation of lexical-semantic information in the brain. Poldrack et al. (1999) found a dissociation for semantic and phonological processing in the frontal cortex. Some regions appeared to be specifically elicited by semantic processing, while others displayed a significant amount of overlap for semantic as well as phonological processing. The authors conclude that semantic processing of words automatically engages phonological processing as well.

Damasio et al. (1996) studied the neural correlates for lexical retrieval. They found activations related to specific categorical retrieval as well as areas for lexical processing in general. The authors conclude that "the neural systems subserving conceptual and word-form knowledge for the same entity, are, in the very least, partly segregated" (Damasio et al. 1996: 505) with different mediating regions engaged depending on the semantic category. Similarly Pulvermüller (1999) – supported by several imaging studies on the processing of words – postulates that words in the brain are represented in widely distributed neural networks, mainly in the left hemisphere, connecting neurons in the perisylvian area with neurons in other cortical areas depending on the semantic content of the word. Within this network, distinct category-related regions were established for words denoting colours compared to action words (Martin et al. 1995), for body parts and numbers (Le Clec'H et al. 2000), as well as for animals and tools, and the living/non-living distinction (Cappa et al.1998; Perani et al.1999a; see Martin and Chao 2001 for a review). Not only category specificity but also the emotional valence of a word influences the pattern of activated structures by e.g. evoking activity in a subcortical structure such as the amygdala (Isenberg et al. 1999; Perani et al. 1999b). Le Clec'H et al. (2000) showed that a subset of the elicited network is stimuli-independent, and according to Martin and Chao (2001: 194) "information about object-specific features may be stored within the same neural systems" accessed in language comprehension as well as in speech production.

Perani et al. (1999b) studied syntactic category as an organisational principle of the lexical knowledge in the brain. The study revealed common areas for the processing of verbs and nouns and hence failed to delineate distinct regions, which are selectively activated by word class. The authors explain that because of the overlapping semantic content of the stimuli (verbs and nouns were matched for semantic category) the differences related to word class may have been minimised. Nonetheless, additional regions were found for verbs only. The authors reason that "the differential activations associated with verb processing might thus be, at least in part, related to the automatic access of structural (syntactic) information associated with active verbs" (Perani et al. 1999b: 2341). These findings may be interpreted as indicative for the larger amount of structural information stored with verbs than with nouns (Aitchison 1990: 101).

In sum, the exact correlation between brain structures and the components of the linguistic system is still under debate. There exists, however, consensus that our knowledge of language is represented in subsystems in the brain and that each component is independent to a certain degree. The very rough distinction into frontal areas (including Broca's area) being involved in syntactic, morphological, and phonological processing as well as in language production, and temporal and parietal areas subserving lexical-semantic aspects still holds true.

2.3. Studies with Bi- and Multilinguals

2.3.1.Language Production

Word Generation. One of the very first studies on bilinguals with neuroimaging techniques was carried out by Klein et al. (1994, 1995). They tested single word processing in two languages in three lexical task conditions. English-French bilinguals who had learned their L2 after the age of 5 were instructed in the first test condition to generate a synonym, in the second to give a translation equivalent, and in the third to produce a rhyming word. Essentially identical activation patterns were found across tasks "independent of the search requirement and irrespective of whether the search took place in the first or second language" (Klein et al. 1995: 29). Producing a translation equivalent in L2 revealed superior activation in a subcortical structure, the left putamen. The authors reason that speaking in a language learned later in life imposes increased articulatory demands and that therefore "additional neural processes within this structure are required for production of L2 as compared to L1" (Klein et al. 1995: 31).

In a more recent study, Klein et al. (1999) investigated cerebral organisation in Mandarin Chinese subjects, who had learned English in adolescence, during a verb generation task. Similarly to the preceding investigation, this study revealed shared neural substrates even for such contrasting languages as Chinese and English. However, the authors did not find any difference in subcortical structures as in the first study.

Chee et al. (1999a) studied the activation patterns during a word completion task in two groups of Mandarin Chinese-English bilinguals. The subjects were divided into an early (exposed to both languages before the age of 6) and a late bilingual group (L2: English, learned only after the age of 12). Stimuli were presented in Latin script for English and in the ideographic script for Chinese words. Similar to Klein et al. (1994, 1999), Chee et al.'s (1999a) findings yielded overlapping cortical areas independent of age of acquisition and of input modality. All three studies were conducted with PET.

In a first pilot study on three languages, Yetkin et al. (1996) used word generation to assess fluency effects on brain activation in the form of number of pixels activated by a language. The subjects were fluent in two languages and not fluent in a third language. The authors make no indications about the age of acquisition of the languages. The results show that a higher number of pixels is activated by the non-fluent language compared to the languages in which the subjects were fluent. Thus, activation decreases as fluency in a language increases.

Story Production. In a fMRI study, Kim et al. (1997) established different organisation patterns in early bilinguals, who had acquired their two languages simultaneously, and in late bilinguals, who had learned their L2 as adolescents. The subjects had various combinations of languages and were fluent in the languages tested. They were instructed to describe events which had occurred the day before. The analysis of Broca's area revealed activity in distinct cortical areas within this structure for the two languages of late bilinguals, whereas the two languages of early bilinguals tended to be represented in the same field. Interestingly, in Wernicke's area, the prominent area envisaged as being involved in semantic and lexical processing, no age of acquisition effect was revealed.

Investigating the representation of three languages in the brain with a similar task as in Kim et al.'s study, Wattendorf et al. (2001) took their results a step further. Multilingual subjects were divided into early bilinguals, who had been exposed to two languages before the age of 3 and had learned a third language after the age of 10, and late multilinguals, who had grown up monolingually and had learned their L2 and L3 after the age of 10. All subjects were highly fluent in the languages tested and used (at least) three languages regularly in their everyday life. The task consisted of describing events of the previous day (morning, noon/afternoon, evening). Participants were asked to imagine they were speaking to a person they know. This is supposed to create a situation that approaches normal everyday interaction. The analysis of Broca's area showed that in early bilinguals the two L1s recruit more and overlapping neural substrate in Broca's area, whereas in late multilinguals L1 and L2 engaged adjacent regions with only partial overlap. Differences were also found in the processing of L3. When speaking in their L3, early bilinguals activate less neural substrate in BA 44 compared to the first two languages, while no difference was found in BA 45 for early and late languages. Similarly to L2, for late multilinguals speaking in their L3 requires noticeably more neural substrate in BA 44. Furthermore, in BA 45 the activation patterns among the late multilingual subjects displayed higher variability for early and late languages. The authors conclude that in early bilinguals the network in BA 44 is "sufficiently adaptable to allow the integration of later learned languages" (Wattendorf et al. 2001: 624). Conversely, in late multilinguals, L2 and L3 have to recruit new neural substrate. The results also show that the two sub-fields of Broca's area are not only spatially but also functionally distinct.

On the one hand, word generation studies revealed overlapping regions for the processing of single words in various languages independent of the age of acquisition, the language, and the input modality. Kim et al.'s (1997) findings of overlapping activations in Wernicke's area are in agreement with these results. On the other hand, in both story production studies, BA 44 appeared to be more sensitive to the various languages of a multilingual speaker with respect to age of acquisition. As mentioned above BA 44 proved to subserve syntactic processing (Friederici et al. 2000a, b; Dapretto and Bookheimer 1999), while BA 45 is involved in (lexical) search and retrieval processes in general (Klein et al. 1994), in addition to semantic processing (Friederici et al. 2000a, b).

2.3.2. Language Comprehension

Sentence Comprehension. Written sentence comprehension in Mandarin Chinese and English was investigated in a fMRI study by using a set of conceptually similar sentences (Chee et al. 1999b). The two languages were chosen because of their difference in orthography, phonology and syntax. Subjects were fluent English-Mandarin Chinese bilingual speakers who were exposed to both languages before the age of 6. The findings showed that in proficient early bilinguals common neural substrate is activated in written sentence processing irrespective of the difference in surface features.

Neville et al. (1997) studied the representation of American Sign Language (ASL) and English while subjects either viewed ASL signs forming sentences or read English sentences. Native speakers of English and native signers, both hearing and deaf, displayed substantially similar activation patterns in the left hemisphere. The authors conclude that dedicated neural systems mediate language processing in native users independent of the modality through which the language is acquired. Yet, the nature of sensory input, the specific processing requirements as well as the age of acquisition do have a determinant effect on language representation in the brain. Early acquisition of ASL showed the engagement of the right hemisphere in both deaf and hearing native signers. Late learners of ASL displayed only very weak activation of the right hemisphere when processing ASL.

Listening to Stories. In three studies Perani and collaborators used story listening to investigate the effects of age of acquisition and proficiency, and the inter-subject variability of cortical representation of L1 and L2. In Perani et al. (1996), a PET study, subjects listened to stories in L1 (Italian), in L2 (English, learned almost exclusively at school after the age of 7), and in an unknown language (Japanese). While they had a fair, but not excellent command of English, none had any knowledge of Japanese. The activation patterns displayed a large set of areas significantly more active for L1, whereas a reduced set of language areas was active for L2. No difference in active regions was found between L2 and the unknown language. The authors highlight that the largest differences between L1 and L2 were found in areas related to sentence-level processing and conclude that their results support the hypothesis of (at least) partially distinct representation of languages in the brain depending on the age of acquisition.

In a follow-up study, Perani et al. (1998) recruited a group of highly proficient Italian-English late bilinguals to be compared to the group of late bilinguals with moderate command of English in the 1996 study, and a third group of highly proficient Spanish-Catalan early bilinguals for a comparison with the group of proficient late bilinguals. The differing cortical representation displayed in the 1996 study was not found in either of the two high proficiency groups. Indeed, the latter showed similar sets of active regions for the two languages of a speaker. From the comparison of the two studies the authors conclude that the level of proficiency is a critical determinant of the representation of L2 in the brain.

Deheane et al. (1997), in a fMRI study, tested French native speakers who had learned English as L2 at school after the age of 7. In all subjects, L1 activated a consistent set of areas in the left hemisphere, whereas L2 displayed patterns of activation in both hemispheres that varied highly from subject to subject. According to the authors, the results confirm that L1 acquisition relies on a dedicated cerebral network in the left hemisphere, while late acquisition of L2 causes high variability in the cortical representation. In individuals, L2 may be represented completely in the left hemisphere, in both hemispheres, or only in the right hemisphere.

Taken together, the comprehension studies indicate that attained proficiency and age of acquisition are both crucial factors in shaping the representation of languages in the brain. The level of proficiency, however, appears to be the more critical determinant. They also show that language engages a dedicated neural network independent of the stimuli presentation or of the modality through which a language was acquired.

2.3.3. Semantic Judgements

Illes et al. (1999) investigated the integration or separation of semantic processing systems in Spanish-English speakers who had learned their L2 after the age of 10. Subjects performed a semantic decision task (concrete/abstract word) and a non-semantic decision task (uppercase/lowercase). The authors identified a shared frontal lobe system for semantic processing for both languages and conclude that "learning a new language, even after the age of 10, does not require the addition of a new semantic processing system or the recruitment of new cortical regions for semantic processing" (Illes et al. 1999: 360).

Chee et al. (2001) examined proficiency effects on the localisation of semantic processing in two groups of bilinguals. The first group consisted of English-Mandarin Chinese bilinguals, who had been exposed to both languages before the age of 5; the second group was composed of Mandarin Chinese-English bilingual speakers, who had learned English at school after the age of 12. In this PET study, participants were administered a semantic judgement and a character size judgement task. The group of early bilinguals showed overlapping regions of activation despite the difference in the relative proficiency. The late bilingual participants displayed a broadly similar pattern of activation as the early bilinguals. However, several additional active regions, including areas in the frontal lobes of the right hemisphere, were found for the less proficient language. Hence the higher level of difficulty of the task in the less proficient language leads to the recruitment of additional brain regions. In agreement with the results of word generation studies (Klein et al. 1994, Chee et al. 1999a), the studies using semantic judgement show that the two languages of a bilingual person access a common semantic system independent of age of acquisition and attained proficiency.

2.3.4. Translation and Selective Access

Price et al. (1999) and Hernandez et al. (2000, 2001) investigated the organisation of languages in bilinguals by administering the subjects a translation task and one requiring selective access to one language (picture naming). As in the other studies using single-word stimuli these studies found that a bilingual's languages are represented in overlapping areas irrespective of the time of acquisition and attained proficiency. Furthermore, Price et al. (1999) showed that translating activated regions specifically associated with semantics and articulation, while selective access modulated activity in areas engaged in word processing at a phonological level.

2.4. Generalizable Outcomes of Neuroimaging Studies on the Multilingual Brain

Besides technical aspects, in comparing the results of the studies on the bilingual brain, it is important to pay attention to at least two other aspects: the experimental task, and the language biography of the subjects. The findings on overlapping or distinct cortical areas cannot be taken as general statements about the organisation of languages in the brain, but have to be interpreted in dependency with the experimental task. Tasks using single words as stimuli led to the hypothesis that languages are represented in overlapping areas in the cerebral cortex. Conversely, tasks using sentences or stories activated distinct cortical areas resulting in the claim that languages are represented separately. However, we rather see the first as giving indications on the representation of semantic or lexical processing, and the additional involvement of syntactic (and maybe also pragmatic) processing in the latter may explain the difference.

Onset time of acquisition proved to be an important factor. Nonetheless, the age of acquisition for the second language in early bilinguals ranges from prior to 2 to 6 years. Fluency was not checked for in the early studies and crystallized only later as another determinant factor. Many other aspects of the participants are hardly ever accounted for, such as the actual use of the various languages in everyday life, ways of L2 learning, emotional impact, and so on. It can be hypothesised that these factors – alongside age of acquisition and attained proficiency- might have an impact on shaping the network of regions subserving the different languages, just as different experiences with specific aspects of a language do. In this context, Paulesu et al. (2000) speak about "cultural effect". They tested a group of English and a group of Italian students, each of which was asked to read only in their native language. In addition to a common brain system active during reading, the investigators identified language-related differences. Reading English activated additional areas associated with object and word naming, and semantic processes. The authors theorise that reading in an inconsistent and complex orthography such as English requires access to the orthographic lexicon for the selection of the correct pronunciation. In contrast, reading Italian displayed enhanced activity in areas linked to phonological processing. This is suggested to reflect a different reading procedure, which takes advantage of the consistent mapping between orthography and phonology.

In sum, different organisational principles such as age of acquisition and attained proficiency differentially affect the representation of the systems for syntactic and lexical-semantic processing in multilinguals. With respect to the neural systems subserving lexical-semantic aspects, age of acquisition and proficiency did not appear to be critical determinants. Rather, evidence has accumulated suggesting that the various languages of a multilingual speaker access a common semantic system which is also independent of the language and of the modality of presentation (e.g. Latin script vs. Chinese ideographs). In fact, it has been proposed above that the same neural systems storing semantic information are active in language comprehension and speech production. A recent study by Rodriguez-Fornells et al. (2002), however, stresses the importance of the phonological processing for avoiding interferences between languages. They instructed Spanish-Catalan early bilinguals and Spanish-only native speakers to press a button when reading a Spanish word and to ignore Catalan and pseudowords. Both groups performed equally well (see also Scarborough et al. 1984), but in fMRI bilinguals showed enhanced activation in those perisylvian areas considered to be engaged in the 'sublexical', phonological processing of words. Together with the analysis of EEG-data, the authors conclude that the meaning of non-target words was not assessed by the bilingual subjects and that they "use an indirect phonological access route to the lexicon of the target language" (Rodriguez-Fornells et al 2002: 1026).

In contrast to lexical-semantic processing, the representation of syntactic knowledge appears to be influenced by age of acquisition and proficiency effects. Finally, neither language modality nor typological distance appeared to affect the localisation of syntactic processing (see Cenoz, this volume).

3. FINAL REMARKS

Such an important distinction in linguistics as the typological distance between languages proved not to be a prominent categorizational need for the brain. Rather, it shows a higher sensitivity towards age of acquisition and fluency in the different languages. A high proficiency attained in a late learned L2 masks in some studies the differences with respect to the onset time of acquisition. Therefore we may assume that "automatization" is the main functional principle of the nervous system, leading to an efficient recruitment of neuronal resources and resulting in lower activation (this also holds true for other activities and is not language-specific). This fact may explain some contrasting results between age and fluency: to be a fluent, competent speaker of a late learned L2 means to handle it like someone who has learned it in childhood. The actual activation, hence, can be similar. The relative importance of these categories is still under debate.

Paradis (2000) has tried to present "Generalizable Outcomes of Bilingual Aphasia Research". He concludes that no function is exclusively available for bilinguals only. Monolingual (or monodialectal) abilities should be seen as being located at one end of a continuum and the abilities of a highly proficient multilingual speaker at the other end: in his terms, the difference is the degree of use the speaker makes of the cerebral system. He rejects the various hypotheses and pleads for the "Subsystem Hypothesis": each of a speaker's languages forms a subsystem within the larger language system (Paradis 2000: 56). Therein, dissociations are possible, but also simultaneous access to more than one language (or dialect), as fluent mixing behaviours, switching, translating etc. show. Thus, a monolingual's registers correspond to the various languages of a bi- or multilingual. No qualitative difference holds between the brain of a monolingual and a bilingual.

What appears evident is the inappropriateness of speaking generally about 'the language' or 'the languages' of a bi- or multilingual person, as well as "to postulate the existence of neural mechanisms specific of bilinguals" (Fabbro 2001: 213). It seems to be a false manner of questioning if a bilingual acts differently than others (i.e. 'normals') or has, e.g., 'one' or 'two' lexicons. Rather, we should ask, in what circumstances the lexicon is differentiated in sub-parts, how they are connected and can be deactivated for specific tasks, e.g. for speaking 'only a language X', correctly to a person. The possibilities to control monolingual and bilingual modes in terms of Grosjean await further research.

If we want to construe a type of 'universal grammar' for multilingual processes – a brain grammar (BG) – we have to model the shared and/or distinct (language-specific) treatment of the language systems in contact. So far we can say that syntax, albeit different in various languages, uses the same neural networks (at least in early bilinguals), whereas phonology requires distinct networks for processing. Semantics, and in particular lexicon, appear to be based on more common ground among languages (some 'concepts' need not be re-established when a new language is learned[vi]). Perhaps, at the lexical level the differences among multilingual processes do exist, but cannot be revealed with the above mentioned macroscopic techniques.

The few studies concerned with the pragmatic level appear to go into the same direction as semantics: we can assume more shared substrate in performing such tasks with the right hemisphere being involved to a higher degree (Chantraine et al. 1998; Pulvermüller 1999).

To see separate areas among languages, sentence and textual tasks must be tested. But here also, early and late, proficient bilinguals proved to activate almost the same areas, whereas late acquisition and low proficiency leads to a higher variability and more diffuse patterns of activation over the two hemispheres.

As we hope to have shown, it is of extreme importance to pay attention to the linguistic stimuli presented in these test situations: many discrepancies between studies dealing with similar questions can be tracked back to differences in paradigm architecture and task-design. Not only do we have to distinguish the classical production, comprehension, and reading tasks, but also the crude physical form of the input: e.g. visual or auditory input in comprehension tasks leads to differences in co-activated brain structures. Hence, depending on the stimuli, activation images may differ. Then only what is consistent and stable throughout different tasks with respect to a specific ability (e.g. 'syntactic recognition'), can be conceived as a generalizable result (e.g. for a BG).

Many questions still remain open. Here, we will mention only a few, which are interesting from a linguistic point of view:

- It is not evident if the detected language areas subserve exclusively language or other systems as well. Broca's area was not only active in syntactic tasks, but also when detecting anomalies e.g. in musical syntax (Maess et al. 2001). This non domain-specificity of areas raises many questions.

- The role of the cerebellum as a fine-tuning control centre might be more pronounced in a linguistic skill such as production.

- The role of subcortical areas is a large field for future research (see for bilinguals: Fabbro and Paradis, 1995).

- The relationship between language and the limbic system – mainly concerned with appraisal and evaluation, and emotion – is a topic in focus for the next years (see Damasio 1999; Schumann 1998). Attitudes and emotions towards languages can be established in in-depth interviews and should be correlated with brain activations.

- What is missing – but the field is too young to expect such research – are longitudinal studies. We know that networks are established for a certain time, not necessarily forever. How does language knowledge (implicit and explicit) change over time, when individuals learn a language (at school or in the country, where the language is spoken)? Is it possible for adults (or nearly impossible, as Paradis 1994 states) to transfer explicit to implicit knowledge? Moreover, learning effects by language training is a branch in which investigations are necessary which distinguish learning per se and the specificity of language learning.

- Similar questions arise when analysing the role of memory (declarative and procedural) and the specificity of language memorisation sub-systems: What are the interdependencies, what is the specificity of language memory?

- The individual factor is a not very appreciated topic in 'hard science', where generalizable, stable result are preferred. Nevertheless, biographical background and contextual factors may explain differences as well. A multimethodological approach is needed to know more about learning contexts of the different languages, old and actual competencies, and attitudes towards the different languages[vii].

- Very little is known about differences in brain activations between dialectal varieties and fully standardised languages. Dialectal varieties are acquired typically orally, as first languages with relatives or in closed networks, and have a high identity value, whereas standardised languages can be learned with additional visual input (scriptural system), the support of institution, and with explicit tutoring. This topic can be used to test the hypothesis, if informal settings of language learning in contrast to formal settings make a difference in fluent early bilinguals.

Last but not least, the quality of the answers the imaging techniques can furnish to linguists depends heavily on the quality of the questions. In this debate, linguists have to play a role.

ACKNOWLEDGEMENTS

Section 1 and 3 were originally written by Rita Franceschini, section 2 by Daniela Zappatore. Of course, all authors take the responsibility for the final version of this paper. We profited enormously from our regular discussions in our research group „Multilingual Brain": E. Wattendorf, B. Westermann and E.W. Radü, in particular, gave extremely important input concerning the new imaging methods, and G. Lüdi and S. Marienberg made valuable contributions. We also want to thank A. Mecklinger (Saarland University) and D. Weniger (University Hospital Zurich).

Saarland University (Germany)
University of Basle (Switzerland)

NOTES

[i] Neural function depends on electrochemical processes. The electrical potentials can be recorded on the surface of the scalp by means of electroencephalography (EEG). Activity of neurons also produces a magnetic field, which can be recorded by magnetoencephalography (MEG). Both these techniques are used in cognitive neuroscience to elucidate how neural activity changes over time in response to a particular task by extracting evoked responses, or event-related potentials (ERPs), from the global EEG or MEG signal. These techniques provide a precise time record, but only a rough indication of the brain structures producing the signal. The neuroanatomical map of brain regions involved by a specific task is better obtained with functional imaging techniques such as PET and fMRI. Unlike EEG and MEG, these two techniques do not record neural events, but measure changes in metabolism or blood flow correlated with neural activity. They provide a helpful tool for exactly localizing differences in neuronal activity between two different tasks, a reference task and the experimental task, the temporal resolution, however, is poor compared to EEG and MEG.

[ii] Combinations of the two techniques are being tested; first results are promising (Kruggel et al. 2000).

[iii] From the linguistic point of view, regular debates on the topic are published mainly in *Bilingualism: Language and Cognition*, see in particular the special issue on the *Cognitive Neuroscience of bilingualism*, 4 (2), 2001, edited by Green; see also Milroy and Muysken 1995, Grosjean 1998, Müller 1996, besides many others.

[iv] Handedness plays - at least to some extent - a role in the hemispheric specialization for language. Right-handers have a left-hemisphere dominance for language, whereas left-handers revealed a higher individual variability, with the majority displaying a standard left lateralization, and a smaller number a right-hemispheric dominance or symmetry of both hemispheres (Kandel et al. 1996: 364-365). For this reason, the subjects recruited in the neuroimaging studies on language are almost exclusively right-handers.

[v] In the beginnings of the 20th century, K. Brodmann created a map of the cortex by dividing it into areas depending on the arrangement of different cell types (so called cytoarchitectonics).

[vi] The role or simply the existence of concepts remains a controversial issue, see the discussion in Pavlenko (2000) on concepts in bilingual memory, and, more generally, Caramazza 1996.

[vii] This approach has been chosen in our research group "Multilingual Brain", see www.unibas.ch/multilingualbrain.

DAVID SINGLETON

PERSPECTIVES ON THE MULTILINGUAL LEXICON:
A CRITICAL SYNTHESIS

1. INTRODUCTORY

The starting point of this concluding synthesis is that the current locus of discussion in respect of the multilingual lexicon is the issue of the relationship between the operations of the mental lexicons associated with the different languages known to the multilingual individual. The article begins by examining some arguments that have hitherto been put with regard to the question of the degree to which such lexical operations are separate or integrated; it goes on to look at a founding model of this discussion; and, finally, it attempts to situate the various contributions to this volume in respect of the different perspectives which have emerged from previous debate.

2. THE MENTAL LEXICONS OF THE MULTILINGUAL: SEPARATION OR INTEGRATION

The received wisdom used to be that the L1 mental lexicon was qualitatively different from, and therefore, by implication, separate from, the mental lexicons associated with any additional languages (see, e.g., Laufer, 1989; Meara, 1984). This notion of a qualitative difference between mental lexicons in terms of organization and functioning is one against which it is relatively easy to find arguments, as indeed it is relatively easy to find arguments in favour of a high degree of interlexical connectivity (see, e.g., Singleton 1994, 1999; Singleton and Little, 1991). Some of the voices raised against the idea that the L1 mental lexicon is quintessentially different and separate from the mental lexicons of additional languages have advocated precisely the contrary point of view. Thus, for example, Cook (e.g. 1992) has proposed the notion of "holistic multicompetence", i.e., the complete integration of language competence, including lexical competence, across languages. A similarly radical point of view is that offered by "integrational linguists" (see, e.g., Harris, 1998), whose questioning of the very concept of individual languages as a self-contained systems would appear to imply a continuity between knowledge and processes associated with what have traditionally been seen as different languages.

J. Cenoz, B. Hufeisen & U. Jessner (eds.), The Multilingual Lexicon, 167—176.

With regard to arguments against the integration of the L1 mental lexicon with the lexicons associated with additional languages, one such argument derives from a theoretical standpoint which is diametrically opposed to the integrationist view, namely the modularity hypothesis (cf. Singleton, 1998), which sees the mind not as a seamless, unitary whole, but as comprising - perhaps in addition to some general-purpose structures – "a number of distinct, specialized, structurally idiosyncratic modules that communicate with other cognitive structures in only very limited ways" (Garfield, 1987: 1). Within the Chomskyan school in particular it is claimed that one of these "structurally idiosyncratic modules" is devoted to language (see, e.g., Fodor, 1983). Modularists differ on the question of which aspects of lexical operations fall within the domain of the language module. However, at least some suggest that a substantial part of the functioning of the L1 mental lexicon is intramodular (see, e.g., Emmorey and Fromkin, 1988; Smith and Wilson, 1979) and at least some hold that any L2 competence acquired beyond the childhood years is extramodular (see, e.g., Bley-Vroman, 1989). Taken together, these two positions imply that, in the case of post-pubertal learner of additional languages, the lexical operations of these languages proceed in isolation from those of the L1.

A fairly persuasive argument of a more empirical stamp against full integration derives from the existence of marked formal differences between languages. It appears that an individual faced with the task of working out the morphological structure of unfamiliar words will refer to the phonological composition of more familiar items and then analogize (see Bybee, 1988; Stemberger and MacWhinney, 1988). Since the languages known to such an individual may be highly divergent in phonological terms, the implication is that the search on which such analogizing tactics depend runs through the lexicon of each language separately.

Other evidence in favour of separation comes from studies of language loss and aphasia in multilinguals (see, e.g., Fabbro, 1999: Chapters 12-16). In the case of language loss, the languages known to the individual may be recovered selectively. Grosjean (1982: 260), for example, cites the case of a native speaker of Swiss German who had lost all language as the result of a head injury. The first language this individual recovered was French, a language he had learned as an adult; he subsequently recovered High German; but he never recovered his L1, Swiss German. Whitaker (1978: 27) likewise reports the case of an English classics scholar who recovered Greek, Latin, French and English in that order. With regard to aphasia, multilinguals sometimes exhibit language disorders affecting just one of their languages. For instance, Paradis and Goldblum (1989) give an account of a trilingual subject who, following a brain operation, evidenced disorders typical of Broca's aphasia in Gujarati (his native language) but no deficits in his other languages, Malagasi and French.

A further point worth making is that users of more than one language mostly keep their languages apart when using them - to the extent that where, for one reason or another, the expectation is that language x is being spoken but where, in fact, it turns out that language y is being used, comprehension may actually be blocked, even where both languages are familiar to the individual in question – as in the following experiences retailed by the Finnish psychologist Elisabet Service:

My sister, while studying in France was once addressed on the street in Finnish. Only after several attempts by the speaker did she understand her own native language, the point being that she was expecting French. I have had a very similar experience trying to make Finnish out of something that was easy enough to understand when I realized it was English.
(Service: personal communication)

Cross-linguistic influence seems to be limited in nature and effects; many errors produced in languages other than the first "seem to have little, if any, connection with the mother tongue" (Dušková, 1969: 19). Such influence admittedly appears to increase in situations where the languages involved are perceived as close (see. e.g, Kellerman, 1977, 1979, 1983; Ringbom, 1987; Singleton, 1987; Singleton and Little 1984); however, the very fact of this "psychotypological" dimension runs counter to the notion of straightforward total integration within the mental lexicon, because, precisely, it implies a degree of selectivity in relation to consultation of the languages represented.

None of the foregoing undermines the notion of a very high degree of connectivity and dynamic interplay between the L1 mental lexicon and additional mental lexicons. The fact that cross-linguistic influence exists at all demonstrates such connectivity beyond doubt, and, of course, evidence of cross-linguistic influence abounds, as the contributions to this volume eloquently demonstrate. Probably the best-known model of the relationship between the L1 and the L2 mental lexicon is Weinreich's (1953) account in terms of "subordinative", "compound" and "co-ordinate" categories: according to this account, in subordinative bilingualism L2 word forms are connected to L1 meanings via primary connections to L1 forms; in compound bilingualism the L1 and L2 forms are connected at the meaning level; and in co-ordinate bilingualism separate systems of form-meaning links exist for each language. Weinreich suggests that these different types of bilingualism are associated with different kinds of learning experience, although he also acknowledges that a person's bilingualism need not be of a single type. Subsequent research and discussion have suggested that different types of relationship between L1 and L2 may co-exist in the same mind-brain (see, e.g., De Groot, 1993, 1995). A further question is whether lexical organization is affected by increasing levels of proficiency. De Groot and Kroll (e.g. De Groot, 1995; Kroll and De Groot, 1997; Kroll and Tokowicz, 2001) cite studies which indicate that subordinative structure is associated with low proficiency in additional languages and compound structure with higher proficiency. Woutersen's (1997) research also suggests that subordinative, compound and co-ordinate organization are at least in part associable with different stages of bilingual development (see also Jiang, 2000).

Many of the models which are on offer in the current literature can be seen as developments of Weinreich's proposals. However, none of the various kinds of bilingualism defined by Weinreich and referred to in more recent work will very frequently be found in nature in its "pure" form. More plausible is Cieślicka's (2000) notion of "variable interconnection", which posits that formal-associative and conceptual links typically exist in some measure between the L1 and L2 mental lexicons in all learners but that "associative links linking various nodes will vary in

strength according to the type of a bilingual person's experience in his or her L2"
(Cieślicka, 2000: 33).

Even in its various modified and qualified versions, however, Weinreich's
model has the disadvantage that it does not really address the question of what
happens when more than two languages are involved. For example, let us take the
case of a co-ordinate bilingual who goes on to learn an L3. If we accept the notion
that subordinative organization is characteristic of the earlier stages of the
acquisition of an additional language, we are then faced with the problem of
determining with which of the two established mental lexicons the L3 mental
lexicon associates itself. One possibility, following the idea of psychotypology, is
that the L3 mental lexicon first becomes subordinate to and subsequently enters into
a compound relationship with the mental lexicon of the language perceived as
typologically closer. An alternative possibility is that an L3 mental lexicon initially
enters into an association with the lexicons of both established lexicons but to
different degrees. Further possibilities can be envisaged within this framework. For
example, the mental lexicons of the first two languages may not be co-ordinately
organized, but may be in a subordinative, compound or (following De Groot, see
above) mixed relationship. In the light of such possibilities, the scope for the
conception of organizational arrangements becomes very much larger, and vastly
complex, especially if one takes account of Cieślicka's notion of "variable
interconnection".

3. THE ARTICLES IN THIS VOLUME

Let us turn now to the contributions to the present volume. We shall take a brief and
rather general look first at the evidence provided in the various preceding chapters of
interaction between the lexical processing operations relating to different languages;
then we shall consider what appears at first sight to be very strong evidence of full
integration from certain of the contributions; finally we shall explore the various
models proposed.

3.1 Evidence of cross-lexical interaction

It is noteworthy that every single article in this book provides evidence and/or
arguments in favour of interaction between the lexical processes bearing on the
different languages used by an individual. Jessner presents data elicited from
German/English bilinguals studying English as L3 which reveal interaction across
all three languages and show that both German and Italian were used as support for
word retrieval in the L3. Similarly, Cenoz's data demonstrate that primary school
children learning English as L3 made use of both their L1 (Spanish) lexical
resources and their L2 (Basque) lexical resources when narrating stories in English.
Interestingly, it emerges that Basque lexical resources were mostly drawn on in the
context of "interactional strategies" – i.e, looking for help -, which Cenoz explains
in terms of the situation (a Basque-medium school) where the data were being
elicited, while Spanish resources were mostly drawn on in "transfer lapses" – i.e.,

non-intentional borrowing and foreignizing -, which she explains in terms of psychotypology.

Psychotypological factors also surface in the contributions of Gibson and Hufeisen, of Müller-Lancé and of Hall and Ecke. Gibson and Hufeisen found that multilingual language learners confronted with the task of translating a passage in Swedish, a language they did not know, tended to seek assistance in the lexicons of languages they knew which they perceived as most similar to Swedish – namely, German and English. Müller-Lancé, in a wide-ranging study of cross-linguistic strategies based on questionnaire and think-aloud data, found that in the production of Romance foreign languages (Spanish and Italian) native German speakers avoided drawing on their L1, whereas native speakers of Romance languages drew on their L1 quite intensely. Müller-Lancé also found evidence, however, of a proficiency factor and of individual learning experience factors in the nature and extent of cross-lexical consultation. Hall and Ecke, for their part, looked at cross-linguistic aspects of the productions in German of L1 speakers of Spanish who also had intermediate to high levels of proficiency in English as an L2 and who were learning German as an L3; they discovered evidence of cross-linguistic influence from both Spanish and English, but found that most cross-linguistic influence at the conceptual level and the greatest overall cross-linguistic effect was from the L2, English, a fact which they explain partly in psychotypological terms.

With regard to conceptual dimensions of cross-lexical interactions, Schönpflug concludes from an analysis of the results of a word fragment completion task performed by L1 speakers of Polish in a procedure involving both their L2 (German) and their L3 (English) that, while trilingual speakers with a high level of proficiency in their L2 and their L3 have later uniqueness points irrespective of language (because of the effect of cross-lexical consultation), conceptual features like concreteness and number of translations also play a decisive role in correct word completions and error rates. Also in the broadly conceptual area, Wei's exploration of data from two native speakers of Chinese - one with native-like L2 proficiency in English and Japanese as L3 and the other with native-like L2 proficiency in Japanese and English as L3 - reveals clear influence in L3 from the lexical-conceptual structure, the predicate-argument structure and the morphological realization patterns of the L2.

A very particular approach to cross-linguistic interaction is taken in Spöttl and McCarthy's exploration of the problems posed by formulaic utterances in a multilingual context. One might perhaps note in passing that it is not at all clear that we yet have a satisfactory operational definition of the notion of formulaic utterance. However, it is perfectly evident that lexical units (cf. Cruse, 1986: Chapter 2) have to be seen as including sequences of words, even if a rigorous characterization of what a lexical unit actually is remains elusive (cf. Singleton, 2000: 56ff.). To return to the question of cross-linguistic interaction, although there is certainly evidence in Spöttl and McCarthy's data of such interaction at individual word level, they claim that there is little evidence of cross-lexical consultation at the formulaic level. They explain this essentially in terms of the learning experience and degree of idiomatic competence of their subjects not having been such as to promote such cross-formulaic consultation. Interestingly, other studies show that, where there is an obvious parallelism between L1 and non-L1 formulas, cross-formulaic consultation plays a major role (see, e.g., Cieślicka, 2002).

Cross-lexical issues are also very much to the fore in Dijkstra's contribution, based on the findings of experimental psycholinguistics, and in that of Franceschini, Zappatore and Nitsch, which provides a neurobiological perspective. Dijkstra's chapter discusses the results of experiments which appear to indicate that a given form triggers all similar forms available to the subject, whatever the language affiliation of the forms in question, and which seem, therefore, to point to a "non-selective access". As for Franceschini *et al.*'s contribution, this notes that lexical-semantic aspects of language processing for all languages known to an individual appear to be localized in the same areas of the brain, irrespective of age of acquisition and proficiency levels of the languages in question. Such evidence suggests that the lexical operations associated with the multilingual's various languages have a very close relationship with each other.

3.2. Evidence of full integration of the multilingual lexicon

A number of the foregoing chapters advocate a view of multilingual lexical operations which may be taken to posit or imply an integrated multilingual mental lexicon. However, while, as we have seen, all of the contributions furnish evidence of a high level of cross-lexical connectivity, which is what, in fact, most of the authors mean by *integration*, only two appear to provide empirical support for a stronger view of *full* integration, namely those of Dijkstra and Franceschini *et al.*

To take the last-mentioned first, as has been indicated, Franceschini et al.'s conclusion from their review of a range of brain-imaging studies is that lexical-semantic aspects of the processing of all languages known to an individual are subserved by essentially the same areas of the cortex. This certainly suggests very close connections between lexical operations relating to the languages in question, but there are grounds for treating with some caution Franceschini *et al.*'s inference that lexical-semantic processing draws on a common system across languages. It is worth mentioning in this context the continuing debate among neurolinguists (cf., e.g., Obler and Gjerlow, 1999: 9-12) between the "localizationalists" who talk about "language centres" in the brain in a fairly traditional sense and "connectionists" and "interactionists" who see the functioning of the brain more holistically and who see patterns of connections as more important than location in the cortical "map" delivered by current technologies – with all their limitations. As Obler and Gjerlow comment, "cortical topography is at best the surface component of a multidimensional set of systems – cortical linked with subcortical – that enable us to use language" (Obler and Gjerlow, 1999: 168). What this implies is that, at the very least, we need to beware of over-interpreting topographical evidence.

With regard to Dijkstra's contribution, as has already been mentioned, this reviews findings from a range of experimental studies which he interprets as indicating that when a particular word form is activated similar word forms known to the individual in question are activated also, whatever the language affiliation of the words in question (at least beyond a certain proficiency level). One notes that the evidence in question largely derives from experimental situations where the stimulus words were decontextualized and that in many instances the stimuli were presented in orthographic form. These conditions may be particularly favourable to the activation of formal "neighbours" across languages. The question of whether a suitably constraining context in normal linguistic interaction can effectively prevent the activation of one language or another has, as Dijkstra recognizes, not really been explored with any rigour. One can draw an analogy, as Dijkstra indeed does, with research relating to activation of meanings of polysemous/homonymous words in context. While early work involving weak to moderate contextual predisposition appeared to show that contextual factors did not inhibit the activation of meanings which were not relevant to the context (see, e.g., Swinney, 1979), more recent research has demonstrated that, when contexts are strongly constraining, only the contextually relevant meaning of ambiguous items appears to be activated (see, e.g., Moss and Gaskell, 1999; Simpson and Krueger, 1991; Tabossi Colombo and Job, 1987). However, even if it is the case that parallel activation occurs in ordinary contextualized language use, this does not of itself constitute proof of the essential unitariness of the multilingual lexicon. It can be equally well explained in terms of a very high level of connectivity between the lexicons associated with the different languages.

In fact, Dijkstra does not go all the way in relation to the question of the lexical integration. He accepts that, depending on circumstances, specific languages as sets can be at different levels of activation. His proposed model incorporates "language nodes", which essentially constitutes an acknowledgment that the lexical items and processes associated with each of the languages known to an individual may be activated and/or de-activated as a set. The issue of precisely how and to what extent the language nodes in question interact with bottom-up factors (phonetic/phonological/orthographic features, etc.) and with top-down factors (linguistic and non-linguistic context) remains an empirical question, but - at least for Dijkstra - the more basic question of the differentiability between lexicons as in some sense separable entities appears to be settled.

3.3 The models proposed

We now turn to the models proposed by the various contributors to this volume. To begin with Dijkstra's Multilingual Interactive Activation model, this assumes that in word recognition there is parallel activation of word candidates from all languages known (beyond a certain level of proficiency) to the individual. However, the model does recognize that neighbour effects will be influenced by subject frequency factors, which implies that items from additional languages in which proficiency and usage levels are lower may have smaller effects on L1 processing than vice versa. Interestingly, Schönpflug comes to rather similar conclusions to Dijkstra's regarding the impact of proficiency in relation to word identification. She takes as her starting point the transfer-appropriate-processing approach, which claims that individuals tend to be faster or more efficient at performing a task on a stimulus when they have had previous experience of performing that task on the same stimulus. As has already been indicated, she finds evidence to support her hypothesis that the more competent speakers are in their various languages the later will be the uniqueness points in word fragment completions.

To return to Dijkstra's model, it also allows for the fact that distinctions in script and other language specific cues will rapidly reduce the pool of word candidates. The model provides, moreover, for the suppression of the activation of the whole set of words associated with a given language via the influence of context, although Dijkstra seems to be fully convinced only by the notion that linguistic context can have this kind of impact. Even in relation to linguistic context effects, however, the model is vague, which is a weakness, but one which is inevitable, given the paucity of pertinent evidence which is available.

Two models proposed, those of Müller-Lancé and of Wei, are closely linked to Levelt's (1989) and Levelt, Roelofs and Meyer's (1999) model. Müller-Lancé and Wei adapt the model in various ways in order to render it capable of dealing multilingual processing. However, the conceptualization remains Leveltian. Notably, the lexicon is represented as a store of declarative (essentially static) knowledge which is separate from "knowledge of the world" and from grammatical encoding procedures. The representation of lexical knowledge as purely declarative is out of keeping with the widely acknowledged dynamism of the lexicon. For example, the lexicon contains provision for word-formation or "lexical redundancy" (see, e.g., Cruse 1986: 50), making possible the generation of a potentially infinite number of new forms. Since lexical creativity based on such possibilities involves a process and a goal, the psychological correlates of lexical redundancy rules must surely be classed as procedural knowledge. The separation in the model of lexical meaning from "encyclopedic meaning" is also problematic. Most linguists, including Chomsky (e.g., Chomsky, 1972: 11; 1980: 62), recognize that it is extremely difficult to find a principled way of distinguishing what is purportedly linguistic meaning from other kinds of meaning. As for the notion that lexical operations are entirely separate from grammatical processing, many linguists may well find this latter proposal difficult to swallow in the light of mounting evidence in favour of lexico-syntactic interpenetration (see, e.g., Singleton, 1999: Chapter 1; 2000).   .

While Spöttl and McCarthy are not principally concerned with model-building, what they have to say about the formulaic dimension of lexical knowledge constitutes a useful prophylactic against a simplistic view of the mental lexicon which might see it in terms merely of a list of individual words. Furthermore, their endorsement of Sinclair's idiomaticity principle and of Wray's standpoint on the essentially dynamic nature of the manner in which formulaic language is deployed in response to the challenges of language use is heavy with implications for the above-discussed Leveltian claims about the separation of lexical and grammatical processing and about the static nature of lexical knowledge. Also important to note is their well-reasoned resistance to the idea – despite scant evidence in their study of cross-formulaic consultation (see above) – that the mental lexicons associated with different languages known to an individual operate in isolation from each other.

Wei, for his part, talks about full integration in the multilingual lexicon, but, in fact he sees the lexemes in this lexicon as "tagged" for language, which clearly implies separability at the word form level. At the lemma level he posits – in a way which bears some resemblances to Weinreich's notion of compound organization (see above) – that, where the lemma for a given lexeme in language x has not been acquired, a lemma from another language may fill the gap. When the appropriate lemma for language x is subsequently acquired, according to this model, recourse to the lemmas of other languages is no longer had. Clearly, this whole scenario carries the implication of the differentiability of the two lexicons at lemma level too. If Wei's model relates to Weinreich's conception of compound bilingualism, the "parasitic" model proposed by Hall and Ecke is reminiscent of Weinreich's proposals regarding subordinative bilingualism, postulating as it does the initial connection of word forms in a new language with the closest matches in formal terms in previously acquired languages, and the subsequent use of contextual clues to probe the plausibility of the connection. This is also, in essence, the model which emerges from Gibson and Hufeisen's study. The obvious reason for the emphasis on the establishment of lemma-level rather than formal connections in Wei's study is the relative absence of cognates across the three languages under scrutiny in the study in question.

In the case of Cenoz's study, the picture that emerges from "transfer lapses" is of a reliance in English L3 production principally on the Spanish L1 lexicon, which is formally closer to the L3 than that of the L2 (Basque). This clearly fits well with the proposals of Hall and Ecke and of Gibson and Hufeisen. On the other hand, Cenoz's findings in respect of "interactional strategies", where the L2 lexicon comes to the fore, is that, even where formal "parasitism" is a major factor, the specific circumstances in which a language is being used and the specific functions of given utterances can trigger other kinds of cross-lexical interaction. Jessner's dynamic systems approach can accommodate such variability in relation to lexical sources very well. In situating her model within dynamic systems theory, Jessner cites Van Geert's (1994) definition of systems in terms of the mutual interaction of all of their components: "each variable affects all the other variables in a system" (p. 50). Interestingly, this definition does not lead Jessner to posit total unitariness within the multilingual lexical system, but rather to conceive of this system as made up of a number of separate but connected and highly interactive language-particular systems.

Finally, let us consider Franceschini *et al.*'s proposals relating to the possibility of, on the one hand, a common lexical-semantic system across languages which is separate from the syntactic system, and, on the other hand, differences across languages in the syntactic system which relate to age of acquisition. With regard to this latter point, some researchers (e.g., Bialystok & Hakuta, 1999; Marinova-Todd, Marshall, & Snow, 2000) point out that no clear relationship has yet been established between neurological differences and differences in language proficiency and argue that, accordingly, it is legitimate to speculate that younger and older L2 acquirers may, for example, "localize their learning differently without showing different levels of learning" (Marinova-Todd, Marshall, & Snow, 2000: 17). Concerning the notion of the separation of lexis and syntax, this obviously chimes well with psycholinguistic models such as Levelt's which postulate just such a separation, but flies in the face of a very great deal of evidence which points in the opposite direction. Clearly this issue requires further investigation. In the light of the above-discussed problems surrounding the interpretation of brain-imaging evidence, such evidence certainly cannot be taken as having settled the matter. Concerning the notion of a common lexical-semantic system, just such a system appears to be evidenced as lower levels of proficiency in additional languages, but there is also evidence that, as proficiency in additional languages increases, each develops a semantic system which has a degree of autonomy. Once again, it would be premature to see neurolinguistics as having said the last word on this question; more research is clearly called for.

4. SOME CONCLUDING REMARKS

A number of the studies reported in the present volume support earlier studies in suggesting that when we encounter new languages we rapidly make judgments about their relationship to languages we already know and in processing terms exploit the lexical resources in those already established languages accordingly, typically prioritizing those languages which we deem to be most useful and making more selective use of those which we see as less relevant. Such prioritization would appear to be incompatible with a position which would claim that lexical knowledge is radically unitary. With regard to evidence in favour of the notion of an integrated multilingual mental lexicon, the fact that lexical stimuli in one language also automatically activate words in other languages known to an individual – at least in some circumstances - is a powerful argument for integration in the sense of a very high degree of cross-lexical connectivity and interaction, but does not entitle us to dismiss evidence of differentiation. As for the neurobiological evidence pointing to a common location across languages for lexical-semantic processing, given the uncertainties surrounding the interpretation of such evidence, and given the existence of contrary evidence from other sources, this should at the very least be treated with a high degree of circumspection.

Trinity College (Ireland)

REFERENCES

Abunuwara, E. (1992). The structure of the trilingual lexicon. *European Journal of Cognitive Psychology*, 4, 311-322.

ACTFL Proficiency Guidelines (1986). Yonkers, NY: ACTFL.

Ahukanna, J.G.W., Lund, NJ, & Gentile, J.R. (1981). Inter- and intra-lingual interference effects in learning a third language. *Modern Language Journal*, 65, 281-287.

Aitchison, J. (1987). *Words in the Mind: An Introduction to the Mental Lexicon.* Oxford: Blackwell.

Albert, R. (1998). Das bilinguale mentale Lexikon. *Deutsch als Fremdsprache*, 35, 90-97.

Altenberg, B. (1998). On the phraseology of spoken English: The evidence of recurrent word combinations. In A. P. Cowie (Ed.), *Phraseology: Theory Analysis and Applications* (pp. 101-122). Oxford: Oxford University Press.

Andersen, J. (1983). Syllable simplification in the speech of second language learners. *Interlanguage Studies Bulletin*, 7, 4-36.

Baayen, R.H., & Schreuder, R. (1996). Modelling the processing of morphologically complex words. In A. Dijkstra & K. De Smedt (Eds.), *Computational Psycholinguistics: AI and Connectionist Models of Human Language Processing* (pp. 166-191). London: Taylor & Francis.

Backus, A. (1999). Evidence for lexical chunks in insertional codeswitching. InB. Brendemoen, E. Lanza & E. Ryen (Eds.) *Language Encounters in Time and Space* (pp. 93-109). Oslo: Novus.

Baddeley, A., Gathercole, S., & Papagno, C. (1998). The phonological loop as a language learning device. *Psychological Review*, 105, 158-173.

Baddeley, A., Papagno C., & Vallar, G. (1988). When long-term learning depends on short term storage. *Journal of Memory and Language*, 27, 586-595.

Baker, C. (2001). *Foundations of Bilingualism and Bilingual Education.* Clevedon: Multilingual Matters.

Bartelt, G. (1989). The interaction of multilingual constraints. In H. W. Dechert & M. Raupach (Eds.), *Interlingual Processes* (pp. 151-177). Tübingen: Narr.

Baschek, I.L., Bredenkamp, J., Oehrle, B., & Wippich, W. (1977). Bestimmung der Bildhaftigkeit (I), Konkretheit (C) und der Bedeutungshaltigkeit (M) von 800 Substantiven. *Zeitschrift für Experimentelle und Angewandte Psychologie*, 24, 353-396.

Basden, B.H., Bonilla-Meeks, J.L., & Basden, D.E. (1994). Cross-language priming in word fragment completion. *Journal of Memory and Language*, 33, 69-82.

Berman, R.A., & Slobin, D.I. (1994). *Relating Events in Narrative: A Cross-linguistic Developmental Study.* Hillsdale, NJ, Erlbaum.

Bialystok, E., & Hakuta, K. (1999). Confounded age: Linguistic and cognitive factors in age differences for second language acquisition. In D. Birdsong (Ed.), *Second Language Acquisition and the Critical Period Hypothesis* (pp. 162-181). Mahwah, NJ: Erlbaum.

Bierwisch, M., & Schreuder, R. (1992). From concepts to lexical items. *Cognition*, 41, 23-60.

Blaxton, T.A. (1989). Investigating dissociations among memory measures: Support for a transfer-appropiate processing framework. *Journal of Experimental Psychology: Learning, Memory, and Cognition*, 15, 657-668.

Bley-Vroman, R. (1989). What is the logical nature of foreign language learning? In S. Gass & J. Schachter (Eds.), *Linguistic Perspectives on Second Language Acquisition* (pp. 41-68). Cambridge: Cambridge University Press.

Bock, K., & Levelt, W.J.M. (1994). Language production: Grammatical encoding. In M.A. Gernsbacher (Ed.), *Handbook of Psycholinguistics* (pp. 945-984). New York: Academic Press.

Bolinger, D. (1976). Meaning and memory. *Forum Linguisticum*, 1, 1-14.

Bond, Z., & Garnes, S. (1980). Misperceptions of fluent speech. In R. Cole (Ed.), *Perception and Production of Fluent Speech* (pp. 115-132). Hillsdale, NJ: Erlbaum.

Bouvy, C. (2000). Towards de construction of a theory of cross-linguistic transfer. In J. Cenoz & U. Jessner (Eds.) *English in Europe: The Acquisition of a Third Language* (pp. 143-156). Clevedon: Multilingual Matters

Bransford, J.D. (1979). Some general constraints on learning and memory research. In L.S. Cermak & F.I.M. Craik (Eds.), *Levels of Processing in Human Memory* (pp. 331-354). Hillsdale, NJ: Erlbaum.

Bybee, J. (1988). Morphology as lexical organization. In M. Hammond & M. Noonan (Eds.), *Theoretical Morphology* (pp. 119-141). London: Academic Press.

Bygate, M. (1988). Units of oral expression and language learning in small group interaction. *Applied Linguistics*, 9, 59-82.

Campaña Rubio, E. B., & Ecke, P. (2001). Un estudio experimental sobre la adquisición y recuperación (parcial) de palabras en una lengua extranjera. In G. López Cruz & M. Morúa Leyva (Eds.), *Memorias del V Encuentro Internacional de Lingüística en el Noroeste* (pp. 63-84). Hermosillo, Mexico: Editorial Unison.

Cappa, S. F., Perani, D., Schnur, T., Tettamanti, M., & Fazio, F. (1998). The effects of semantic category and knowledge type on lexical-semantic access: A PET study. *NeuroImage*, 8, 350-359.

Caramazza, A. (1996). The brain's dictionary. *Nature*, 380, 485-86.

Carroll, S. E. (1992). On cognates. *Second Language Research*, 8, 93-119.

Carton, A.S. (1971). Inferencing: A process in using and learning language. In P. Pimsleur & T. Quinn (Eds.), *The Psychology of Second Language Learning* (pp. 45-58). Cambridge: Cambridge University Press.

Celce-Murcia, M., Dörnyei, Z., & Thurrell, S. (1995). A pedagogically motivated model with content specifications. *Issues in Applied Linguistics*, 6, 5-35.

Cenoz, J. (2000). Research on multilingual acquisition. In J. Cenoz & U. Jessner (Eds.), *English in Europe: The Acquisition of a Third Language*, (pp. 39-53). Clevedon: Multilingual Matters.

Cenoz, J. (2001). The effect of linguistic distance, L2 status and age on cross-linguistic influence in L3 acquisition. In J. Cenoz, B. Hufeisen & U. Jessner (Eds.), *Cross-linguistic Influence in Third Language Acquisition: Psycholinguistic Perspectives* (pp. 8-20). Clevedon: Multilingual Matters.

Cenoz, J., & Genesee, F. (Eds.) (1998a). *Beyond Bilingualism. Multilingualism and Multilingual Education*. Clevedon: Multilingual Matters.

Cenoz, J., & Genesee, F. (1998b). Psycholinguistic perspectives on multilingualism and multilingual education. In J. Cenoz & F. Genesee (Eds.), *Beyond Bilingualism: Multilingualism and Multilingual Education* (pp. 16-32). Clevedon: Multilingual Matters.

Cenoz, J., Hufeisen, B., & Jessner, U. (Eds.) (2001a). *Cross-Linguistic Influence in Third Language Acquisition: Psycholinguistic Perspectives.* Clevedon: Multilingual Matters.

Cenoz, J., Hufeisen, B., & Jessner, U. (Eds.) (2001b). *Looking Beyond Second Language Acquisition. Studies in Tri- and Multilingualism.* Tübingen: Stauffenburg.

Cenoz, J., Hufeisen B., & Jessner, U. (2001c). Introduction. In J. Cenoz, B. Hufeisen & U. Jessner (Eds.), *Cross-Linguistic Influence in Third Language Acquisition. Psycholinguistic Perspectives* (pp. 1-8). Clevedon: Multilingual Matters.

Cenoz, J., & Jessner, U. (Eds.) (2000). *English in Europe: The Acquisition of a Third Language.* Clevedon: Multilingual Matters.

Cenoz, J., & Valencia, J.F. (1994). Additive trilingualism: Evidence from the Basque Country. *Applied Psycholinguistics*, 15, 195-207.

Chaffin, R. (1997). Associations to unfamiliar words: Learning the meanings of new words. *Memory & Cognition*, 25, 203-226.

Challis, B.H., & Brodbeck, D.R. (1992). Level of processing affects priming in word fragment completion. *Journal of Experimental Psychology: Learning, Memory, and Cognition*, 18, 595-607.

Chantraine, Y., Joanette, Y., & Cardebat, D. (1998). Impairments of discourse-level representations and processes. In B. Stemmer & H.A. Whitaker (Eds.), *Handbook of Neurolinguistics* (pp. 262-275). San Diego: Academic Press.

Chee, M. W., Tan, E. W. L., & Thiel, T. (1999). Mandarin and English single word processing studied with functional magnetic resonance imaging. *The Journal of Neuroscience*, 19, 3050-3056.

Chee, M.W., Caplan, D., Soon, C.S., Siriam, N., Tan, E.W.L., Thiel, T., & Weekes, B. (1999). Processing of visually presented sentences in Mandarin and English studied with fMRI. *Neuron*, 23, 127-137.

Chee, M.W., Hon, N., Lee, H.N., & Soon, C.S. (2001). Relative language proficiency modulates BOLD signal change when bilinguals perform semantic judgements. *NeuroImage*, 13, 1155-1163.

Choi, S., & Bowerman, M. (1991). Learning to express motion events in English and Korean: The influence of language-specific lexicalization patterns. *Cognition*, 41, 83-121.

Chomsky, N. (1972). *Language and Mind.* Enlarged edition. New York: Harcourt Brace Jovanovich.

Chomsky, N. (1980). *Rules and Representations.* Oxford: Blackwell.

Cieślicka, A. (2000). The effect of language proficiency and L2 vocabulary learning strategies on patterns of bilingual lexical processing. *Poznan Studies in Contemporary Linguistics*, 36, 27-53.

Cieślicka, A. (2002). Bilingual language users' sensitivity to semantic analyzability of L2 idioms – testing the effect of idiom analyzability in L2 metalinguistic tasks. *Paper presented at the XVth International Conference on Foreign/Second Language Acquisition.* Szyrk, May 2002.

Clyne, M. (1980). Triggering and language processing. *Canadian Journal of Psychology*, 34, 400-406.

Clyne, M. (1997). Some of the things trilinguals do. *The International Journal of Bilingualism*, 1, 95-116.

REFERENCES

Collins, A.M., & Loftus, E. (1975). A spreading activation theory of semantic processing. *Psychological Review*, 82, 407-428.

Cook, V. (1992). Evidence for multicompetence. *Language Learning*, 42, 557-591.

Cook, V. (1993). Wholistic multi-competence - jeu d'esprit or paradigm shift? In B. Kettemann & W.Wieden (Eds.), *Current Issues in European Second Language Acquisition Research* (pp. 3-9). Tübingen: Narr.

Cook, V. (Ed.) (2003). *The Effects of the L2 on the L1.* Clevedon: Multilingual Matters.

Council of Europe. (2001). *Common European Framework of Reference for Languages: Learning, Teaching, Assessment.* Cambridge: Cambridge University Press.

Cruse, D. (1986). *Lexical Semantics.* Cambridge: Cambridge University Press.

Cumming, A. (1988). Writing expertise and second language proficiency in ESL writing performance. Unpublished doctoral thesis, University of Toronto.

Cummins, J. (1991). Interdependence of first- and second language proficiency. In E. Bialystok (Ed.), *Language Processing in Bilingual Children* (pp. 70-89). Cambridge: Cambridge University Press.

Cusack, P. (1993). *Einfluß der ersten Fremdsprache (Französisch) auf die Intersprache der zweiten Fremdsprache (Deutsch) bei Lernenden mit Englisch als Muttersprache.* Unpublished Master's thesis, University of Kassel.

Cusack, P. (2000). Mehr als die Muttersprache: Wird die eigene Intersprache von weiteren Sprachen beeinflußt? Special issue of *Zeitschrift für Interkulturellen Fremdsprachenunterricht* 5, 20 pp. Available: http://www.ualberta.ca/~german/ejournal/cusack.htm [May 1, 2002].

Damasio, A. (1999). *The Feeling of What Happens: Body and Emotion in the Making of Consciousness.* New York: Harcourt Brace.

Damasio, H., Grabowski, Th. J., Tranel, D., Hichwa, R. D., & Damasio, A. R. (1996). A neural basis for lexical retrieval. *Nature*, 380, 499-505.

Dapretto M., & Bookheimer, S. (1999). Form and content: dissociating syntax and semantics in sentence comprehension. *Neuron*, 24, 427-432.

De Angelis, G. (1999). Interlanguage transfer and multiple language acquisition: A case study. *Paper presented at the annual TESOL conference.* New York.

De Angelis, G., & Selinker, L. (2001). Interlanguage transfer and competing linguistic systems in the multilingual mind. In J. Cenoz, B. Hufeisen & U. Jessner (Eds.), *Cross-linguistic Influence in Third Language Acquisition: Psycholinguistic Perspectives* (pp. 42-58). Clevedon: Multilingual Matters.

De Bot, K. (1992). A bilingual production model: Levelt's "Speaking" model adapted. *Applied Linguistics,* 13, 1-24.

De Bot, K. (forthcoming). *The Psycholinguistics of Multilingualism.* Amsterdam/Philadelphia: Benjamins.

De Bot, K., & Schreuder, R. (1993). Word production and the bilingual lexicon. In R. Schreuder & B. Weltens (Eds.), *The Bilingual Lexicon* (pp. 191-214). Amsterdam/Philadelphia: Benjamins.

De Carrico, J. (1998). Syntax, lexis and discourse: Issues in redefining the boundaries. In K. Haastrup & Å. Viberg (Eds.), *Perspectives on Lexical Acquisition in a Second Language* (pp. 127-149). Lund: Lund University Press.

Dechert, H.W., & Raupach, M. (1989a). *Transfer in Language Production.* Norwood, NJ: Ablex Publications.

Dechert, H.W., & Raupach, M. (1989b). Introduction. In Dechert, H. W. & Raupach, M. (Eds.), *Transfer in Language Production* (pp. ix-xvii). Norwood, NJ: Ablex Publications.

De Cock, S. (2000). Repetitive phrasal chunkiness and advanced EFL speech and writing. In C. Mair & M. Hundt (Eds.), *Corpus Linguistics and Linguistic Theory. Papers from ICAME 20* (pp. 51-68). Amsterdam: Rodopi.

De Groot, A. M. B. (1992). Determinants of word translation. *Journal of Experimental Psychology: Learning, Memory, and Cognition*, 18, 1001–1018.

De Groot, A. M. B. (1993). Word-type effects in bilingual processing tasks: Support for a mixed-representational system. In R. Schreuder & B. Weltens (Eds.), *The Bilingual Lexicon* (pp. 27-51). Amsterdam/Philadelphia: Benjamins.

De Groot, A. M. B., & Nas, G. L. J. (1991). Lexical representation of cognates and non-cognates in compound bilinguals. *Journal of Memory and Language*, 30, 90–123.

De Groot, A.M.B. (1995). Determinants of bilingual lexicosemantic organisation. *Computer Assisted Language Learning*, 8, 151-180.

Dehaene, S., Dupoux, E., Mehler, J., Cohen, L., Paulesu, E., Perani, D., Van de Moortele, P. F., Lehéricy, S., & Le Bihan, D. (1997). Anatomical variability in the cortical representation of first and second language. *NeuroReport*, 8, 3809-3815.

Dell, G. S. (1986). A spreading activation theory of retrieval in sentence production. *Psychological Review*, 93, 283-321.

De Moor, W. (1998). *Visuele Woordherkenning bij Tweetalige Personen.* Unpublished Master's Thesis, University of Ghent.

Dewaele, J.M. (1998). Lexical inventions: French interlanguage as L2 versus L3. *Applied Linguistics,* 19, 471-490.

Dewaele, J.-M. (2001). Activation or inhibition? The interaction of L1, L2 and L3 on the Language Mode continuum. In , J. Cenoz, B. Hufeisen & U. Jessner (Eds.), *Cross-linguistic Influence in Third Language Acquisition: Psycholinguistic Perspectives* (pp. 69-89). Clevedon: Multilingual Matters.

Dijkstra, A., De Bruijn, E., Schriefers, H.J., & Ten Brinke, S. (2000). More on interlingual homograph recognition: Language intermixing versus explicitness of instruction. *Bilingualism: Language and Cognition*, 3, 69-78.

Dijkstra, A., & Van Heuven, W.J.B. (2002). The architecture of the bilingual word recognition System. *Bilingualism: Language and Cognition* 5, 175-197.

Dijkstra, T., Timmermans, M., & Schriefers, H.J. (2000). Cross-language effects on bilingual homograph recognition. *Journal of Memory and Language,* 42, 445-464.

Dijkstra, T., & Van Heuven, W.J.B. (1998). The BIA-model and bilingual word recognition. In J. Grainger & A. Jacobs (Eds.), *Localist Connectionist Approaches to Human Cognition* (pp. 189-225). Hillsdale, NJ: Erlbaum.

Dijkstra, T., van Jaarsveld, H., & Ten Brinke, S. (1998). Interlingual homograph recognition: Effects of task demands and language intermixing. *Bilingualism: Language and Cognition,* 1, 51-66.

Duffy, S., Morris, R., & Rayner, K. (1988). Lexical ambiguity and fixation times in reading. *Journal of Memory and Language*, 27, 429-446.

Dufour, R., & Kroll, J.F. (1995). Matching words to concepts in two languages: A test of the concept mediation model of bilingual representations. *Memory and Cognition,* 23, 166-180.

Dulay, H., & Burt, M. (1974). You can't learn without goofing. In J. Richards (Ed.), *Error Analysis: Perspectives on Second Language Acquisition* (pp. 95-123). London: Longman.

Dušková, L. (1969). On sources of error in foreign language learning. *International Review of Applied Linguistics,* 7, 11-36.

Ecke, P. (1997). Tip of the tongue states in first and foreign languages: Similarities and differences of lexical retrieval failures. In L. Díaz, & C. Pérez (Eds.), *Proceedings of the EUROSLA 7 Conference* (pp. 505-514). Barcelona: Universitat Pompeu Fabra.

Ecke, P. (2001). Lexical retrieval in a third language: Evidence from errors and tip-of-the-tongue states. In J. Cenoz, B. Hufeisen & U. Jessner (Eds.), *Cross-linguistic Influence in Third Language Acquisition: Psycholinguistic Perspectives* (pp. 90-114). Clevedon: Multilingual Matters.

Ecke, P., & Garrett, M. F. (1998). Lexical retrieval stages of momentarily inaccessible foreign language words. *Cognitive Perspectives on the Acquisition/Learning of Second/Foreign Languages,* 35, 157-183.

Ecke, P., & C. J. Hall (1998). Tres niveles de la representación mental: Evidencia de errores léxicos en estudiantes de un tercer idioma. *Estudios de Lingüística Aplicada*, 28, 15–26.

Ecke, P., & Hall, C. J. (2000). Lexikalische Fehler in Deutsch als Drittsprache: Translexikalischer Einfluss auf drei Ebenen der mentalen Repräsentation. *Deutsch als Fremdsprache,* 37, 30-36.

Ellis, N.C. (1996). Sequencing in SLA: Phonological memory, chunking and points of order. *Studies in Second Language Acquisition,* 18, 91-126.

Ellis, N. C. (1997). Vocabulary acquisition: Word structure, collocation, word-class, and meaning. In N. Schmitt & M. McCarthy (Eds.), *Vocabulary: Description, Acquisition, and Pedagogy* (pp. 122-139). Cambridge: Cambridge University Press.

Ellis, N. C. (2001). Memory for language. In Peter Robinson (Ed.), *Cognition and Second Language Learning* (pp. 33-69). Cambridge: Cambridge University Press.

Ellis, N. C., & Beaton, A. (1993). Psycholinguistic determinants of foreign language vocabulary learning. *Language Learning,* 43, 559-617.

Ellis, R. (1985). *Understanding Second Language Acquisition*. Oxford: Oxford University Press.

Elston-Gütler, K., & Williams, J.N. (submitted). Bilingual ambiguities: Sentence context effects on processing interlingual homographs and translated L1 homographs in the L2.

Emmorey, K., & Fromkin, V. (1988). The mental lexicon. In F. Newmeyer (Ed.), *Linguistics: The Cambridge Survey. Volume III. Language: Psychological and Biological Aspects* (pp. 124-149). Cambridge: Cambridge University Press.

Engbrant-Heider, E., Rising Hintz, G., & Wohlert, M. (1986) (3rd ed.). *Svenska för Nybörjare. Del 1.* Stockholm: Svenska Institutet.

Ericsson, A., & Simon, H. (1984). *Protocol Analysis: Verbal Reports as Data.* Cambridge, MA: MIT Press.

Fabbro, F. (1999). *The Neurolinguistics of Bilingualism: An Introduction.* Hove: Psychology Press.

Fabbro, F. (2001). The bilingual brain: cerebral representation of languages. *Brain and Language,* 79, 211-222.

Fabbro, F., & Paradis, M. (1995). Differential impairments in four multilingual patients with subcortical lesions. In: M. Paradis (Ed.), *Aspects of Bilingual Aphasia* (pp. 139-176). Oxford: Pergamon Press.

Faerch, C., & Kasper, G. (1986a). One learner – two languages: Investigating types of interlanguage knowledge. In J. House & S. Blum-Kulka (Eds.), *Interlingual and Intercultural Communication* (pp. 211-228). Tübingen: Narr.

Faerch, C., & Kasper, G. (1986b). Transfer and second language speech processing. In E. Kellerman & M. Sharwood Smith (Eds.), *Crosslinguistic Influence in Second Language Acquisition* (pp. 49-65). New York: Pergamon.

Faerch, C., & Kasper, G. (Eds.) (1987). *Introspection in Second Language Research.* Clevedon: Multilingual Matters.

Fay, D., & Cutler, A. (1977). Malapropisms and the structure of the mental lexicon. *Linguistics Inquiry,* 8, 505-520.

Firth J. R. (1951/1957). Modes of meaning. *Papers in Linguistics 1934-151* (pp.190-215). Oxford: Oxford University Press.

Fodor, J. (1983). *The Modularity of Mind: An Essay on Faculty Psychology.* Cambridge, MA: MIT Press.

Forster, K., & Jiang, N. (2001). The nature of the bilingual lexicon: Experiments with the masked priming paradigm. In J. Nicol (Ed.), *One Mind, Two Languages: Bilingual Language Processing* (pp. 72-83). Oxford: Blackwell.

Franceschini, R., & Zappatore, D. (2001). Language-learning strategies in the course of a life: A language-biographic approach. Paper given at 2nd International Conference on Third Language Acquisition and Trilingualism. Leuwaarden, Sept. 13-15.

Friederici, A.D., Opitz, B., & Von Cramon, D.Y. (2000a). Segregating semantic and syntactic aspects of processing in the human brain: An fMRI investigation of different word types. *Cerebral Cortex,* 10, 698-705.

Friederici, A.D., Meyer, M., & Von Cramon, D.Y. (2000b). Auditory language comprehension: An event-related fMRI study on the processing of syntactic and lexical information. *Brain and Language,* 74, 289-300.

Fries, C. (1945). *Teaching and Learning English as a Foreign Language.* Ann Arbor: University of Michigan Press.

Garfield, J. (1987). Introduction: Carving the mind at its joints. In J. Garfield (Ed.), *Modularity in Knowledge Representation and Natural-Language Understanding* (pp. 1-13). Cambridge MA: MIT Press.

Garrett, M.F. (1993). Errors and their relevance for models of speech production. In G. Blanken, J. Dittmann, H. Grimm, J.C. Marshall, & C.-W. Wallesch (Eds.), *Linguistic Disorders and Pathologies* (pp. 72-92). Berlin: Walter de Gruyter.

Gass, S. (1984). A review of interlanguage syntax: Language transfer and language universals. *Language Learning*, 34, 115-132.

Gass, S., & Selinker, L. (1992). *Language Transfer in Language Learning*. Amsterdam/Philadelphia: Benjamins.

Gass, S. & Selinker, L. (1994). *Second Language Acquisition: An Introductory Course*. Amsterdam: John Benjamins.

Gass, S.M., & Selinker, L. (2001). *Second Language Acquisition: An Introductory Course*. Mahwah, NJ: Erlbaum.

Gathercole, S., Frankish, C.R., Pickering, S.J., & Peaker, S. (1999). Phonotactic influence on short-term memory. *Journal of Experimental Psychology*, 25, 84-95.

Genesee, F. (1998). A case study of multilingual education in Canada. In J. Cenoz & F. Genesee (Eds.) *Beyond Bilingualism: Multilingualism and Multilingual Education* (pp. 243-258). Clevedon: Multilingual Matters.

Gerard, L., & Scarborough, D. (1989). Language-specific lexical access of homographs by bilinguals. *Journal of Experimental Psychology: Learning, Memory and Cognition*, 15, 305-315.

Gibbs, R. (1986). Skating on thin ice: Literal meaning and understanding idioms in conversation. *Discourse Processes*, 9, 17-30.

Gibbs, R., & O'Brien, J. (1990). Idioms and mental imagery: The metaphorical motivation for idiomatic meaning. *Cognition*, 36, 35-68.

Gibson, M., & Hufeisen, B. (2001). 'Sich konzentrieren *an': Prepositional verb errors by second language versus third language learners of German. In Siv Björklund (Ed.), *Language as a Tool. Immersion Research and Practices* (pp. 176-195). Vaasa (Finland): Proceedings of the University of Vaasa Reports 83.

Gibson, M., & Hufeisen, B. (2002). Production of locative prepositions by learners of German as a second foreign language. In H. Barkowksi. & R. Faistauer (Eds.), *Deutsch als fremde Sprache unter fremden Sprachen.* (pp. 73-90). Hohengehren: Schneider.

Gibson, M., B. Hufeisen, & Libben, G. (2001). Learners of German as an L3 and their production of German prepositional verbs. In J. Cenoz, B. Hufeisen & U. Jessner (Eds.), *Cross-Linguistic Influence in Third Language Acquisition. Psycholinguistic Perspectives* (pp. 219-234). Clevedon: Multilingual Matters.

Graf, P., & Ryan, L. (1990). Transfer-appropriate processing for implicit and explicit memory. *Journal of Experimental Psychology: Learning, Memory, and Cognition*, 16, 978-992.

Grainger, J., & Dijkstra, T.H. (1992). On the representation and use of language information in bilinguals. In R. J. Harris (Ed.), *Cognitive Processing in Bilinguals* (pp. 207–220). Amsterdam: North Holland.

Grainger, J., & Segui, J. (1990). Neighborhood frequency effects in visual word recognition: A comparison of lexical decision and masked identification latencies. *Perception & Psychophysics*, 47, 191-198.

Granger, S. (1998). Prefabricated writing patterns in advanced EFL writing: Collocations and formulae. In A.P. Cowie (Ed.), *Phraseology: Theory, Analysis and Applications* (pp. 145-160). Oxford: Claredon Press.

Green, D.W. (1993). Towards a model of L2 comprehension and production. In R. Schreuder, & B. Weltens (Eds.), *The Bilingual Lexicon* (pp. 249-277). Amsterdam/Philadephia: Benjamins.

Green, D.W. (1986). Control, activation and resource: A framework and a model for the control of speech in bilinguals. *Brain and Language, 27*, 210-23.

Green, D.W. (1998). Mental control of the bilingual lexico-semantic system. *Bilingualism: Language and Cognition*, 1, 67-81.

Griessler, M. (2001) The effects of third language learning on second language proficiency: An Austrian example. *International Journal of Bilingual Education and Bilingualism*, 4, 50-60.

Green, D.W. (Ed.) (2001). *Cognitive Neuroscience of Bilingualism*. Special Issue of Bilingualism: Language and Cognition, 4.

Grosjean, F. (1982). *Life with Two Languages: An Introduction to Bilingualism*. Cambridge, MA: Harvard University Press.

Grosjean, F. (1985). The bilingual as a competent but specific speaker-hearer. *Journal of Multilingual and Multicultural Development*, 6, 467-477.

Grosjean, F. (1988). Exploring the recognition of guest words in bilingual speech. *Language and Cognitive Processes*, 3, 233-274.

Grosjean, F. (1995). A psycholinguistic approach to code-switching: The recognition of guest words by bilinguals. In L. Milroy & P. Muysken (Eds.), *One Speaker, Two Languages: Cross-Disciplinary Perspectives on Code-Switching* (pp. 259-75). Cambridge: Cambridge University Press.

Grosjean, F. (1997). Processing mixed language: Issues, findings and models. In A. de Groot & J. Kroll (Eds.), *Tutorials in Bilingualism: Psycholinguistic Perspectives* (pp. 225-254). Hillsdale, NJ: Erlbaum.

Grosjean, F. (1998). Studying bilinguals: methodological and conceptual issues. *Bilingualism: Language and Cognition*, 1, 131-149.

Grosjean, F. (2001). The bilingual's language modes. In J. Nicol (Ed.), *One Mind, Two Languages: Bilingual Language Processing* (1-25). Oxford: Blackwell.

Hall, C.J. (1992). Making the right connections: Vocabulary learning and the mental lexicon. Universidad de las Américas - Puebla. (*ERIC Document Reproduction Service* No. ED 363 128).

Hall, C.J. (1996). La estrategia parasítica: Un modelo psicolingüístico del aprendizaje de vocabulario. In S. Cuevas & J. Haidar (Eds.), *La Imaginación y la Intelegencia en el Lenguaje: Homenaje a Roman Jakobson* (pp. 229–238). Mexico City: INAH.

Hall, C.J. (1997). Palabras concretas, palabras abstractas y rasgos categoriales en el léxico mental bilingüe. In R. Barriga Villanueva & P. M. Butrageño (Eds.), *Varia Lingüística y Literaria: 50 Años del CELL, Tomo 1. Lingüística* (pp. 363–381). Mexico City: El Colegio de México.

Hall, C.J. (2002). The automatic cognate form assumption: Evidence for the Parasitic Model of vocabulary development. *International Review of Applied Linguistics* in Language Teaching, 40, 69-87.

Hall, C.J., & Schultz, M. (1994). Los errores de Marco Sintáctico: Evidencia del modelo parasitario del léxico mental en un segundo idioma. *Memorias del II Congreso Nacional de Lingüística* (Special issue of Estudios en Lingüística Aplicada), (pp. 376–389). Mexico City: UNAM, INAH and ECM.

Halliday M.A.K. (1966). Lexis as a linguistic level. In C.E. Bazell, J.C. Catford, M.A.K. Halliday & R.H. Robins (Eds.), *In Memory of J.R. Firth* (pp. 148-62). London: Longman.

Hamilton, M., & Rajaram, S. (2001). The concreteness effect in implicit and explicit memory tests. *Journal of Memory and Language,* 44, 96-117.

Hammarberg, B. (1998). The learner's word acquisition attempts in conversation. In D. Albrechtsen, B Henriksen, I.M. Mees & E Poulsen (Eds) *Perspectives on Foreign and Second Language Pedagogy: Essays Presented to Kirsten Haastrup on the Occasion of the Sixtieth Birthday* (pp. 177-190). Odense: Odense University Press.

Hammarberg, B. (2001). Roles of L1 and L2 in L3 production and acquisition. In J. Cenoz, B. Hufeisen, & U. Jessner (Eds*.), Cross-Linguistic Influence in Third Language Acquisition. Psycholinguistic Perspectives* (pp. 21-41). Clevedon: Multilingual Matters.

Harley, B. (1995). The lexicon in second language research. In B. Harley (Ed.), *Lexical Issues in Language Learning* (pp. 1-28). Amsterdam/Philadelphia: Benjamins.

Harris, R. (1998). *Introduction to Integrational Linguistics*. Kidlington: Elsevier.

Harris, R. J. (Ed.) (1992). *Cognitive Processing in Bilinguals*. Amsterdam: North-Holland.

Haugen, E. (1953). *The Norwegian Language in America: A Study in Bilingual Behavior*. Philadelphia: University of Pennsylvania Press.

Henning, G. H. (1973). Remembering foreign language vocabulary: Acoustic and semantic parameters. *Language Learning*, 23, 185-196.

Herdina, P., & Jessner, U. (1994). The paradox of transfer. Paper presented at IRAAL-Conference. Dublin, 23-25 June.

Herdina, P., & Jessner, U. (2000). The dynamics of third language acquisition. In J. Cenoz & U. Jessner (Eds.), *English in Europe: The Acquisition of a Third Language* (pp. 84-98). Clevedon: Multilingual Matters.

Herdina, P., & Jessner, U. (2002). *A Dynamic Model of Multilingualism: Perspectives of Change in Psycholinguistics*. Clevedon: Multilingual Matters.

Hernandez, A.E., Martinez, A., & Kohnert, K. (2000). In search of the language switch: An fMRI study of picture naming in Spanish-English bilinguals. *Brain and Language,* 73, 421-431.

Hernandez, A.E., Dapretto, M., Mazziotta, J., & Bookheimer, S. (2001). Language switching and language representation in Spanish-English bilinguals: An fMRI study. *NeuroImage,* 14, 510-520.

Herwig, A. (2001). Plurilingual lexical organisation: Evidence from lexical processing in L1-L2-L3-L4 translation. In J. Cenoz, B. Hufeisen, & U. Jessner (Eds.), *Cross-Linguistic Influence in Third Language Acquisition: Psycholinguistic Perspectives* (pp. 115-137). Clevedon: Multilingual Matters.

Hinger, B., & Spöttl, C. (2001). A multilingual approach to vocabulary acquisition. *Papers Presented at the Second International Conference on Third Language Acquisition*. Leeuwarden, 13-15 September 2001 (CD-Rom).

Howarth, P. (1998). Phraseology and second language proficiency. *Applied Linguistics,* 19, 24-44.

Huebner, T. (1985). System and variability in interlanguage syntax. *Language Learning*, 35, 141-163.

Hufeisen, B. (1991). *Englisch als erste und Deutsch als zweite Fremdsprache. Empirische Untersuchung zur fremdsprachlichen Interaktion.* Frankfurt/Main: Lang.

Hufeisen, B. (1993). Fehleranalyse: Englisch als L2 und Deutsch als L3. *International Review of Applied Linguistics*, 31, 242-256.

Hufeisen, B. (1998). L3- Stand der Forschung - Was bleibt zu tun? In B. Hufeisen & B. Lindemann (Eds.) *Tertiärsprachen: Theorien, Modelle, Methoden.* (pp. 169-184). Tübingen: Stauffenburg.

Hufeisen, B. (2000a). A European perspective - tertiary languages with a focus on German as L3. In Rosenthal, J. W. (Ed.), *Handbook of Undergraduate Second Language Education: English as a Second Language, Bilingual, and Foreign Language Instruction for a Multilingual World* (pp. 209-229). Mahwah, NJ: Erlbaum.

Hufeisen, B. (2000b). How do foreign language learners evaluate various aspects of their multilingualism? In Dentler, S., B. Hufeisen & B. Lindemann (Eds.), *Tertiär- und Drittsprachen. Projekte und empirische Untersuchungen.* (pp. 23-39). Tübingen: Stauffenburg.

Hufeisen, B., & Lindemann B. (Eds.) (1998). *Tertiärsprachen. Theorien, Modelle, Methoden.* Tübingen: Stauffenburg.

Illes, J., Francis, W.S., Desmond, J.E., Gabrieli, J.D.E., Glover, G.H., Poldrack, R.A., Lee, C.J., & Wagner, A.D. (1999). Convergent cortical representation of semantic processing in bilinguals. *Brain and Language*, 70, 347-363.

Isenberg, N., Silberzweig, D., Engelien, A., Emmerich, S., Malavade, K., Beattie, B., Leon, A. C., & Stern, E. (1999). Linguistic threat activates the human amygdala. *Proceedings of the National Academy of Sciences*, 96, 10456-10459.

Jackendoff, R. (1991). Parts and boundaries. *Cognition*, 41, 9-45.

Jacobson, R. (1990). *Codeswitching as a Worldwide Phenomenon.* New York: Lang.

Jake, J. L. (1998). Constructing interlanguage: Building a composite matrix language. *Linguistics*, 36, 334-377.

James, C. (1992). Awareness, consciousness and language contrast. In Mair, C. & Markus, M. (Eds.), *New Departures in Contrastive Linguistics. Vol. II.* (pp. 183-198). Innsbruck: University of Innsbruck.

James, C. (1998). *Errors in Language Learning and Use.* London: Longman.

Jessner, U. (1997). Towards a dynamic view of multilingualism. In M. Pütz (Ed.), *Language Choices: Conditions, Constraints and Consequences* (pp. 17-30). Amsterdam/Philadelphia: Benjamins.

Jessner, U. (1999). Metalinguistic awareness in multilinguals: Cognitive aspects of third language learning. *Language Awareness*, 8, 201-209.

Jessner, U. (2000). Metalinguistisches Denken beim Drittsprachgebrauch – Bilingualismus ist kein doppelter Monolingualismus. In A. James (Ed.), *Aktuelle Themen im Zweitspracherwerb. Österreichische Beiträge* (pp. 77-88). Wien: Edition Präsens.

Jessner, U. (2001). Drittspracherwerb: Implikationen für einen Sprachunterricht der Zukunft. In S. Kuri & R. Saxer (Eds.), *Deutsch als Fremdsprache an der Schwelle zum 21. Jahrhundert. Zukunftsorientierte Konzepte und Projekte* (pp. 54-64). Innsbruck: Studienverlag.

Jessner, U., & Herdina, P. (1996). Interaktionsphänomene im multilingualen Menschen: Erklärungsmöglichkeiten durch einen systemtheoretischen Ansatz. In A. Fill (Ed.), *Sprachökologie und Ökolinguistik* (pp. 217-30). Tübingen: Stauffenburg.

Jiang, N. (2000). Lexical representation and development in a second language. *Applied Linguistics,* 21, 47-77.

Jin, Y.-S. (1990). Effects of concreteness on cross-language priming in lexical decision. *Perception and Motor Skills*, 70, 1139–1154.

Johnston, M. (1985). Syntactic and morphological progressions in learner English. Research report. Department of Immigration and Ethnic Affairs, Commonwealth of Australia.

Juhasz, J. (1970). *Probleme der Interferenz*. Munich: Hueber.

Kandel, E.R., Schwartz, J.H., & Jessel, T.H. (1996). *Neurowissenschaften*. Heidelberg: Spektrum Akademischer Verlag.

Kasper, G., & Kellerman, E. (Eds.) (1999). *Communication Strategies: Psycholinguistic and Sociolinguistic Perspectives*. London: Longman.

Kecskes, I., & Papp, T. (2000). *Foreign Language and Mother Tongue*. Mahwah, NJ: Erlbaum.

Kellerman, E. (1977). Towards a characterization of the strategy of transfer in second language learning. *Interlanguage Studies Bulletin*, 2, 58-145.

Kellerman, E. (1978). Giving learners a break: Native language intuitions as a source of predictions about transferability. *Working Papers on Bilingualism* 15, 59-92, 309-15.

Kellerman, E. (1979). Transfer and non-transfer: Where are we now? *Studies in Second Language Acquisition*, 2, 37-57.

Kellerman, E. (1983). Now you see it, now you don't. In S. Gass & L. Selinker (Eds.), *Language Transfer in Language Learning* (pp. 112-134). Rowley, MA: Newbury House.

Kellerman, E. (1984). The empirical evidence for the influence of the L1 in interlanguage. In A. Davies, C. Criper, & A. P. R. Howatt (Eds.), *Interlanguage* (pp. 98-122). Edinburgh: Edinburgh University Press.

Kellerman, E. (1986). An eye for an eye: Cross-linguistic constraints on the development of the L2 lexicon. In E. Kellerman & M. Sharwood Smith (Eds.), *Cross-linguistic Influence in Second Language Acquisition* (pp. 35-48). New York: Pergamon.

Kellerman, E. (1995). Crosslinguistic influence: Transfer to nowhere? *Annual Review of Applied Linguistics,* 15, 125-150.

Kellerman, E. (2001). New uses for old language: Cross-linguistic influence in the depiction of motion and emotion. In J. Cenoz, B. Hufeisen & U. Jessner (Eds.), *Cross-linguistic Influence in Third Language Acquisition: Psycholinguistic Perspectives* (pp. 170-191). Clevedon: Multilingual Matters.

Kellerman, E., & Sharwood Smith, M. (Eds.) (1986). *Crosslinguistic Influence in Second Language Acquisition*. New York: Pergamon.

Kempen, D., & Huijbers, P. (1983). The lexicalization process in sentence production and naming: Indirect election of words. *Cognition*, 14, 185-209.

Kim, K.H.S., Relkin, N.R., Lee, K.-M., & Hirsch, J. (1997). Distinct cortical areas associated with native and second languages. *Nature*, 388, 171-174.

Klein, D., Milner, B., Zatorre, R.J., Meyer, E., & Evans, A.C. (1994). The neural substrates underlying word generation: A bilingual functional-imaging study. *Proceedings of the National Academy of Sciences*, 92, 2899-2903.

Klein, D., Zatorre, R.J., Milner, B., Meyer, E., & Evans, A.C. (1995). The neural substrates of bilingual language processing: Evidence from positron emission tomography. In M. Paradis (Ed.), *Aspects of Bilingual Aphasia* (pp. 23-36). Oxford: Pergamon.

Klein, D., Milner, B., Zatorre, R.J., Zhao, V., & Nikelski, J. (1999). Cerebral organization in bilinguals: A PET study of Chinese-English verb generation. *Neuroreport*, 10, 2841-2846.

Klein, E. (1995). Second versus third language acquisition: Is there a difference? *Language Learning*, 45, 419-465.

Klein, H. (1999). Interkomprehension in romanischen Sprachen. *Grenzgänge*, 6, 17-29.

Köberle, B. (1998). Positive Interaktion zwischen L2, L3, L4 und ihre Applikation im Fremdsprachenunterricht. In Hufeisen, B. & Lindemann, B. (Eds.), *Tertiärsprachen: Theorien, Modelle, Methoden.* (pp. 89-109). Tübingen: Stauffenburg.

Krashen, S. (1981). *Second Language Acquisition and Second Language Learning.* Oxford/New York: Pergamon Press.

Krashen, S., & Scarcella, R. (1978). On routines and patterns in language acquisition and performance. *Language Learning*, 28, 283-300.

Kroll, J.F., & de Groot, A. (1997). Lexical and conceptual memory in the bilingual: Mapping form to meaning in two languages. In A. de Groot & J. Kroll (Eds.), *Tutorials in Bilingualism* (pp. 169-200). Mahwah, NJ: Erlbaum.

Kroll, J.F., & Dijkstra, A. (2002). The bilingual lexicon. In R. Kaplan (Ed.), *Handbook of Applied Linguistics* (pp. 301-321). Oxford: Oxford University Press.

Kroll, J.F., & Stewart, E. (1994). Category interference in translation and picture naming: Evidence for asymmetric connections between bilingual memory representations. *Journal of Memory and Language*, 33, 149-174.

Kroll, J.F., & Tokowicz, N. (2001). The development of conceptual representation for words in a second language. In J. L. Nicol (Ed.), *One Mind, Two Languages: Bilingual Language Processing* (pp. 49-71). Oxford: Blackwell.

Kruggel, F., Wiggins, C.J., Herrmann, C.S., & Von Cramon, D.Y. (2000). Recording of event-related potentials during functional MRI at 3.0 tesla field strenght. *Magnetic Resonance in Medicine*, 44, 277-282.

Lado, R. (1957). *Linguistics Across Cultures.* Ann Arbor: University of Michigan Press.

Lasagabaster, D. (2000). Three languages and three linguistic models in the Basque educational system. In J. Cenoz & U. Jessner (Eds.) *English in Europe: The Acquisition of a Third Language* (pp. 179-197). Clevedon: Multilingual Matters.

Laufer, B. (1988). The concept of 'synforms' (similar lexical forms) in vocabulary acquisition. *Language and Education*, 2, 113-132.

Laufer, B. (1989). A factor of difficulty in vocabulary learning: Deceptive transparency. *AILA Review*, 6, 10-20.

Laufer, B. (1991). Some properties of the foreign language learner's lexicon as evidenced by lexical confusions. *International Review of Applied Linguistics*, 29, 317-330.

Laufer, B. (1998). The development of passive and active vocabulary in a second language: same or different? *Applied Linguistics*, 19, 255-271.

Laufer, B., & Eliasson, S. (1995). What causes avoidance in L2 learning: L1-L2 difference, L1-L2 similarity or L2 complexity? *Studies in Second Language Learning*, 15, 35-48.

Le Clec'H, G. , Dehaene, S., Cohen, L., Mehler, J. , Dupoux, E., Poline, J. B., Lehéricy , S, Van de Moortele, P. F., & Le Bihan, D. (2000). Distinct cortical areas for names of numbers and body parts independent of language and input modality. *NeuroImage*, 12, 381-391.

Levelt, W.J.M. (1989). *Speaking: From Intention to Articulation*. Cambridge, MA: MIT Press.

Levelt, W.J.M. (1995). The ability to speak: From intention to spoken words. *European Review*, 3, 13-23.

Levelt, W.J.M., Roelofs, A., & Meyer, A. S. (1999). A theory of lexical access in speech production. *Behavioral and Brain Sciences*, 22, 1–75.

Levenston, E. (1979). Second language lexical acquisition: issues and problems. *Interlanguage Studies Bulletin*, 4, 147-160.

Levin, B., & Pinker, S. (1991). Introduction. Special issue of *Cognition on Lexical and Conceptual Semantics*. Cognition, 41, 1-7.

Lucas, M. (1999). Context effects in lexical access: A meta-analysis. *Memory and Cognition*, 27, 385-398.

Lüdi, G. (1996). Mehrsprachigkeit. In H. Goebl, P. Nelde, Z. Starý & W. Wölck (Eds.), *Kontaktlinguistik: ein internationales Handbuch zeitgenössischer Forschung* (pp. 233-245). Berlin: de Gruyter.

MacWhinney, B. (1987). The competition model. In B. MacWhinney (Ed.), *Mechanisms of Language Acquisition* (pp. 249-308). Hillsdale, NJ: Erlbaum.

MacWhinney, B. (1997). Second language acquisition and the competition model. In A. M. B. de Groot & J. F. Kroll (Eds.), *Tutorials in Bilingualism* (pp. 113-142), Mahwah, NJ: Erlbaum.

Mägiste, E. (1984). Learning a third language. *Journal of Multilingual and Multicultural Development*, 5, 415-421.

Maess, B., Koelsch, S., Gunter, Th.C., & Friederici, A.D. (2001). Musical syntax is processed in Broca's area: An MEG study. *Neuroscience*, 4, 540-545.

Malakoff, M. (1992). Translation ability: A natural bilingual and multilingual skill. In Harris, R. (Ed.), *Cognitive Processing in Bilinguals* (pp. 515-529). Amsterdam: North Holland.

Marinova-Todd, S.H., Marshall, D.B., & Snow, C.E. (2000). Three misconceptions about age and L2 learning. *TESOL Quarterly*, 34, 9-34.

Martin, A., Haxby, J.V., Lalonde, F.M., Wiggs, C.L., & Ungerleider, L.G. (1995). Discrete cortical regions associated with knowledge of color and knowledge of action. *Science*, 270, 102-105.

Martin, A., & Chao, L.L. (2001). Semantic memory and the brain: structure and processes. *Current Opinion in Neurobiology*, 11, 194-201.

Marx, N. (2001). Models of multilingualism. Paper presented at the Second International Conference on Third Language Acquisition and Trilingualism, Leeuwarden, 13-15 September.

Mathey, S., & Zagar, D. (2000). The neighborhood distribution effect in visual word recognition: Words with single and twin neighbors. *Journal of Experimental Psychology: Human Perception and Performance*, 26, 184-205.

Matz, K.-D., Teschmer, J., & Weise, G. (1988). Angewandte Fremdsprachenpsychologie und ihr Beitrag für die Effektivierung des Lernens und Lehrens von Fremdsprachen. *Deutsch als Fremdsprache*, 25, 224-230.

Mayer, M. (1969). *Frog, where are you?* New York: Dial Press.

McCarthy M. J. (1998). *Spoken Language and Applied Linguistics*. Cambridge: Cambridge University Press.

McClelland, J.L., & Rumelhart, D.E. (1981). An interactive activation model of context effects in letter perception, Part 1: An account of basic findings. *Psychological Review*, 88, 375-405.

McElree, B., Jia, G., & Litvak, A. (2000). The time course of conceptual processing in three bilingual populations. *Journal of Memory and Language*, 42, 229-254.

McLaughlin, B., & Nayak, N. (1989). Processing a new language: Does knowing other language make a difference? In Dechert, H. & Raupach, M. (Eds.), *Interlingual Processes* (pp. 5-16). Tübingen: Narr.

Meara, P. (1983). Word associations in a foreign language: A report on the Birkbeck Vocabulary Project 2. *Nottingham Linguistic Circular*, 2, 29-37.

Meara, P. (1984). The study of lexis in interlanguage. In Davies, C. Criper, & A.P.R. Howatt (Eds.), *Interlanguage* (pp. 225-235). Edinburgh: Edinburgh University Press.

Meara P.M. (1996). The dimensions of lexical competence. In G. Brown, K. Malmkjaer & J. Williams (Eds.) *Performance and Competence in Second Language Acquisition* (pp. 35-50). Cambridge: Cambridge University Press.

Meara, P. (1999). Self-organisation in bilingual lexicons. In P. Broeder & J. Muure (Eds.), *Language and Thought in Development: Crosslinguistic Studies* (pp. 127-144). Tübingen: Narr.

Meisel, J. (1983). Transfer as a second language strategy. *Language and Communication*, 3, 11-46.

Meissner, F.-J. (1998). Transfer beim Erwerb einer weiteren romanischen Fremdsprache: Das mehrsprachige mentale Lexikon. In F.-J. Meissner & M. Reinfried (Eds.), *Mehrsprachigkeitsdidaktik. Konzepte, Analysen, Lehrerfahrungen mit romanischen Fremdsprachen* (pp. 45-67). Tübingen: Narr.

Milroy, L., & Muysken, P. (Eds.) (1995). *One Speaker, Two Languages. Cross-Disciplinary Perspectives on Code-Switching*. Cambridge: Cambridge University Press.

Missler, B. (1999). *Fremdsprachenlernerfahrungen und Lernstrategien. Eine empirische Untersuchung*. Tübingen: Stauffenburg.

Missler, B. (2000). Previous experience of foreign language learning and its contribution to the development of learning strategies. In S. Dentler, B. Hufeisen & B. Lindemann (Eds.), *Tertiär- und Drittsprachen. Projekte und empirische Untersuchungen* (pp. 7-22). Tübingen: Stauffenburg.

Möhle, D. (1989). Multilingual interacion in foreign language production. In H.W. Dechert & M. Raupach (Eds.), *Interlingual Processes* (pp. 179-94). Tübingen: Narr.

Moon, R. (1998). *Fixed Expressions and Idioms in English*. Oxford: Claredon Press.

Moro, A., M. Tettamanti, D. Perani, C. Donati, S.F. Cappa, & Fazio, F. (2000). Syntax and the brain: Disentangling grammar by selective anomalies. *NeuroImage*, 13, 110-118.

Moss, H.E., & Gaskell, M.G. (1999). Lexical semantic processing during speech comprehension. In S. Garrod & M. Pickering (Eds.), *Language processing* (pp. 59-99). Hove: Psychology Press.

Müller, N. (Ed.) (1996). *Two Languages, Two Grammars? Studies in Second-Language and Bilingual First-Language Acquisition*. Berlin: Mouton de Gruyter. Special Issue of Linguistics 34.

Müller-Lancé, J. (2000a). Estrategias de inferencia en el aprendizaje del español o italiano por germanohablantes. Paper read at Universidad Complutense de Madrid on 18th June, 1999.

Müller-Lancé, J. (2000b). Zugänge zum Wortschatz Romanischer Sprachen im Tertiärsprachenerwerb. Habilitationsschrift, Albert-Ludwigs-Universität Freiburg.

Müller-Lancé, J. (2000c). Mehrsprachiges Assoziieren und das Inferieren von Bedeutungen. In K. Aguado & A. Hu (Eds.), *Mehrsprachigkeit und Interkulturalität* (pp. 145-158). Berlin: Pädagogischer Zeitschriftenverlag.

Müller-Lancé, J. (2001). 'Das kenn' ich doch aus dem Lateinischen': Zur Nutzung von Kompetenzen aus weiteren Fremdsprachen bei der Hin- und Herübersetzung. In J. Albrecht & H.-M. Gauger (Eds.), *Sprachvergleich und Übersetzungsvergleich - Leistung und Grenzen, Unterschiede und Gemeinsamkeiten* (pp. 150-180). Frankfurt/Main: Lang.

Müller-Lancé, J. (2003). *Der Wortschatz Romanischer Sprachen im Tertiärsprachenerwerb*. Tübingen: Stauffenburg.

Murray, D.J. (1986). Characteristics of words determining how easily they will be translated into a second language. *Applied Psycholinguistics*, 7, 353-372.

Myers-Scotton, C., & Jake, J.L. (2001). Explaining aspects of codeswitching and their implications. In , J. Nicol (Ed.), *One Mind, Two Languages: Bilingual Language Processing* (pp. 91-125). Oxford: Blackwell.

Näf, A., & Pfander, D. (2001). <Springing of> a <bruck> with an elastic <sail> - Deutsches im Englisch von französischsprachigen Schülern. *Zeitschrift für Angewandte Linguistik*, 35, 5-37.

Nation, I.S.P. (2001). *Learning Vocabulary in Another Language*. Cambridge: Cambridge University Press.

Nation, R., & McLaughlin, B. (1986). Experts and novices: An information-processing approach to the "good language learner" problem. *Applied Psycholinguistics*, 7, 51-56.

Nattinger, J.R., & De Carrico, J. (1992). *Lexical Phrases in Language Teaching* Oxford: Oxford University Press.

Neville, H.J., Coffey, S.A., Lawson, D.S., Fischer, A., Emmorey, K., & Bellugi, U. (1997). Neural systems mediating American sign language: Effects of sensory experience and age of acquisition. *Brain and Language*, 57, 285-308.

Obler, K., & Gjerlow, K. (1999). *Language and the Brain*. Cambridge: Cambridge University Press.

Odlin, T. (1989). *Language Transfer: Cross-Linguistic Influence in Language Learning*. Cambridge: Cambridge University Press.

Paivio, A., Yuille, J.C., & Madigan, S. (1968). Concreteness, imagery and meaningful values for 925 nouns. *Journal of Experimental Psychology Monograph Supplement*, 76.

Paradis, M. (1981). Neurolinguistic organization of a bilingual's two languages. In J. E. Copeland & Davis, P. W. (Eds.), *The Seventh LACUS Forum* (pp. 486-494). Columbia, SC: Hornbeam Press.

Paradis, M. (1987). *The Assessment of Bilingual Aphasia*. Hillsdale, NJ: Erlbaum.

Paradis, M. (1994). Neurolinguistic aspects of implicit and explicit memory: Implications for bilingualism and SLA. In N.C. Ellis (Ed.), *Implicit and Explicit Learning of Languages* (pp. 393-419). London: Academic Press.

Paradis, M. (2000). Generalizable outcomes of bilingual aphasia research. *Folia Phoniatrica et Logopaedica*, 52, 54-64.

Paradis, M., & Goldblum, M.C. (1989). Selective crossed aphasia in a trilingual aphasic patient followed by reciprocal antagonism. *Brain and Language*, 36, 62-75.

Paulesu, E., McCrory, E., Fazio, F., Menoncello, L., Brunswick, N., Cappa, S.F., Cotelli, M., Cossu, G., Corte, F., Lorusso, M., Pesenti, S., Gallagher, A., Perani, D., Price, C., Frith, C. D., & Frith, U. (2000). A cultural effect on brain function. *Nature Neuroscience*, 3, 91-96.

Pavlenko, A. (2000). What's in a concept? *Bilingualism: Brain and Cognition*, 3, 31-36.

Pawley, A., & Syder, F.H. (1983). Two puzzles for linguistic theory: Nativelike selection and nativelike fluency. In J.C. Richards & R.W. Schmidt (Eds.), *Language and Communication* (pp. 191-226). New York: Longman.

Peal, E., & Lambert, W. (1962). The relation of bilingualism to intelligence. *Psychological Monographs*, 76, 1-23.

Perani, D., Dehaene, S., Grassi, F., Cohen, L., Cappa, S. F., Dupoux, E., Fazio, F., & Mehler, J. (1996). Brain processing of native and foreign languages. *NeuroReport*, 7, 2439-2444.

Perani, D., Paulesu, E., Galles, N. S., Dupoux, E., Dehaene, S., Bettinardi, V., Cappa, S. F., Fazio, F., & Mehler, J. (1998). The bilingual brain: Proficiency and age of acquisition of the second language. *Brain*, 121, 1841-1852.

Perani, D., Schnur, T., Tettamanti, M., Gorno-Tempini, M., Cappa, S. F., & Fazio, F. (1999a). Word and picture matching: A PET study of semantic category effects. *Neuropsychologia*, 37, 293-306.

Perani, D., Cappa, S. F., Schnur, T., Tettamanti, M., Collina, S., Rosa, M. M., & Fazio, F. (1999b). The neural correlates of verb and noun processing: A PET study. *Brain*, 122, 2337-2344.

Perdue, C. (1993). *Adult Language Acquisition: Cross-linguistic Perspectives. Vol I: Field Methods*. Cambridge: Cambridge University Press.

Perecman, E. (1989). Bilingualism and jargonaphasia: Is there a connection? *Brain and Language, 36,* 49-61.

Peters, A. (1983). *The Units of Language Acquisition.* Cambridge: Cambridge University Press.

Pienemann, M. (1984). Psychological constraints on the teachability of languages. *Studies in Second Language Acquisition,* 6, 186-214.

Pienemann, M. (1998). *Language Processing and Second Language Development. Processability Theory.* Amsterdam/Philadelphia: Benjamins.

Poldrack, R.A., Wagner, A.D., Prull, M.W., Desmond, J.E., Glover, G.H., & Gabrieli, J.D.E. (1999). Functional specialization for semantic and phonological processing in the left inferior prefrontal cortex. *NeuroImage,* 10, 15-35.

Posner M.I., & Raichle, M.E. (1996). *Bilder des Geistes: Hirnforscher auf den Spuren des Denkens.* Heidelberg: Spektrum Akademischer Verlag.

Poulisse, N. (1990). *The Use of Compensatory Strategies by Dutch Learners of English.* Dordrecht: Foris.

Poulisse, N. (1997a). Language production in bilinguals. In A. De Groot & J. Kroll (Eds.), *Tutorials in Bilingualism* (pp. 201-224). Mahwah, NJ: Erlbaum.

Poulisse, N. (1997b). Some words in defence of the psycholinguistic approach. *The Modern Language Journal,* 81, 324-328.

Poulisse, N. (1999). *Slips of the Tongue: Speech Errors in First and Second Language Production.* Amsterdam/Philadelphia: Benjamins.

Poulisse, N., & Bongaerts, T. (1994). First language use in second language production. *Applied Linguistics,* 15, 36-57.

Price, C., Green, D.W., & Von Studnitz, R. (1999). A functional imaging study of translation and language switching. *Brain,* 122, 2221-2235.

Pulvermüller, F. (1999). Words in the brain's language. *Behavioral and Brain Sciences,* 22, 253-336.

Ransdell, S.E., & Fischler, I. (1987). Memory in a monolingual mode: When are bilinguals at a disadvantage? *Journal of Memory and Language,* 26, 392-405.

Raupach, M. (1984). Formulae in second language speech production. In H. Dechert, D. Möhle & M. Raupach (Eds.), *Second Language Productions* (pp. 114-137). Tübingen: Narr.

Ringbom, H. (1978). The influence of the mother tongue on the translation of lexical items. *Interlanguage Studies Bulletin,* 3, 80-101.

Ringbom, H. (1982). The influence of other languages on the vocabulary of foreign language learners. In G. Nickel & D. Nehls (Eds.), *Error Analysis, Contrastive Linguistics and Second Language Learning.* Papers from the 6th Congress of Applied Linguistics, Lund, (pp. 85-96). (Special Issue of International Review of Applied Linguistics).

Ringbom, H. (1983). Borrowing and lexical transfer. *Applied Linguistics,* 4, 207-212.

Ringbom, H. (1986). Crosslinguistic influence and the foreign language learning process. In E. Kellerman, & M. Sharwood Smith (Eds.), *Crosslinguistic Influence in Second Language Acquisition* (pp. 150-162). New York: Pergamon.

Ringbom, H. (1987). *The Role of the First Language in Foreign Language Learning*. Clevedon: Multilingual Matters.

Ringbom, H. (2001). Lexical transfer in L3 production. In J. Cenoz, B. Hufeisen, & U. Jessner (Eds.), *Cross-Linguistic Influence in Third Language Acquisition: Psycholinguistic Perspectives* (pp. 59-68). Clevedon: Multilingual Matters.

Rodriguez-Fornells, A., Rotte, M., Heinze, H.-J., Nösselt, T., & Münte, Th.F. (2002). Brain potential and functional MRI evidence for how to handle two languages with one brain. *Nature*, 415, 1026-1029.

Roediger, H.L. III, & Blaxton, T.A. (1987). Effects of varying modality surface features, and retention interval on priming in word fragment completion. *Memory and Cognition*, 15, 379-388.

Roediger, H.L. III, Weldon, M.S., & Challis, B.H. (1989). Explaining dissociations between implicit and explicit memory: A processing account. In H.L. Roediger III & F.I.M. Craik (Eds.), *Varieties of Memory and Consciousness: Essays in Honor of Endel Tulving* (pp. 3-41). Hillsdale, NJ: Erlbaum.

Roediger, H.L. III, Weldon, M.S., Stadler, M.A., & Riegler, G.H. (1992). Direct comparison of two implicit memory tests: Word fragment and word stem completion. *Journal of Experimental Psychology: Learning, Memory and Cognition*, 18, 1251-1269.

Roelofs, A. (1992). A spreading-activation theory of lemma retrieval in speaking. *Cognition*, 42, 107-142.

Rosch, E. (1978). Principles of categorization. In E. Rosch & B.B. Lloyd (Eds.), *Cognition and Categorization* (pp. 27-48). Hillsdale, NJ: Erlbaum.

Rumelhart, D.E., McClelland, J.L., & the PDP Research Group (1986). *Parallel Distributed Processing: Explorations in the Microstructure of Cognition, Vol. 1, Foundations*. Cambridge: MIT Press.

Sánchez Casas, R.M., Davis, C.W., & García-Albea, J.E. (1992). Bilingual lexical processing: Exploring the cognate/noncognate distinction. *European Journal of Cognitive Psychology*, 4, 293–310.

Scarborough, D., Gerard, L., & Cortese, C. (1984). Independence of lexical access in bilingual word recognition. *Journal of Verbal Learning and Verbal Behavior*, 23, 84-99.

Schachter, J. (1983). A new account of language transfer. In S. Gass, & L. Selinker (Eds.), *Language Transfer in Language Learning* (pp. 98-111). Rowley, MA: Newbury House.

Schmid, S. (1993). Learning strategies for closely related languages: On the Italian spoken by Spanish immigrants in Switzerland. In B. Kettemann & W. Wieden (Eds.), *Current Issues in European Second Language Acquisition Research* (pp. 405-418). Tübingen: Narr.

Schmidt, R., & Frota, S. (1986). Developing basic conversational ability in a second language: A case study of an adult learner of Portuguese. In R. Day (Ed.), *Talking to Learn: Conversation in Second Language Acquisition* (pp. 237-326). Rowley, MA: Newbury House.

Schönpflug, U. (2000). Word fragment completions in the second (German) and third (English) language: A contribution to the organisation of the trilingual speaker's lexicon. In Cenoz, J. & Jessner, U. (Eds.), *English in Europe. The Acquisition of a Third Language* (pp. 121-142). Clevedon: Multilingual Matters.

Schreuder, R. & Weltens, B. (Eds.) (1993). *The Bilingual Lexicon*. Amsterdam/Philadelphia: John Benjamins.

Schulpen, B., Dijkstra, A., Schriefers, H.J., & Hasper, M. (submitted). Recognition of interlingual homophones in bilingual auditory word recognition.

Schumann, J. (1998). *The Neurobiology of Affect in Language.* London: Blackwell.

Schwartz, A., Kroll, J.F., & Diaz, M. (2000). Reading Spanish words with English word bodies: Activation of spelling-to-sound correspondences across languages. Paper presented at the Second International Conference on the Mental Lexicon, Montreal, 18-20 October 2000.

Schwartz, B.L. (2002). *Tip-of-the-Tongue States: Phenomenology, Mechanism, and Lexical Retrieval.* Mahwah, NJ: Erlbaum.

Selinker, L., & Baumgartner-Cohen, B. (1995). Multiple language acquisition: "Damn it, why can't I keep these two languages apart?" In M. Bensoussan, & I. Berman (Eds.), *Language Culture and Curriculum* (special issue), 8, 1-7.

Shanon, B. (1991). Faulty language selection in polyglots. *Language and Cognitive Processes,* 6, 339-350.

Sharwood-Smith, M. (1994). *Second Language Learning: Theoretical Foundations.* London: Longman.

Sharwood-Smith, M., & Kellerman, E. (1986). Crosslinguistic influence in second language acquisition: An introduction. In E. Kellerman & M. Sharwood Smith (Eds.), *Crosslinguistic Influence in Second Language Acquisition* (pp. 1-9). New York: Pergamon Press.

Simpson, G.B., & Krueger, M.A. (1991). Selective access of homograph meanings in sentence context. *Journal of Memory and Language,* 30, 627-643.

Sinclair, J. Mc H. (1966). Beginning the study of lexis. In Bazell C.E., Catford J.C., Halliday M.A.K. & Robins R.H. (Eds.), *In Memory of J R Firth* (pp. 410-430). London: Longman.

Sinclair, J. Mc H. (1991). *Corpus, Concordance, Collocation.* Oxford: Oxford University Press.

Singh, R., & Carroll, S. (1979). L1, L2 and L3. *Indian Journal of Applied Linguistics,* 5, 51-63.

Singleton, D. (1987). Mother and other tongue influence on learner French. *Studies in Second Language Acquisition,* 9, 327-46.

Singleton, D. (1994). Learning L2 lexis: a matter of form? In G. Bartelt (Ed.), *The Dynamics of Language Processes: Essays in Honor of Hans W. Dechert* (pp. 45-57). Tübingen: Narr.

Singleton, D. (1996). Crosslinguistic lexical operations and the L2 mental lexicon. In T. Hickey & J. Williams (Eds.), *Language, Education & Society in a Changing World* (pp. 246-252). Clevedon: Multilingual Matters.

Singleton, D. (1997). Learning and processing L2 vocabulary. *Language Teaching,* 30, 213-225.

Singleton, D. (1998). *Lexical Processing and the "Language Module".* Dublin: Trinity College, Centre for Language and Communication Studies (*CLCS Occasional Paper* 53), and Alexandria,Virginia (*ERIC Reports* ED 421 856).

Singleton, D. (1999). *Exploring the Second Language Mental Lexicon.* Cambridge: Cambridge University Press.

Singleton, D. (2000). *Language and the Lexicon: An Introduction.* London: Arnold.

Singleton, D., & Little, D. (1984). A first encounter with Dutch: Perceived language distance and language transfer as factors in comprehension. In L. Mac Mathúna & D. Singleton (Eds.), *Language Across Cultures* (pp. 259-270). Dublin: Irish Association for Applied Linguistics.

Singleton, D., & Little, D. (1991). The second language lexicon: Some evidence from university-level learners of French and German. *Second Language Research*, 7, 61-82.

Smith, E.E., & Medin, D.L. (1981). *Categories and Concepts*. Cambridge, MA: Harvard University Press.

Smith, N., & Wilson, D. (1979). *Modern Linguistics: The Results of Chomsky's Revolution*. Harmondsworth: Penguin.

Smith, V. (1994). *Thinking in a Foreign Language. An Investigation into Writing and Translation by L2 Learners*. Tübingen: Narr.

Söderman, T. (1993). Word associations of foreign language learners and native speakers: The phenomenon of a shift in response type and its relevance for lexical development. In H. Ringbom (Ed.), *Near-Native Proficiency in English* (pp. 91-182). Åbo: Åbo Akademi University.

Srinivas, K. (1996). Size and reflection effects in priming: A test of transfer-appropriate processing. *Memory and Cognition*, 24, 441-452.

Srinivas, K., & Roediger, H.L. (1990). Classifying implicit tests: Category association and anagram solution. *Journal of Memory and Language*, 29, 389-412.

Stedje, A. (1977). Tredjespråksinterferens i fritt tal - en jämförande studie. In R. Palmberg & H. Ringbom (Eds.), *Papers from the Conference on Contrastive Linguistics and Error Analysis. Stockhom and Åbo, 7-8 February, 1977* (pp. 141-58). Åbo: Åbo Akademi.

Stemberger, J., & MacWhinney, B. (1988). Are inflected forms stored in the lexicon? In M. Hammond & M. Noonan (Eds.), *Theoretical Morphology* (pp. 101-116). London: Academic Press.

Swain, M. (1997). The influence of the mother tongue on second language vocabulary acquisition and use. In N. Schmitt & M. McCarthy (Eds.), *Vocabulary: Description, Acquisition and Pedagogy* (pp. 156-180). Cambridge: Cambridge University Press.

Swinney, D.A. (1979). Lexical access during sentence comprehension: (Re)considerations of context effects. *Journal of Verbal Learning and Verbal Behaviour*, 18, 645-659.

Tabossi, P., Colombo, L., & Job, R. (1987). Accessing lexical ambiguity: Effects of context and dominance. *Psychological Research*, 49, 161-167.

Tabossi, P., & Zardon, F. (1993). Processing ambiguous words in context. *Journal of Memory and Language*, 32, 359-372.

Talamas, A., Kroll, J.F., & Dufour, R. (1999). From form to meaning: Stages in the acquisition of second-language vocabulary. *Bilingualism: Language and Cognition*, 2, 45–58.

Talmy, L. (1985). Lexicalization patterns: Semantic structure in lexical forms. In T. Shopen (Ed.), *Language Typology and Syntactic Description (Volume III), Grammatical Categories and the Lexicon* (pp. 57-138). Cambridge: Cambridge University Press.

Tanaka, S. (1987). The selective use of specific exemplars in second language performance: The case of the dative alternation. *Language Learning*, 37, 63-88.

Tanaka, S., & Abe, H. (1984). Conditions on interlanguage semantic transfer. In P. Larson, E. L. Judd, & D. S. Messerschmitt (Eds.), *On TESOL '84: A Brave New World for TESOL*, (pp. 101-120).

Tanenhaus, M.K., Leiman, J. M., & Seidenberg, M. S. (1979). Evidence for multiple stages in the processing of ambiguous words in syntactic context. *Journal of Verbal Learning and Verbal Behaviour*, 18, 427-441.

Tannen, D. (1989). *Talking Voices: Repetition, Dialogue and Imagery in Conversational Dialogue*. Cambridge: Cambridge University Press.

Tarallo, F., & Myhill, J. (1984). Interference and natural language processing in second language acquisition. *Language Learning*, 33, 55-76.

Targonska, J. (in press). Zur Nutzung der Englischkenntnisse beim Erwerb des deutschen Wortschatzes. Eine empirische Untersuchung bei polnischen Schülern. In B. Hufeisen & N. Marx (Eds.), *Beim Schwedischlernen sind Englisch und Deutsch Ganz Hilfsvoll. Untersuchungen zum Multiplen Sprach Enlernen*. Frankfurt/Main: Lang.

Thomas, J. (1988). The role played by metalinguistic awareness in second and third language learning. *Journal of Multilingual and Multicultural Development*, 9, 235-247.

Thomas, J. (1992). Metalinguistic awareness in second- and third-language learning. In Harris, R. J. (Ed.), *Cognitive Processing in Bilinguals* (pp. 531-545). Amsterdam: North-Holland.

Thorndike, E.L., & Lorge, I. (1957). *The Teacher's Wordbook of 30 000 Words*. New York: Columbia University Teachers' College.

Van Geert, P. (1994). *Dynamic Systems of Development. Change between Complexity and Chaos*. New York: Harvester Wheatsheaf.

Van Hell, J., & Dijkstra, T. (2002). Foreign language knowledge can influence native language performance in exclusively native contexts. *Psychonomic Bulletin & Review*, 9, 780-789.

Van Heste, T. (1999). *Visuele Woordherkenning bij Tweetaligen: Selectieve en Niet-Selectieve Activatieprocessen in Functie van de Experimentele Taak*. Unpublished Master's Thesis, University of Leuven.

Van Heuven, W.J.B., Dijkstra, T., & Grainger, J. (1998). Orthographic neigborhood effects in bilingual word recognition. *Journal of Memory and Language*, 39, 468-483.

Wattendorf, E., Westermann, B., Zappatore, D., Franceschini, R., Lüdi, G., Radü, E.-W., & Nitsch, C. (2001). Different languages activate different subfields in Broca's area. *NeuroImage*, 13, 624.

Wei, L. (2000a). Unequal selection of morphemes in adult second language acquisition. *Applied Linguistics*, 21, 106-140.

Wei, L. (2000b). Types of morphemes and their implications for second language morpheme acquisition. *The International Journal of Bilingualism*, 4, 29-43.

Wei, L. (2002). The bilingual mental lexicon and speech production process. *Brain and Language*, 81, 691-707.

Weinert, R. (1995). The role of formulaic language in second language acquisition. *Applied Linguistics*, 16, 180-205.

Weinreich, U. (1953). *Languages in Contact: Findings and Problems*. The Hague: Mouton.

Weldon, M.S., & Roediger, H.L. III (1987). Altering retrieval demands reverses the picture superiority effect. *Memory & Cognition*, 15, 269-280.

Whitaker, H. (1978). Bilingualism: A neurolinguistics perspective. In W. Ritchie (Ed.), *Second Language Acquisition Research: Issues and Implications* (pp. 21-32). New York: Academic Press.

Williams, S., & Hammarberg, B. (1997). *L1 and L2 Influence in L3 Production* Stockholm: Stockholm University, Centre for Research on Bilingualism.

Williams, S., & Hammarberg, B. (1998). Language switches in L3 production: Implications for polyglot speaking model. *Applied Linguistics,* 19, 295-333.

Wode, H. (1980). *Learning a Second Language 1: An Integrated View of Language Acquisition.* Tübingen: Narr.

Wolter, B. (2001). Comparing the L1 and L2 mental lexicon. A depth of individual word knowledge model. *Studies in Second Language Acquisition*, 23, 41-69.

Woutersen, M. (1997a). *The Organisation of the Bilectal Lexicon.* University of Nijmegen: Nijmegen.

Woutersen, M. (1997b). *Bilingual Word Perception.* Nijmegen: Katholieke Universiteit Nijmegen.

Wray, A. (1992). *The Focusing Hypothesis: The Theory of Left Hemisphere Lateralised Language Re-Examined.* Amsterdam/Philadelphia: Benjamins.

Wray, A. (2000). Formulaic sequences in second language teaching: Principle and practice. *Applied Linguistics,* 21, 463-489.

Wray, A. (2002). *Formulaic Language and the Lexicon.* Cambridge: Cambridge University Press.

Yetkin, O., Yetkin, F. Z., Haughton, V. M., & Cox, R. W. (1996). Use of functional MR to map language in multilingual volunteers. *American Journal of Neuroradiology*, 17, 473-477.

Zobl, H. (1980a). The formal and developmental selectivity of L1 influence on L2 acquisition. *Language Learning*, 30, 43-57.

Zobl, H. (1980b). Developmental and transfer errors: Their common bases and (possibly) differential effects on subsequent learning. *TESOL Quarterly*, 14, 469-479.

Zobl, H. (1992). Prior linguistic knowledge and the conservatism of the learning procedure: Grammaticality judgements of unilingual and multilingual learners. In Gass, S. & L. Selinker (Eds.), *Language Transfer in LanguageLearning* (revised ed.) (pp. 176-196). Amsterdam/Philadelphia: Benjamins.

INDEX